EDUCATIONAL DEVELOPMENTS IN MUSLIM WORLD

ENCYCLOPAEDIC SURVEY OF ISLAMIC CULTURE SERIES—3

Educational Developments in Muslim World

Edited by
MOHAMED TAHER

ANMOL PUBLICATIONS PVT. LTD.
New Delhi-110 002

ANMOL PUBLICATIONS PVT. LTD.
Regd. Office: 4360/4, Ansari Road, Daryaganj,
New Delhi-110002 (India)
Tel.: 23278000, 23261597, 23286875, 23255577
Fax: 91-11-23280289
Email: anmolpub@gmail.com
Visit us at: www.anmolpublications.com

Branch Office: No. 1015, Ist Main Road, BSK IIIrd Stage
IIIrd Phase, IIIrd Block, Bangalore-560 085 (India)
Tel.: 080-41723429 • Fax: 080-26723604
Email: anmolpublicationsbangalore@gmail.com

Educational Developments in Muslim World

First Edition 1997

Reprint 2003, 2010
ISBN 81-7488-537-4

PRINTED IN INDIA

Printed at Atul Printers, Delhi.

Preface

The Encyclopaedic Survey of Islamic Culture is a unique reference source. This series seeks to anthologise the most important primary and secondary materials on a wide variety of topics and writers of Islamic culture and civilisation. The scholar, the student and the layman will find in various volumes not only a generous selection of reprinted articles, but original essays, bibliographies, and other materials brought for the first time in a comprehensive and exhaustive fashion.

The need for this collation grew out of our awareness that there is no comprehensive source of information for the study and research of the field. Other published works are too specialised in the topics discussed or neglect the institutional as well the individual role which the Islamic system plays. Few encyclopaedic works do exist, and few anthologies also have appeared. Fewer books, again, have systematically covered such topics as Islam in Africa, Islamic sociology, Islamic polity, Islamic thought, etc. Although these topics have been addressed separately, no attempt has been made to discuss them as part of a united treatment of the literature of the field.

Islam brought a total change in all spheres of life. It revolutionised many societies, both in the east and the west. But this is not always accepted and acknowledged. To quote Major Arthur Leonard from his work: Islam; her moral and spiritual value:

"Never to this day has Europe acknowledged in an honest and whole hearted manner the great and everlasting debt she owes to Islamic culture and civilisation. Only in a lukewarm and perfunctory way has she recognised that when, during the dark ages, her people were sunk in feudalism and ignorance, Muslim civilisation under the Arabs reached a high standard of social and scientific splendour that kept the flickering members of European society from utter decadence."

"Do not we, who now consider ourselves on the top most pinnacle ever reached by culture and civilisation, recognise that, had it not been for the high culture, the civilisation and intellectual, as well as the social splendours of the Arabs and soundness of their school system, Europe would to this day have remained sunk in the darkness of ignorance. Have we forgotten that the Muslim maxim was that, the real learning of a man is of more public importance than any particular religious opinions he may entertain, that Muslim liberality was in striking contrast with the then intolerant state of Europe? Does the magnificent valour of the Arabs, inspired as it was by a theism as lofty as it was pure, not appeal to us? Does not the moderation and comparative toleration shown by them to the conquered, notwithstanding the fierce and burning ardour to regenerate mankind that impelled them onward to conquest, also appeal to us? Does it not all the more appeal to us when we contrast this with the bitterness of the attitude of the Christian sects towards one another? Especially when we consider that in Christendom, as it was then constituted, extortion, tyranny and imperial centralisation, combining with ecclesiastical despotism and persecution, had practically extinguished patriotism, by substitution in its place schismatic and degenerate Church?"

Further the same writer continues to say:

> "Is it possible that Europe is unmindful of, and has the ingratitude to ignore the splendid services of the scientists and philosophers of Arabic? Are the names of Assamh, Abu Othman, Alberuni, Albeithar, Abu Ali Ibn Sina (Avicenna) the great physician and philosopher, Ibn Rushd (Anempace) besides a host of others but dead letters? Is the great work that they have done and the fame they have left behind them in their books to be consigned to the limbo of oblivion, by an ungrateful but antipathetic Europe?

"It cannot be that already we have lost sight of the amazing intellectual activity of the Muslim world during the earlier part of the 'Abbaside' period more especially. It cannot be that we have quite forgotten the irrecoverable loss that was inflicted on Arabian literature, and on the world at large, by the wanton destruction of thousands of books that was promoted by Christian bigotry and fanaticism? It cannot be surely said of Christian Europe that for centuries now she has done her best to hide obligations to the Arabs; yet most assuredly, obligations such as these, are far too sacred to lie much linger hidden."

This is one side of the story. The other side is that the West has definitely absorbed much of the Islamic contributions and is "unaware." To quote Marcus Marby and William Underhill "Bold new visions from ancient landscapes" (Newsweek May 29, 1995): Christian and Islamic civilizations have been in conflict for most of their history. But as often as they have clashed, they have enriched each other. In this ninth century, Moors brought advanced architecture, astronomy and medicine to occupied Spain. While Europe lingered in the Dark Ages, courtly poetry from Persia inspired the troubadours, whose verse evolved into the literature of the early French Renaissance. Even whiling away hours over coffee and conversation—the basis for the cafe—came from Arab culture... France's most popular dish today is not escargots but couscous. French slang is peppered with Arab words like kif-kif (50-50) and Insha Allah (God willing). The hottest new music is Arab-inspired rai" (p. 28). The list of Arabic borrowed words in English and Western usages are many more, not mere algebra, alchemy, azimuth, albatross, timbal, zenith, etc.

There is, in short, a lot of misinformation and incorrect representation about Islam. And more so there is a need today to describe and interpret the issues and express in clear terms what this thought actually deals with. Due to social and cultural changes, the salient aspects of the field require examination. The post cold war era has left the world with a unipolar political system. Islam is a system which promises the world that if applied in toto it would solve the multi-dimensional problems of the modern era. But is there any one who wishes to test this module and try it in a space and time to see the truth of the statement?

The primary purpose of this encyclopaedic survey is to serve as a basic handbook on significant topics of Islamic culture. To facilitate an understanding of the field, the series presents a survey and an analysis of the various socio-cultural forces that shape both the structure and functions of the field as well as by the way this society has changed. We also analyse the larger forces outside the community, such as assimilation and acculturation, and forces inside the community, like, role of the leadership, role of the social and cultural groups and the so much alleged 'imbalance' in the theory and practice of the faith.

We are confident that this work will make a permanent and significant contribution to the study of Islam. Its style is simple, and it is presented in a style accessible to a wide audience. Its target audience is faculty, students, and all concerned with the understanding of the faith of the second largest following in the world. While it has scholarly materials, it is nevertheless also of use to those who have no knowledge of the field, as well as to those who are working in related and allied fields. Most important, we hope that this series will be useful in teaching and learning as an educational resource in the academic world.

The series is planned to be both, multi-volume and multi-facted set, which will run into hundreds of numbers. The compilation of such a huge set is a gigantic task and requires the support and encouragement of all concerned. It requires feed-back and also support from the literary market place and literary circles all over.

A collection of articles, or an anthology, has many benefits, like, it renews our acquaintance with literature which we have neglected, it reveals to us material of which we were ignorant, and it exposes relationships where we did not suppose them to exist. This is the ultimate purpose of our efforts and we wish and pray that this is fulfilled.

A word of acknowledgement is due to the inspiration of the idea of a comprehensive, commulative and compact set of literary works on the Islamic culture. These inspirers are from all walks of life and their efforts must be acknowledged which includes, contributors, authors and editors, as well as the publishers who have graciously contributed to this project and we duly acknowledge their cooperation. The well wishers are many more and listing all the concerned by names is impossible here. Each must be duly rewarded for this gesture, and this is our sincere prayer.

Editor

Contents

1

Some Aspects of the History of the Madrasa

J. PEDERSEN

In the historical tradition Nizam al-Mulk, who from 456 to 485 A.H. was Wazir of the Seljuk sultans, is regarded as the founder of the Madrasa. Some historians, e.g., al-Maqrizi and al Suyuti, object to this tradition rightly that there were madrasas before the time of that great Wazir. As a matter of fact Nizam al-Mulk was not the founder of the Madrasa as an institution, but it was due to his interest that this institution attained such a flowering state in the east that it spread widely over the whole of Mesopotamia. Syria and Egypt. As the work of Nizam al-Mulk, above all his madrasat-al-Nizamiya in Baghdad contributed to the spread of these institutions in Egypt and Syria, where they assumed an immense importance, it is only natural that to those countries he appeared as the founder of the whole institution.

From the beginning, the science of Islam was connected with the mosque. The main points of interest were the Qur'an and Hadith. In the Hadith-collections we see a reflection of the mode of learning, when the Prophet is represented as sitting in the mosque with his halqa of listeners who repeat his words three times in order to memorise them, and people come and ask him about this or that hadith. As some learning about Islam was indispensable to every Muslim, 'Umar sent in the year 17 teachers of the Qur'an in every region, and the people attended their lectures in the mosque every Friday. Lectures of this kind were called *mau'iza*, because there was no real difference between learning and edification. Such edifying instruction was given in the mosques by the qussas. In the time of 'Umar, Tamim al-Daris spoke in the mosque of Medina as qass. As early as 38 or 39 A.H. an official qass was appointed in the 'Amr mosque in Cairo; it was the Qadi Sulaini b. 'Itr al-Tujibi, and after him several Qadis were qussas as well; Ibn Hujayra, d 83, Khayir b. Nu'aim in the year 120, Ibr b. Ishaq al-Qari, d. 204, etc. The qass recited, standing, a part of the Qur'an, and after that explained, sitting on his chair, what he had read, and edified the listeners with his mau'iza or dhikr. The qussas or wu'az acted still for centuries in the mosques; in 580 A.H. Ibn Jubayr listened with keen interest to some famous wu'az in the mosques of Baghdad and even afterwards we hear about them in Cairo. But they were preachers much more than teachers, and beside them other people had taken over the real instruction.

'Umar b. 'Abdal-Aziz sent a learned maula to Egypt in order to teach the Egyptians the sunan, and after that time we find a number of muftis and Qadis sitting in their halqa in the 'Amr mosque and teaching their pupils Islamic Science. It is not possible to trace the evolution of the instruction given in the mosques, in all its details. But in the 3rd century A.H., we find that all the mosques are centres of learning as well as of worship and jurisdiction. The instruction had a very free character. In the year 256 al-Tabari dictated the poems of al-Tirimmah in the 'Amr mosque, sitting near the Bait-al-mal, and some years earlier the great al-Shafi'i spent the most of his time in this mosque. Just after the Sala-tal-Subh he taught the Qur'an; at sunrise Hadith; later, the subject of scientific method (*Mudhakara wal-nazar*), at duha came the ahl al'Arabiya and learned with him grammar and poetry; at noontime he went home. Every teacher had his special seat in the mosque, and after his death it was inherited by another.

When you entered a mosque you witnessed a very motley life. Nasir i-Khosrau, of the 5th century, tells that 5,000 people daily visited the mosque of 'Amr, amongst them teachers, qurra', students, strangers, writers making contracts and bills, etc. You found circles, halaq, of people attending lectures in all kinds of science, especially as told by al-Maqdisi, Fuqaha, Qurra, and Ahl al-Adab wal-Hikma. Since the third century, after al-Shafi'i, it was no more the Hadith, but the more systematical fiqh that was the main subject. Famous scholars gathered a vast audience, like al-Na'ali, (d 380), whose attenders filled up the space of 17 columns. Not only young people attended the lectures. Interested people of all social positions came to get the *baraka* of the great scholars. Discussions were not uncommon, and the great scholar won over the audience of his adversaries. When al-Shafi'i came to Baghdad (195 A.H.) al-Subki tells, there were in the great mosque 20 halaq listening to Hanafitic teachers; but al-Shafi'i's argumentation won over so many of them that only 3 or 4 halaq stayed with the Hanafites.

Beside fiqh, the Hadith, and of course of the Qur'an, formed still a very important subject in the lectures of the mosques. And the Arabic philology never failed to interest the Muslims who were very careful about their rich and difficult language. Some of the Fuqaha, like al-Shafi'i taught philology as well as fiqh, but there were also special philologists, lecturing in their own part of the mosque, as was the case in Basra and a philologist renowned as al-Kisa'i lectured in the mosque named after him in Baghdad. The Mu'tazilite Kalam was taught in the mosque of Mansur in Basra, where al-Ash'ari attended the lectures of al-Jubba'i. But also quite different subjects were treated in the Mosques. Al-Khatib al-Baghdadi read his history of Baghdad in the big mosque of that town. Even medicine, (*Tibb*) was occasionally treated in the mosques. Ibn al-Haytham (d. 430) gave lectures upon that subject in al-Azhar in the time of al-hakim, and when Lajin restored the mosque of Ibn Tulun, he ordered lectures for medicine, a subject that otherwise was taught in the hospitals.

These examples show us to what a great extent the mosques were schools. We know not much about the organization of the instruction and of the teachers in the old time. But we can suggest that the organisation was a very free one. Every Muslim could enter the mosque and attend a lecture, the traveller could always go to the principal mosque in the town he visited to attend a lecture about hadith[16]. There was no examination, but when a pupil had finished a book he got the ijaza of his master, by which he was entitled to teach the book himself. Everyone could lecture on such a book, if anyone would listen to him, but in the big mosques it was necessary to get the permit of the leader in order to give lectures as we are told in the biography of al-Khatib al-Baghdadi. In all mosques there were several waqfs for the professors, and these waqfs gave the background of the appointments. But a ruler or another mighty one of this world could always give an allowance for any scholar, enabling him to spend his time in giving lectures in a mosque. This was very important, as many of the great scholars spent their time in travelling. This is a main feature in the scholarly life of Islam, an inheritance from antiquity. It contributed to make a unity of Islam, and was always stimulating to the studies. In that way al-Shafi'i, al-Ghazali, 'Abdal-Latif, Ibn Khaldun—just to name some few examples—could give their lectures in different parts of the Islamic world without difficulty.

The travelling of the scholars was facilitated in another way. The mosque was not only—to speak in the European way—church and school at once, but also hostel. Pious people could spend day and night in the mosque if they liked to do so, and it is told of some scholars that they never left the mosque. And when poor travellers came to a town it was their right to spend the night in the mosque. Therefore, dwellings were arranged in connection with several mosques.

From the oldest time pious ascetics were living in the minarets, and in the mosque of the 'Umayyads at Damascus al-Ghazali as earlier al-Baghdadi, lived in one of its minarets. And Ibn Jubayr tells us about the well-equipped dwellings that were connected with that mosque, not only for ascetics, but also for scholars and students. According to al-Waqidi, as quoted by al-Suyuti, there was very early a dwelling-house for the qurra' in Medina, in which house 'Abdullah b. Umm Maktum was living. Institutions of that kind may not have been uncommon in connection with a mosque. We know from Egypt in the time of the Fatimids 361 A.H. (i.e. 972 A.D.) that after the building of the Azhar Mosque had been completed the Shi'itic Qadi of the new ruler, 'Ali b. al-Nu'man, lectured about the fiqh-system of his madhab. And in 378 the Caliph al-'Aziz and his wazir Ya'qub b. Killis, inaugurated a foundation for 35 professors, giving them salaries and dwellings in a big house beside the mosque.

All branches of Islamic science found an asylum in the mosque. This was the meeting-place of all learned men, the place of devotion and study, of working and discussion, not strictly organised, open to every Muslim, and at the same time many of the students and teachers found a lodging in the mosque, appropriate to their humble pretensions. The mosque was a very cheap high-school, as the halaq were sitting only on the floor, mostly in the same big hall. A library was the only thing especially wanted for the students.

But science had other refuges besides the mosque. It is well known that al-Ma'mun (198-202) founded an academy, *Bait al-Hikma,* in Baghdad. This institution that reminds us of the older, pre-Islamic one in Qunde Shapur, consisted mainly of a library, an astronomical observatory and dwellings for the scholars; their principal task was to translate the Hellenistic literature into Arabic. A somewhat similar institution was founded much later by al-Mu'tadid (279-289) who built a palace for himself and in connection with it, rooms and dwellings for students of every branch of science, who got salaries for studies and instruction. These institutions were of special importance because they were interested in studies that lay rather far from the main interest of the mosque, where the Qur'an, Hadith and Fiqh always stood in the foreground. The academies were occupied with the Hellenistic sciences like Logic, Philosophy, Mathematics, Astronomy, Music, Medicine and Alchemy that were named "the old sciences" *al-'ulum al-qadima.*

Some wealthy people, scholars themselves, or interested in the studies, founded institutions of a similar kind. 'Ali b. Yahya, named the Astronomer, (*al-Munajjim*) d. 275, was the owner of a palace with a big library, *khizamat al-hikma,* that comprised a large collection of astronomical books; this library was open to every one who wanted to use it, and it was visited by scholars from every country. It is told that Abu Ma'shar the Astronomer arrived there from Khurasan bound for Mecca to fulfil the Hajj. He was then not much versed in astronomical studies, but when he had stayed some time in this institution he was so affected with them that he never more went on pilgrimage and even left Islam. In Mausil ja'far b. Muhammad, (d. 323) founded a "dwelling of science", *dar al-'ilm* with a library, in which the students worked daily in every science and got paper gratuitously. The founder himself read papers to them about poetry. In the 4th Islamic century we get information about several institutions of this kind, founded in the eastern countries. Al Maqdisi gives an account of a library, *khizanat al-Kutub,* arranged in Shiraz by 'Adud al-Daula (367-72) and well organised with a director (wakil), an assistant (khazin) and an inspector (mushrif); every person of consideration could get admittance to it. In those libraries splendid manuscripts of the Qur'an and the classical authors were found. In the library of Baha al-Daula, son of 'Adud al-Daula, probably the same library as that just mentioned, Ibn al-Bawwab found a very precious copy of the Qur'an in 30 parts, written by Ibn Muqla on fine Kaghid paper, with golden letters; as one part was lacking, Ibn al-Bawwab prepared that himself just like the other parts and stipulated as his reward a robe of honour and 100 dinars. In the year 383 the Wazir Sabur b. Aradashir founded a *dar al-'ilm* with a big library for the scholars, and in the same century a friend of science, Ibn Sanwar founded a *dar al-kutub* in Basra and one in Ram Hurmuz with salaries for the scholars; and in basra a Shaikh gave lectures about Mu'tazilite Kalam. In al-Rayy there was at the same time a library comprising more than 400 camel-loads of books, amongst them many of the Shi'a doctrine. In other towns of the east we get information about such more or less public institutions.

In the west the Fatimids founded their renowned institutes on the same lines. Their aim was to support the Sḫi'a doctrine, but not only that. The institutions were real working places of science. In their place in Cairo they had a library disposing of 40 rooms, as al-Maqrizi tells us, and he mentions that there were not less than 1200 copies of Al-Tabari's *Tarikh,* and—as in the east—the Hellenistic sciences, *al-'ulum al-qadima,* were represented by many volumes. The Wazir of al-'Aziz, Ya'qub b. Killis, founded an institute that cost him 1000 Dinars every month; the money was spent on books and salaries for the scholars. And in the year 395 A.H. (*i.e.* 1005 A.D.) al-Hakim founded his famous academy, *dar al-'ilm* or *dar al-hikma,* in the northern part of the western palace in Cairo, containing a big library, a reading room and lecture rooms. A big staff of scholars were busy with studies, with lectures and with the administration of the library, that comprised all kinds of books of Muslim science, a large amount of books treating of Medicine, Astronomy and others of "the old sciences", that were of little interest to studies connected with the mosque.

This splendid institution was in a flourishing state for half a century. During the frightful famine that devastated Egypt under the reign of Al-Mustansir (427-487) every thing fell in disorder and large parts of the rich library were spoiled. But the institution still was preserved until the decline of the Fatimids. When Saladin took the power (567/1171) he put an end to this Shi'a-institute, and all the books were taken off. Some of them were burnt or thrown in the Nile, or heaped up in the sand, making "the Mound of books"; the book-bindings were good enough for boots for the Turkish soldiers. But some of the books were saved, being sold and given over to the new institutions of learning that just then had appeared in Egypt, the *Madaris.* A lot of camel-cargoes were brought to Syria.[34]

In spite of the decay under Al-Mustansir the Hakim institute was still a very important one when it was closed. Abu Shama says the library was the biggest one in Islam; it sounds quite fantastical when he estimates the number of its books as 2 millions.

The institution called *dar al-hikma* or *dar al-'ilm* vanished from Egypt because the Fatimids had connected it with their propaganda, and the director of the institute was the Fatimid head missionary (*da'i'l-du'at*). But as we have seen, it was not solely that, and the institution was itself originally quite independent of doctrinal controversies. There can be little doubt that with these academics Islam carried on old traditions from the Hellenistic period. Not only was the academy of Al-Ma'mun not very different from the pre-Islamic one in Qunde-Shapur, where Hellenistic scholars worked, but Ibn Abi Usaybi'a reckons natural science in Egypt under Islam as a continuation of an older *dar al-'ilm,* where Hellenistic science was taught, and also Al-Maqrizi (Khitat IV 377) mentions the pre-Islamic *dar al-hikma* in Egypt as an institute that, according to the description, was nearly related to the Islamic academy. From other sources we know well the importance of such institutions in Alexandria and Pergamon in the old time.

So we find in the first centuries of Islam two kinds of seats of learning. One is the mosque, that is mainly but not only, interested in the special Muslim learning, and another is the more or less public *dar al-'ilm, dar-al-kutub* or *dar al-hikma,* that often, but not only, serves the interest of physical science, etc., but whose character is determined by its founder and his interests, as it is a quite independent institution. Of course many of these institutions served the same purpose as the Mosque. As the Shi'a Academy, so also the Sunnite *Madrasa* came into existence in close continuation of such institutions.

In his *Tabaqat al Shafi'iya* al Subbi relates of the foundation of institutes with libraries where learned men taught the subjects they were interested in. Some of them were founded in the 4th century. Abu Hatim al-Busti A.H. 277 890 founded such an institute with dwellings and scholarships for students from abroad. Sometimes wealthy people founded a special institute for a renowned scholar, as in Tabaran for al-Hatimi (d. 393/1003) or for al-Isfara'ini (d. 418/1027) in Baghdad or for al-Sa'igh al-Nisaburi (d. 349/960) in Nisabur, where later on a splendid institute of that kind was built for al-Isfara ini. Some scholars were not content with the opportunity they had of giving lectures in the Mosque. If they were able to do so they built a house of their own, where they received the students and gave lectures on fiqh or dictated hadith; we know examples of that in Merw and Nisabur from about 400 A.H.

As mentioned above there were given lectures in many of the institutions called *dar al-'ilm,* but the study in the library was the principal thing. In the institutes here mentioned it was otherwise. Here the instruction was the main purpose, and they were especially interested in subjects of a more practical character, necessary for Muslim education. But that there was no fundamental difference between the two places of learning is seen by the fact that al-Hakim established a Sunnite dar al-'ilm in Cairo 400 A.H. for hadith and Malikite *fiqh,* the scholars living in the institute. They were named madrasa, a word that means place of study and instruction. When al-Maqdisi travelled in the eastern countries in the 4th Islamic century, these institutes were so developed that he can praise the excellent *madaris* of Iranshahr. According to their character these Madaris were very nearly related to the mosques. The subjects taught in them were the same; in both places there were libraries and often dwellings for the students. And we may suppose that the madrasa had that very small apparatus making it fit for a Muslim worship place: the indication of the Qibla in a room large enough for the gathering in the prostrations of the Salat.

The difference between the mosque and the madrasa was that in the first worship was the principal purpose, and also that it had a more public character. Like the above named institutions the madrasa was a private institution; even if the public was admitted in a liberal way, not every one could enter it who liked. Often a madrasa was founded, not separately, but in a mosque, a room being arranged in it and one or more scholars being appointed to give lectures and may be even to live there. There was the case with the Sunnite *dar al-'ilm* founded, but soon again abolished, in Cairo by Al-Hakim. And later on a lot of madaris were founded in the big mosques, as in the mosques of Amr and Al-Azhar in Egypt and the Mosque of the Umayyads in Damascus.

The practice that a scholar founded a madrasa of his own or that an eminent scholar was given a madrasa by others developed to a high degree in the beginning of the 5th century. In the first half of this century there were 4 famous schools of that kind in Nisabur: Al-Bayhaqiya, founded by al-Bayhaqi 441, Al-Sa'idiya by Nasr al-Din Subuktakin, governor of Nisabur 389, one founded by Al-Astarabadhi and one for Al-Isfara'ini. All of these schools were, according to the development of Muslim learning and the needs of the time, above all centres of fiqh-studies.

In this manner there developed from the private institutions of learning besides the mosque a definite type of school related to the mosque in its principal aims. The type was full developed when Nizam al-Mulk became Wazir in the year 456. He saw clearly the importance of the school as an education-place for people determined to be functionaries of the State and leaders of the people. They were moulded on a frankly Sunnite type, and they received in a regular way the necessary Muslim knowledge, in a more regular way than in the mosque. This was important for the unity of the empire and the strength of its administration.

Nizam al-Mulk founded several madaris, called after him al-Nizamiya. We know of one in Nisabur, founded for al-Yuwayni, Imam al-Haramayn, one in Balkh, one in mausil, one in Herat. Like the above mentioned, these also were mostly founded for a special scholar; the madrasa in Herat was destined for al-Shashi (d. 485/

1092), who came from Ghazna. The most famous Nizamiya was that founded in Baghdad. Its construction took two years, and it was inaugurated in the year 459. As its teacher was appointed Abu Ishaq al-Shirazi, who gave lectures in a mosque in Baghdad. It is told, as a proof of his scrupulosity, that he declined to take over the new professorship, because it was rumoured that the ground of the building was taken over by force without justice. Therefore Ibn al-Sabbagh was instituted in his place, but after some few weeks he overcame his mis-givings.

Beside Nizam al-Mulk, many others founded madaris in his time as before him and a great number of them were raised in 'Iraq and the eastern countries, also in the same cities as those in which the great Wazir founded his colleges. Only to mention one, the competitor of Nizam al-Mulk, Taj al-Mulk (d. 484/1093) founded in Baghdad his *Madrasa Tajiya.* But the Nizamiya in Baghdad was the most splendid of them all, and after it had been repaired in 504/1110 it still was the most beautiful of the colleges whose number was about 30, found by Ibn Jubayr in Baghdad when he visited it in the year 581/1185 and also further on until the sumptuous Mustansiriya was founded 631/1234, a few years before the conquest of Baghdad by Hulaqu.

As the madrasa had become a stronghold of Sunni doctrine it is natural that it did not get any importance during the 5th century in Syria and Egypt, where the Fatimids were the rulers. But we find a *dar al-qur'an,* al-Risha'iya in Damascus about 400, arranged like the other *dar al-'ilm,* and in 491 1097 Shuja' al-Daula Sadir founded a madrasa for Hanafi fiqh in the neighbourhood of the mosque of the Umayyads and various other madaris were founded in that city shortly after 500 A.H. The Shafi'ite Aminiya was founded 514, the Hanafite Tarkhaniya 520, another Hanafite madrasa al-Khatuniya outside the town was founded 526, the Hanbalite Sharifiya 536 and Al-'Umariya before 528. Some of them were founded by Turkish officers coming from the East, and when Nur al-Din b. Zanki came to power in Syria 541/1146, he and his Emirs were not less keen on founding madaris than his eastern kinsmen, and his activity was continued by his successor Salah al-Din (570-589).

It is only natural that we find still less traces of the Sunnite madaris in Egypt, the seat of the Fatimids, in the 5th and the first half of the 6th century. With exception of the above mentioned madrasa founded and again abolished by al-Hakim, no Sunnite madrasa was established in that country before Salah al-Din, before whose powerful ruling the Fatimid dynasty vanished. The first ones were the Malikite Rambiya, and the Shafi'ite Nasiriya founded by Salah al-din 566, and some few years later he founded the most splendid of them all, al-Salahiya, that gave occasion for a most enthusiastic outburst of Ibn Jubayr, when he visited it some few years after its foundation. It is well known how splendidly the madrasa developed in Egypt during the next centuries, more than in any other country. At the end of the 6th century, after the fall of the Fatimids, the madrasa was introduced in Hijaz. In Tunis and the Maghrib it did not flourish before the 7th and 8th century; in Spain we do not find it before the 8th century when Yusuf Abu'l-Hajjaj founded a madrasa in Granada in the year 750/ 1349. On the whole the madrasa was not of the same importance in the far West as in the eastern countries.

A look at the history of the madrasa shows us a mighty development. Beginning as a private supplement to the mosque as a school, it grew to be the most important stronghold of Sunnite education. The interest of the rulers for it did not mean that it lost its original character and became a state institution, it only meant that it got better circumstances and a higher appreciation. With this great development the relation between mosque and madrasa became a different one. When the madrasa became bigger, it was not different from the mosque; like the latter it was a prayer-place as well as a school, and the qibla was indicated by a mihrab. From the 5th century there even came a minbar (pulpit) in the big madrasas. In al-Nizamiya in Nisabur a sermon was delivered at its inauguration, and Ibn Jubayr attended a sermon delivered from the minbar of the Nizamiya in Baghdad. Friday-khutba was not given in Cairo in more than one mosque from 569/665 in accordance with the Shafi'ite doctrine, but after that time every big madrasa got its minbar for the weekly Friday service. And we know of many madaris in Cairo that they were used for this service and that a Khutba was delivered in them.

So there was no difference between madrasa and masjid and often the madrasa could be a jami.' In the 8th century Ibn al-Hajj tries to make a distinction between masjid and madrasa, saying that the masjid is more holy (*K. al-Madkhal* II 3.48); this was true in the earliest time of the history of the madrasa, but at the time of Ibn al-Hajj the distinction was quite artificial. The splendid mosques built during the Mameluke time in Cairo were alike prominent as jawami and madaris, as for instance in the 8th century Jami' al-Hasan and in the 9th century Àl-Jami' al-Mu'ayyadi. In the 9th century therefore the word masjid is used by Maqrizi not only in a general sense of all the prayer-places as of old, but also in a special sense of only of quite insignificant small prayer-places.

The identification of madrasa and jami was favoured by the fact that every important mosque still was a school. The development of the madrasa had not checked the interest for the learning in the old mosques, but rather promoted it. At the time of al-Maqrizi there were 8 rooms for fiqh studies in the mosque of 'Amr in Cairo, and in the middle of the 8th century there were more than 40 *Halaqat* in it. In the mosque of Ibn Tulun there was given instruction of fiqh according to the four madhahib after its restoration by Lajin about 700 (op. cit. 41). The same was the case in Al-Azhar, Al-Hakimi, etc., and as in the madaris there were stipends and dwellings for the students.

A madrasa might still be a small building in or near a big mosque, but when it was an independent institution, the only difference between the old great mosque or jami' and the madrasa was in the architecture. When the madrasa had finished its development and had become the same as the mosque, the special interest for it diminished. In Cairo most of the madaris decayed, and it was the Azhar *mosque* that once more became the central seat of learning. In other countries madrasa and mosque remained alike the focus of Muslim learning during the last centuries until new high-schools of a different type have come to existence in our days.

2

Education in the Hijaz
Under Turkish and Sharifian Rule

JAMAL ALAMI

When the Ottoman Sultan Salim I conquered Egypt in 1517 he sent an emissary to the Sharif of Mecca offering to confirm him in office on condition of mentioning the name of the Sultan in the Friday prayers. With the acceptance of the arrangement the Hijaz fell under nominal Ottoman sovereignty. As a token of the connection, the Sultan sent an annual sum of money and other gifts for the Sharif and the people of the Hijaz. Poor in natural resources the Hijaz always depended on supplies from the neighbouring countries, especially Egypt which sent grain. The pilgrims who came from all over the Muslim world provided another source of income. A third source was the donations and gifts of pious and wealthy men and women from all over the world.

The Holy mosques of Mecca and Medina had since the early days of Islam been seats of Islamic education and learning. To them came scholars and students from many Islamic countries for learning, teaching and meditation. Apart from the two mosques, educational facilities in the Hijaz differed very little from those available in other Arabic or Islamic countries. In urban centers the most common type of primary school was the *kuttab* where the elements of reading, writing and some arithmetic were taught, together with memorising portions of or the whole of the Koran. The higher type of *madrasah* existed mostly in Mecca and Medina, generally in the vicinity of the two holy mosques. In the mosques teaching was according to the proverbial *halqa* (circle): learners, listeners and students sitting in a circle round a teacher who discoursed on religious subjects. There was no syllabus and no set rules. Anyone who felt proficient gave lessons and anyone of any age could listen to him. Later on teachers authorized to give a *dars* (discourse) were licensed by the shaikh of al Haram and generally received remuneration for their labour.

More precise information, particularly statistical, is lacking even for comparatively recent times. The scanty references to education in the works of three distinguished Europeans who visited the Hijaz in the nineteenth century — Burckhardt (1814) Burton (1853) and Snouck Hurgronje (1885)—provide no more than mere glimpses, and are not always free from misinterpretation. They found the two mosques the centres of teaching the elements as well as proficiency in the higher Arabic and Islamic sciences. They found that the *kuttab* was still useful for learning the elements whether conducted privately in the house of the teacher or in a corner of the mosque. They found that the traditional Islamic ideal of gratuitous teaching was not dead. They witnessed scholars from other countries residing in or around the two mosques for prayer, meditation and study as *mujawirun.* This phenomenon demonstrated that another Islamic tradition in the quest for learning, the undertaking of a journey (*rihla*), was still alive. They found that students from the Jizaz went for further study to the institutions in Damascus and Cairo. At the latter city the students went to the famous al Azhar, where there were special quarters for them known as *Riwaq al Haramain.*

The only documentary evidence of this traditional system is preserved at the University of Riyadh in the form of a few licenses (sing *ijazah).* A licence was usually issued by a teacher to his pupil testifying that he attained a certain level in a certain subject or subjects and was himself deemed competent to teach it to others.

Such were the conditions when in 1869 the Ottoman Education Law was issued. It comes as a surprise that its provisions were applied, as from the next decade, to the remote provinces of the Yemen and the Hijaz. But it is even more surprising to find that the new state schools in the Hijaz were almost exclusively attended by the children of Turkish officials and soldiers. These were opened in the two holy cities and other urban centres. None, so far as could be discovered, were opened in rural, still less, beduin areas.

Following the nomenclature of the law, the new schools were called *Ibtidaiya* (elementary), *Rushdiya* (higher elementary) and *I'dadiya* (pre-paratory). Children of the local Arabs continued to patronise the traditional schools and some private schools run on more or less modern lines. Only a small number of Arab children attended the state schools, and these were the children of notables, merchants or government officials.

One reason why the Turkish state schools were not popular was the teaching through the medium of Turkish and the fact that the teachers were practically all Turks. The syllabus of the state school was itself a deterrent for it included the teaching of Turkish and Persian in addition to Arabic and some of the modern subjects like geography, history and elementary science. Another reason for not going to the state schools was the usual beduin fear of conscription, for it was assumed that once a boy became literate he was liable to enlistment in the army.

That the new state schools in the Hijaz were a replica of those opened in Turkish and Syrian cities, without adaptation to the local conditions, is clear from the teaching of French, and the opening of a school for crafts (*madrashah sinaiya*). A training school (*dar al mu'allimin*) was however a necessity. But perhaps the most ambitious venture was the plan of a university (*dar al-funun)* at Medina, with the Egyptian savant, Shaikh 'Abdul-Aziz Shawish as Rector. It was instituted by royal decree in 1913, and its foundation stone was actually laid. It was intended to attract students from all over the Arab countries and indeed the Muslim world as a whole. It was named after Saladin as *Salahiyya.* Nothing came of the scheme which was overtaken by the outbreak of the First World War. The name was, however, adopted for a less ambitious college started during the war in Jerusalem with the initiative of Jamal Pasha, Minister of Marine and Commander-in-Chief of the Fourth Army. One of the merits of this college was that it taught through the medium of Arabic and concentrated on the training of teachers.

It must not be forgotten that Arab children continued to attend the traditional schools as well as the private schools, some with the suggestive names of *Najah, Falah* and *Islah.* A number of these were endowed foundations established by non-Arab Muslim residents or by wealthy Muslims in various countries. It was no accident that the first named schools was opened in mercantile Jiddah at the turn of the century.

Teachers of the *kuttab* invariably charged fees and expected gifts from parents at certain stages in the progress of their children. A school of this type was generally a one-teacher's show, but some such teachers employed as monitor (*arif*) one of their 'advanced' pupils. Anyone could open such a school in the absence of a licensing authority, and the teaching was entirely unsupervised or inspected.

An interesting detail noted by Snouck-Hurgronje deserves notice. In a conservative society he saw girls being taught in the lower grade *kuttab* with boys. Girls were, however, withdrawn early before maturity. Well-to-do parents were known to employ private teachers to give instruction to their children, boys and girls at home.

It is a mark of the respect which the Harams of the two cities enjoyed under Turkish sultans that the officially sponsored teaching in the two holy shrines was not restricted to the Hanafi school, their own, but embraced the other three schools of Sunni Islam : the Shafii, Maliki and Hanbali. In 1332/1913 the Sharif Husain Ibn 'Ali, the Amir of Mecca, introduced a new system of teaching in the Harams controlled by a special committee composed of the Muftis of the four schools. Teachers had to prove their proficiency before undertaking the task. Under this system thirteen licensed teachers, each with an assistant, were assigned to the Haram in Mecca and received salaries.

In 1916 four centuries of Ottoman sovereignty came to an end when Husain Ibn 'Ali, the Sharif of Mecca, proclaimed the Arab revolt and quickly occupied Mecca and the rest of the country with the exception of Medina which held out till after the armistice. This is a suitable juncture at which to sum up the educational achievement during the Turkish supremacy.

Foreign travellers particularly Snouck-Hurgronje misinterpreted the transfer of the *madrasahs* from the exterior to the interior of the holy mosques and regarded it as a sign of decline if not the extinction of these schools. That was not so. The teachers concerned preferred the blessing of teaching inside rather than outside the mosques, and Islamic tradition confirmed them in this preference. So by the end of the Turkish era both the *kuttab* and the *madrasah* type of schooling was dispensed more often inside rather than outside the mosques in Mecca and Medina. But there were such schools conducted outside the mosques as in Taif and Jiddah.There was nothing unusual in this development nor was it as supposed by foreign writers a retrograde step. The main point to bear in mind about these institutions is that they were supported by *waqf* (a religious foundation) in almost every case. The supervision of the trust was in the hands of the Ulama or the Shaikh of the Haram, when it was in Mecca or Medina.

Towards the close of the Ottoman period, about four years before the outbreak of the First World War, 'Abbas II, the Khedive of Egypt, performed the pilgrimage to Mecca and Medina. In his entourage was Muhammad Labib al Batanuni who wrote a rambling account of the journey under the title of *ar Riha al-Hijaziya* There are casual references in it to some of the educational facilities noted at random by an author who was not an educationist. Here are the most important of these notes recorded according to the Khedive's itinerary.

1. In Jiddah two schools are mentioned : *al-Islah* private school with eighty pupils and a *Rushdiya* state school with 120 pupils taught the elements of reading and writing Arabic and Turkish and arithmetic.
2. In Mecca two private schools are mentioned without details except that one was established by a local notable and the other by an Indian. In the Haram the teaching was mainly *tafsir* (exegesis) of the Koran and Arabic. The number of students was put at several hundred and the *active* teachers at thirty. The pay, that came from official sources, was insufficient, so that teachers supplemented it by taking additional employment. (Elsewhere the author gives the total number of *mudarrisin* as 107. These were probably part-time teachers who each gave an occasional *dars* (lecture)

in the mosque to a circle of interested listeners and received some remuneration).

3. As in Mecca exegesis and jurisprudence were taught at al-Haram in Medina. There is a mention of a *madrasah* called *al majidiya* (? after Sultan 'Abdul Majid) at the northern entrance of the Haram, but no details are given about it. In the same location there were two schools of the *kuttab* type for the teaching of the Koran. Another school of this type taught arithmetic in addition to the Koran. The city contained seventeen *maktabs* (which indicates Turkish state nomenclature), but no details as to number of pupils and teachers are given.
4. Apart from the numerous copies of the Koran, both manuscript and printed, that the author saw near the Prophet's tomb, he noted three libraries : a) the library of 'Arif Hikmat, Shaikh al Islam, with 5,404 books ; b) a library named after Sultan Mahmud II contained 4,569 books; c) a library named after Sultan 'Abdul-Hamid contained 1,659 books. These and other libraries at the gates of the Haram contained about 30,000 books, some very rare.

So much for the eye-witness Batanuni. A well-known Arab educationist, Sati al-Husri, was director of the cultural department of the Arab League and editor of its cultural annual (*Hauliya).* In the second volume issued in 1949 he stated, on the basis of official Turkish statistics published in 1915, that the province of Hijaz had 78 state schools. Neither the number of pupils nor of teachers was given. So it is difficult to assess the accuracy of what seems to be an incredible figure, considering the fact that Turkish state schools existed only in urban centres where Turkish officials and soldiers were stationed.

Be that as it may, attention must now be turned to the new educational set up under the Arab Hashemite government proclaimed by the Sharif who some four months after the revolt was styled 'King of the Arab Nation or King of the Arab countries' but to his British allies he remained only 'King of the Hijaz.' It is remarkable that amidst the daunting war with the Turks, the new government took immediate steps to establish an Arabic school system using the buildings and equipment left by the Turks. Otherwise everything was new : Arabic replaced Turkish as the medium of instruction, the syllabus was reformed and Arab teachers were recruited largely locally and partly from Syria.

A ministry of education was formed with the Sharif's eldest son 'Ali as the first minister. But since he was a commander of an army in the field it fell to his father to be the effective minister with the Syrian Shaikh Kamil al-Qassab as deputy minister. The Sharif was of course in charge of everything from military operations to dictating or writing ordinary letters. He personally controlled all expenditure. The new ministry was given the Arabic Turkish name *Nazarah* . Early in 1917 regulations were formulated for its schools under the title of *Nizam Madaris al-Hukumah al-Arabiya al Hashimiya.* Under these Regulations an education board (*Majlis al Maarif*) was instituted for the routine supervision and administration of the schools. (The early establishment of a military academy under Syrian officers must not be taken as strictly a school under the ministry of education, for its purpose was to produce as quickly as possible junior officers for the regular army of the Sharif.)

No schools for girls were opened. The Turkish teachers training school did not survive under the Arabic system. The schools were as under the Turks conducted in urban centres, and the beduins were not served except possibly when their camps happened to be near an urban school. Nor were the private schools much affected by the change. They continued to flourish beside the new state schools as under the Turks.

The Turkish nomenclature was abandoned and the Arabic schools were styled *Tahdiriya* (elementary), *Raqiya* (intermediate) and *'Aliya* (secondary). During the first year there were fourteen schools of the first category, four of the second and one of the third.

It seems all three were started simultaneously, pupils of different standards recruited from private schools, the *kuttab* and remnants of the Turkish schools. Admission to the first type was either from the *kuttab* or the private schools, and the length of the course was three years. The length of the course in the second type was four years, and three years in the third.

Reliable statistics are lacking, but it is possible with a patient search in the pages of *al-Qiblah,* the official organ of the Sharif, to glean some information. For example a notice in No. 35 (18 Safar, 1335) signed by the editor described a visit to the newly established Hashimiya School in Mecca. It was in a spacious building where only Arbic poetry, prophetic tradition and the Koran were taught by the old method of committing everything to memory. All other subjects, which were not named, were, taught according to the method of 'deduction and application.

It must have been a difficult task not to follow the natural course of development. The number of pupils is very difficult to determine, but considering that according to the regulations each elementary school had five teachers it may be assumed that such schools had over two hundred pupils.

The syllabus was less ambitious than that of the Turkish schools. No foreign languages were taught, and in addition to the usual Arabic and Islamic subjects arithmetic, elementary science and geometry were taught. Of particular interest was an agricultural school started at Jarwal in 1920, under a qualified Syrian headmaster. But taking the system as a whole there was only quantitative development in the next five years before the Sharifian era came to an end.

3

Objectives of Education in the Pakistani Society before Colonial Rule

N. A. BALOCH

Pakistan, as a modern state, was established in August 1947, but it encompasses within its boundaries territories which have had an ancient history and cultural traditions. Herein flourished the Indus Valley civilization in the pre-historic times with its centres at Moenjodaro and Harrapa, and the Buddhist civilization later with its centres at Taxila and further north in the Gandhara country. These ancient societies had their own ways of instructing the young which enabled them to attain a high level of cultural advancement. The Buddhist monastries had arrangement for instructing the young monks in the Buddhist religion. The Vedas of the early nature worshipping Aryans composed in the valleys of the Indus and its five tributaries, were memorized and transmitted to the posterity and became later on the scriptures of the Hindu religion.

An organized system of education with the modern objective of universal literacy became a feature of the Muslim society which, in the Hindustan sub-continent, was established and consolidated first in Sind by the Muslim Arabs in the 8th century. Sind was conquered by Muhammad b. al-Qasim al-Thaqafi in A.D. 711 and the administrative boundaries of the Al-Sind Province were extended subsequently (8th-9th centuries) to include most of the present territories of Pakistan plus the Indian territories in the East and South of Sind. Except the latter and the northern parts which changed hands, the remaining regions remained under the Arabs up to the end of the 10th century followed by the local Muslim dynastic rule.

First Phase : The Sindo Muslim Society

During the first century of Islam, development of education in the Arab-Muslim Society was motivated by the Quranic injunctions and the prophet's teachings, and the mosques became important centres of formal instruction. Simultaneously, higher education became the concern of the more qualified scholars who taught individually or together. The institution of *Ashab al-Suffah*, approved and commended by the Prophet, came to be the prototype for institutions of higher learning with the main objective of free discussion and further inquiry into all fields of knowledge.

The educational institutions and procedures developed during the first century of Islam were adopted and continued in Sind. The tradition of elementary education — consisting of reading, writing, instruction in faith and personal guidance of the learner — was institutionalized through the *maktab* school. In the higher scholarly circles and institutions, the search for new knowledge was extended, at the initial stage, mainly in the direction of language learning, because the Arab Muslims who had settled down in Sind permanently, felt the need of knowing the local languages, Sindhi in the first instance. The learning of other native languages was also dictated by administrative and diplomatic needs and the Umayyed Governor, Junaid b. Abd al-Rahman al-Murri (A.D. 724-729), appointed one Bukair b. Mahan, an accomplished linguist from Kufah, as his official translator. Bukair was so very highly paid for his specialized knowledge of the local languages that he made a fortune out of his services in Sind.

This official recognition of the language proficiency encouraged scholars not only to learn the spoken languages but also to study Sanskrit, the repository of the written record. The new capital city of al-Mansurah founded in the Lower Indus Valley during A.D. 730-735, soon became a centre of higher learning and research. It was here that the Sanskrit works were studied and translated some three decades before the founding of Baghdad (762). The two important astronomical works of Brahmagupta (an astronomer of the city of Bhilmal in the neighbouring Gurjara country in the S.E. of Sind, born in 598 and died in the last quarter of the 7th century), viz. *Karana Khanda-Khadyaka* and *Brahama Sphute Siddhanta,* were the first to be translated into Arabic most probably by Ibrahim b. Habib al-Fazari and his Sindhian associates; the former translated in the year 109 of the Sindhian era (117 A.H./ A.D. 735) became widely known as *Alarkand,* and the latter translated thereafter (A.D.735-754) came to be known as *Sindhind.*

It would appear that Mathematics, Pharmacology and Medicine were among the other subjects, besides Astronomy, studied at the Mansurah institutions, and both the Arab and the local scholars participated in these studies. Pharmacology remained a popular subject of study up to the end of the 4th/10th century when Bishr. b. Abd al-Wahhab al-Fazari, on the basis of his studies in Sind, incorporated the Sindhian and the Indian names of a number of herbs and drugs in his book *Tafasir al-Adviyyah.*

On the social side, the study of History received attention and both the local history and the earlier history of Islam came under study. The details of Muhammad b. al-Qasim's campaign and conquest of Sind. (in A.D. 711) were carefully recorded and preserved. Also inquiries were extended into the pre-Islamic period of Sind history and a fairly detailed account of the previous two dynasties was recorded. These are the earliest historical records of any part of the Hindustan sub-continent which have survived to this day. Study of the early history of Islam received equal attention and, Abu Ja'far al-Daibuli (of Debal) was probably the first author to have compiled the letter of the Prophet in his book entitled *Makatib al-Mursalin.*

Mansurah and the port city of Debal had developed the institutions wherein inquiry-based broad general education, including both the study of Islam and its developing tradition and the search for all new useful knowledge, became the main objective of higher learning.

In a distant land like Sind, it was but natural that the new Sindo-Muslim community remained concerned with the original sources of Islamic law. Judging from the contributions of scholars from the two cities of Mansurah and Debal during the 3rd and 4th centuries. A.H., it would appear that the study of Quran and Hadith had become the core of 'Islamic learning.' To enable the local Muslim community and other to understand the meaning of the Quran, the Holy Book was translated probably into more than one language. In the 3rd century, one translation was made at the request of the King of Kashmir. Abu Ja'far al-Sindi and other scholars from Sind had specialized in *Hadith* and written standard works on the subject. The Qadi of Mansurah, Abu al-Abbas Ahmad b. Muhammad b. Salih al-Tamimi in the 4th century A.H. and al-Imam Amad al-Din Husain Ibn Shaibah al-Sindi later, became the most renowned faqihs in the world of Islam in their own days. Abu al-Abbas belonged to the city of Mansurah, as recorded by al-Samani (*K. al-Ansab*) who had the occasion to meet him. Also Bashshari al-Maqdisi (*Ahsan al-Taqasim*) met him sometime in 357 A.H. and found him to be the *imam* of the Dawudiyyah/ Zahiriyyah school and an author of many standard works. According to al-Bashshari, the study of Hadith was then popular in Sind. Ibn Nadim (*K.al-Fihrist)* confirmed later that the School of Dawud in Fiqh flourished in Mansurah, and that Abu al-Abbas was an authority on the subject and had authored voluminous works of great merit such as *Kitab al-Misbah al-Kabir, Kitab al-Hadi,* and *Kitab al-Nayyir.*

The Dawudiyyah school was founded by Aby Sulaiman Dawud b. Khalaf al-Isfahani (d. 270 H./884) who had held that the obvious literal meaning of Quran and Hadith, instead of *qiyas* (reasoning by analogy), be followed as a guide for formulating the laws of *Shariah* and that the principle of *Ijma* be restricted to the consensus of the Prophet's companions only. In the lands far distant from Arabia, this view was dictated by reasons of security and authenticity — to preserve for the correct guidance of the Muslim community the principles and practices exactly as they were underlined in the Quran and Hadith. Later, in the 4th/5th century A.H. these principles of the Dawudiyyah/ Zahiriyyah School of Jurisprudence and Theology had gained popularity not only in Iran but also in Spain and Sind. Abu al-Abbas became its exponent in Sind and Ibn Hazm in Spain.

The study of the Zahiriyyah School of Jurisprudence spread from the educational institutions of southern Sind to those of the northern province of Multan from where it was extended farther north to the regions of Hind which were conquered by Sultan Mahmud of Ghazna in the early 11th century. Writing in the 5th century, Ibn Hazm (d. 456

H/1064) observed that the vast territories in Hind, adjacent to Sind, conquered by Sultan Mahmud (d. A.D. 1030) 'are now inhabited by Muslims, the study of the Quran and Hadith flourishes there and the Zahiriyyah *madhab* (school) is predominant there.

For want of adequate record, it is not clear how far studies in Science and Technology had advanced after the initial stage of research which centered on Sanskrit works. The circumstantial evidence, however, leads to the conclusion that Astronomy, Mathematics, Medicine and other subjects had remained under study down to the 5th/11th century. It is indicated that the scholars of Sind and Multan who were the contemporaries of Al-Beruni (d. 443/1051) had met him, were interested in his researches, and had possibly supplied him with relevant information including the translations of some original Sanskrit works. Technological skills were also advanced. The bulk of the army, including engineers and technicians, accompanying Muhammad b. al-Qasim (A.D. 711) had settled down in Sind. His victories in Sind were mainly due to the use of superior technology, viz. the ability to employ the *manjaniq* (catapult) and to construct quickly a boat bridge on the Indus during the flood season. Later on, the founding of the huge capital city of Mansurah, expansion of commercial highways and the extension of agriculture which took place, during the Arab rule in Sind, indicate the development of technical skills which go with town planning, building and architecture, construction of roads and bridges, and agricultural technology. During the Caliphate of al-Mu'tasam (A.D. 833-842), Imran b. Musa al-Barmai, the Governor of Sind, constructed an irrigation dam in the territory of the Meds which became known as 'Sakr al-Med' (The Dam of the Med). This name would indicate that the Dam was built on the section of the Indus where the modern Sukkur Barrage was completed in 1932. 'Sukkur', which is now the name of the city, is most probably a reminiscent of the early historical *Sakr (dam).*

In conclusion, it may be stated that basically, the process of education in the Sindo-Muslim society, as elsewhere in the Islamic world during this period, had generated an abiding interest in *tahqiq*, i.e. 'search for reality' through scientific studies and inquiries into all fields of knowledge.

Second Phase : The Indo Muslim Society

The conquests of Sultan Mahmud of Ghazna initiated the development of the second phase of the Muslim society in Hind. The first phase in Sind, during the 8th/10th centuries, had Arab influence as its basic component and was essentially Sindo-Muslim (Arab-Sindhian) in character. The second phase commencing from the 11th century had Turkish-Iranian influences as its basic component, and it was Indo-Muslim in character. The educational institutions during the second phase were patterned mainly after those of Khurasan, Iran and Transoxiana which had developed under the Samanid, Ghaznawid, Seljuq and the Ghaurid rules. Persian, instead of Arabic of the Sindo-Muslim period, became the State language and also the medium of instruction.

It was a long period of educational activity (11th/17th century) over vast regions covering practically the whole of Hind. Unlike Sind, where most of the population had embraced Islam, in Hind the Muslim and Hindu communities lived side by side. For some three centuries, each community lived in isolation maintaining its own educational institutions with different objectives. After the spread of the Indo-Muslim system of education, the elementary school with its emphasis on reading, writing, general education and personal guidance of the pupil, developed into a common school where children of both the communities could study together. At the higher level, Persian language and literature, Philology, Poetry, Secretarial Writing (Insha) and Tibb (Medicine) became the common subjects of study.

'Islamic learning', as such, gradually became a distinct field of study and specialization for Muslim scholars. Until the 12th/13th century, the study of Quran and Hadith was continued in Hind under the influence of the educational institutions of Sind and Multan; thereafter the study of Hadith became gradually weaker, till its revival in the 18th century. The study of the Hanafite School of Jurisprudence was advanced during this period, a number of works were written and a considerable body of *Fatawa* literature was produced for the application and administration of law. *Nahv, Tasawwuf, Mantiq, Kalam* and *Adab* were the other principal subjects of study, but from the 9th/14th century onwards the study of *al-Ulum al-Aqliyyah,* mainly *Mantiq*

(Logic) and *Hikmat* (Philosophy), became the main objectives of higher education and the very heart of the Islamic Studies curriculum.

In contrast with the principle of *tahqiq* which had motivated the process of learning during the first phase, Education in the Indo-Muslims society during the second phase gradually became more specific in content and circumscribed in objectives.: *taqlid* instead of *tahqiq* became its governing and guiding principle. Consequently, criticism of the subject-ridden curriculum became more pronounced in scholarly circles and curriculum revisions were affected in different parts of the country. The last one which was accepted and followed widely was brought about by Mulla Nizamuddin Sihalawi (d. 1161/ 1768). Known as *'Dars-i Nizami'*, it was broader in scope and based on a carefully selected series of text-books for each of the twelve subjects of study (*Sarf, Nahv, Balaghah, Mantiq, Hikmat, Riyaziyyah* (Arithmetic, Geometry) *Fiqh, Usulal-Fiqh, Kalam, Tafsir, Hadith* and *Munazirah*). It aimed at depth study, comprehension and self-direction on the part of the student at the advanced stage.

Dars-i Nizami and other curriculum reforms elsewhere were still within the traditional pattern and confined 'Education' to a limited concept of 'Islamic Studies'. It was in the 16th century that *two* major viewpoints emerged which underlined the all-inclusive objective of Education, viz., to pursue knowledge in all its branches, with differing emphasis but without any compartmentalization of 'Islamic Studies'.

First it was during 1556-1566 that an eminent educator Ja'far al-Bubakani wrote his *Nahj al-Ta'llum*, in which besides expressing his advanced viewpoints about the teaching-learning process and teacher-pupil relationship, he underlined the expanding scope of knowledge and consequently, the need for an all-inclusive objective of Education. He categorised the fields of knowledge into (i)Religious Sciences (ii) Polite literature and (iii) Physics and Philosophy. The latter was sub-divided into Practical and Theoretical--the Practical including Political Science (*Tadbir al-Mudn*), Economics (Tadbir al-Munzil) and Ethics (*Ilm al-Akhlaq* or *Tasawwuf*); and the Theoretical consisting of (i) Natural Sciences (Tabi'i) including the study of Matter and its changing conditions (i.e.,'when it is at rest and in motion'), Medicine, Anatomy,

Chemistry etc.; (ii) Computational Sciences (*Riyazi*), including Geometry, Astronomy, Algebra, Music, Perspective (*'Ilm al-Manazir*, Mechanics (*lm-i-Jarr-i'athqal*, Moving Spheres (*ukar-i Mutaharraka*); and (iii) Metaphysics (*Ilhai*). He suggested a broad-based curriculum consisting of Compulsory, Optional, Additional or Preferable, and Voluntary subjects. Under the first category, he included the knowledge and God and His Unity the basic principles of Islam and the study of human feelings and conduct (*ma'rafat-i ahwal-i qalb wa akhlaq-i hamidah wa dhamimah*). Under the remaining parts, he included, among others, Medicine, Anatomy, Hygiene necessary for maintaining health, Mathematics, Study of Space and Time, and Observation of Skies, History etc. He explained that in individual choice, priority should be given in accordance with the need, interest and ability of the learner.

This far-sighted statement of educational objectives and of the curriculum design emerged in Sind before it became a part of the Mughal Empire (1599). No record is available of the actual educational practice which followed subsequently, but this new concept influenced the educational thinking during the second half of the 16th century. As a result a new Educational Policy was enunciated in the reign of Emperor Akbar (1556-1605). This Policy as explained by Abu al-Fadi Allami in *Ain-i-Akbari* (1601), required that among others:

> Every boy ought to read books on morals, arithmetic the notation particular to arithmetic, agriculture, mensurational geometry, astronomy, physiognomy, household matters, the rules of government medicine logic, the *tabii riyazi* and ilahi sciences and history, all of which may be gradually acquired. No one should be allowed to neglect those which the present time requires.

The introduction of such subjects as ethics, mathematics, accounts, agriculture and the art of administration, in the curriculum shows that the main objective was to prepare the student for the practical needs of life and living. Due to the curriculum change that followed, the schools had shown progress and the colleges became 'the light and ornament of the empire'. According to Abu al-Fadi. 'all civilized nations had schools for the education of youth, but Hindustan was particularly famous for its seminaries.' It has been recognized that at 'its (education's) height, the Indian Muslim Universities were thronged by thousands of students and a professor had often hundreds of hearers.

The main advance which came through the State Educational Policy of Emperor Akbar consisted in integrating vocational and technical education with general education. This had not happened during the previous era (11th to 16th century), though considerable progress was made in vocational skills and in engineering and technology. Planning of towns, extension of highways, construction of bridges, erection of minarets and monumental buildings, advances in military technology, building of irrigation dams and canals, development of agriculture, and achievements in arts, crafts-music and architecture confirm this. However, the objectives of formal education had remained isolated from those of vocational and technical training. Workmanship (*San'at*) qualifying for the industry (*Sina'at*) was motivated by economic advantages of ready employment and better remunerations and was promoted by the guilds of artisans in their own workshops and further standardized during the period of apprenticeship in the State-owned or Private *Karkhanas* (factories).

This had been the established practice from early times. In fact, despite the great advances made in the theory and practice of education in the Islamic worlds an 'inquiry-based all-inclusive concept of Education', which was developed under the inspiration of the Quranic injunctions and the Prophetic teachings had its impact mainly during the first few centuries of Hijra. Later on, 'Education' gradually became limited to 'learning in particular Islamic subjects' and the spirit of scientific inquiry was replaced by adherence to the specific tradition.

The idea of integrating religious and technical education into common curriculum had, for the first time, emerged in the Indo-Muslim society by the turn of the 16th century. The key note of this new approach was that 'no one should be allowed to neglect those things which the present times require.' This development which promised the emergence of a progressive system of education suited to the requirements of modern times, would have become effective and productive later during the 17th century, but it did not happen because of the weakening of the Mughal Empire by the turn of the 17th century and its eventual downfall. The growing foreign influence and the gradual occupation of the country by the British during the 17th/18th century curtailed the growth and development of the indigenous institutions including Education.

4

Higher Education in the Arab World

M. M. MORSI

The Arab world has a population of about 130 million of whom about 70% are illiterate. This represents a major educational problem. Modern education is relatively new in the Arab world, and was introduced on European lines at the beginning of the nineteenth century. Egypt had a longer history of such education and consequently a more developed educational system than other Arab countries. Public education in the Arab world is provided at present for a period ranging from 11 to 12 years and embraces the age group between 6 to 18. It is divided into the three stages: primary, intermediate and secondary. The most common pattern of school organization is 6-3-3. Education is provided free in state schools and even in universities in all Arab countries. Schooling is compulsory in most Arab systems of education but only in the primary stage between the ages of 6 and 12. There is a general tendency to raise the school leaving age up to 15, and Jordan was the first to have done so.

At present there are more than 15 million pupils in all public schools in the Arab world and about 75% of them are in primary schools. The main problems of public education, are: the pressure of the ever increasing social demand on education, the strain caused by social mobility from rural to urban areas, the great and largely unsuccessful efforts to eradicate illiteracy the slow rate of educational expansion especially for women, the comparatively low standard and quality of education, the inadequacy of school building and equipment, the shortage of teachers especially of mathematics, science and foreign languages and finally the high rates of drop-out and wastage.

Higher education represents the tertiary level of education (i.e. post-secondary education). It consists of two types of institutions—universities and institutes.

The universities enjoy higher prestige than institutes even when they grant the same degrees. At present there are 26 universities in all the Arab world, nine of them are in Egypt alone including al-Azhar which has developed into a modern university from the traditional college and mosque under the same name. They are generally similar in their organization, but they vary in size and the number of faculties. Some follow the commonly known graded course system, others follow the credit hours system widely known in American universities. The faculties or colleges which are the main type of institution may be divided into two main categories—humanities and science and technology. The academic year comprises 30 weeks. The courses of study comprise four years in humanities leading to the B.A. and four years in science, five years in pharmacy and engineering, and six and a half years in medicine (plus one year training) leading to B.Sc. All faculties have their own system of research and post-graduate studies leading to M.A. and Ph.D., and this is particularly true of Egyptian universities.

The Institutes are the second type of higher education. Their courses and period of study vary considerably from one country to another and even within the same country. In general they are mainly technical and polytechnical institutes which aim at training professionals and technicians in commerce, agriculture, Industry, and special careers such as social work and hotel management. The duration of study varies from two years leading to a diploma to four or five years leading to a diploma or a B.Sc.

Under higher education come also teacher training institutes for primary school teachers. Their courses of study comprise two years after secondary education or five years after preparatory education.

There was considerable increase, especially in university enrollment. In Egypt alone, the number of students attending universities has more than doubled in the last ten years. About half the total number of students receiving higher education are in Egyptian universities. In

1973 their number was more than 200,000.

Arab higher education suffers generally from a certain shortcoming including lack of coherent and planned policy, a predominantly abstract character, verbal teaching, quantitative expansion not always matched by high quality, insufficient research, inadequacy of facilities, shortage of staff and equipment, too high expansion in humanities and as a result in ability to cope with social and economic demands of society.

The growing demand on higher education varies of course from one country to another, but it amounts to pressure in Egypt. The pressure began in 1953 when a system was introduced according to which certain students may register without being allowed to attend lectures. They have to study the courses privately, and sit for the examination at the end of the year. This system which is similar to non-campus colleges in the U.S.A. is allowed only in arts, law, and commerce colleges.

The difference between theory and practice in admission is great. Thus in 1974 the estimated number of admissions into Egyptian universities was 40,000 students, but the actual number admitted was 66.000. One of the main challenges confronting all Arab educational systems is demographic. Apart from the higher birth rate, more than half the population is under 24 years of age, and there is now higher expectation of life due to improved living standards. This problem is common to all Arab educational systems and constitutes a constant strain on education at all levels including higher education.

Higher education, especially in universities, enjoys high esteem and prestige. Hence the great demand on it as a free social service, provided without any discrimination on social, financial or religious grounds. But it is interesting to note that a research conducted on the changing social origins of students in Egyptian universities found that more than half the sample of the students of the prestigious colleges of medicine came from peasant origins and low income families.

National pride is one of the main factors contributing to the unplanned expansion of higher education, particularly universities.

Several rich Arab countries have established their own universities without regard to cost or the needs of society. With more thought and coordination, central or regional colleges might have served the Arab world as a whole. The Arab League Association of Universities aims at introducing some co-ordination and overcoming such wastage.

Large universities in Egypt are matched by small ones in Libya and Kuwait. And yet with her limited resources Egypt must discharge her obligations towards the Arab world by supplying Arab universities and institutions with the teaching staff and other personnel. While Egyptian universities suffer from acute shortage of staff, many of the best Egyptian professors are seconded every year to various Arab universities.

Institutions of higher education in the Arab world as in other countries accept in principle that one of their functions is to undertake research in order to promote knowledge and advance culture. In practice such research suffers from insufficiency of essential facilities such as new books, periodicals and laboratory equipment. The problem is aggravated by a shortage of skilled technicians who can operate or maintain sophisticated equipment. Hence, when such equipment is available it is sometimes not used. Obsolete concepts and stringent administrative measures also hinder research and training.

It may sound strange in this democratic age to remark that Arab universities seem to contain at present more students than can profit from higher education. This is not only a waste of public money but also of manpower. This overcrowding at the universities is bound to hinder the raising of academic standards.

There is still a considerable amount of teaching in Arab universities through the medium of a foreign language, mostly English. There is still some teaching through the medium of French at a lower level in the schools of the Arab states in North Africa that were formerly under French control. The problem of Arabicizing education by teaching through the sole medium of the national language, while providing for the teaching of foreign languages for facilitating study and research is still awaiting a solution.

Reference has been made above to Egypt's practice of seconding some of its best professors for service in Arab universities. This is at once a lesson in self-denial and inter-Arab cooperation in education. In this sense it does not constitute a 'brain drain'. But there is unfortunately such a drain in other directions: the loss of Arab talent to countries in the west that can do without it. This is a problem common to all developing countries. It is by no means uncommon for students from those countries training in western institutions to be attracted by the better living conditions and higher pay to stay in western countries instead of going back to help develop their own countries. Because of the greater need of their native land this kind of desertion is almost like that of a soldier from the battle field.

5

Elementary Schools in Hijaz

ABDUL LATIF BIN DUHAISH

The growth and development of Islamic education is closely associated with the advent of Islam which paid due attention to the study of the holy Qur'an as the basic source of knowledge and the codified Islamic law. For this purpose, since the very beginning of Islamic period, there existed two basic academic institutions, *viz.*, elementary schools and mosques. Both of these shouldered the responsibility of teaching the holy Qur'an and other Islamic and Arabic sciences.

While the elementary schools took the responsibility of teaching the youngsters the holy Qur'an, the "reading," "writing" and "arithmetic," the mosques held the academic circles (*halaqat al-dars*) to teach the specialized branches of Islamic learning like exegesis (*tafsir*), Prophetic traditions (*Hadith*), jurisprudence (*fiqh*), syntax (*nahw*), literature (*adab*) etc.

During the 4th century after the Hijrah/9th century A.D., a third kind of academic institution came into existence which was known as Islamic Schools or Nizamiyah Schools. These schools were reserved for teaching specified subjects and were identified by their definite fields of study and their special system. They were normally attached either to the mosques or to some special buildings near it.

The present article deals mainly with one of these institutions, namely, elementary schools. We shall first of all make a general study of these institutions and thereafter provide as much material as we can about the elementary schools of the Hijaz during the first half of the 14th century.

Elementary Schools

Al-kuttab (pl. *katatib*), a place of reading and writing, was one of those important academic centres of the Muslim society wherein the youngsters were trained mentally and morally through Islamic teachings.

According to Baladhuri, *al-kuttab* (the elementary school) was known popularly even before the advent of Islam. The great number of businessmen in Makkah, who had acquired knowledge of reading and writing for their trade purposes, is a proof of the presence of such kinds of institutions. It is mentioned that there were seventeen persons among the Qurayshites who knew reading and writing at the advent of Islam which is also a clear proof that the elementary schools existed at Makkah in those days.

This, however, has been refuted by 'Abd al-Rahman Salih 'Abd Allah who says, "In fact arriving at such a conclusion is not so natural since the Qurayshites had a close relation with the neighbouring nations on account of trade and commerce. It is most likely, therefore, that they had learnt reading and writing from those who they came in contact."

Nevertheless, the fact remains that the centres of teaching did exist before Islam, whether in Makkah or elsewhere. Often they were known by names other than the popular name of *al-kuttab* or elementary school. The sole purpose of their existence was teaching "reading" and "writing" and the teachers who were engaged in these elementary schools for teaching had not embraced Islam yet.

With the expansion of Islam, learning began to be imbued with the Islamic spirit and new centres grew for the spread of Islamic teachings. These centres were none but the elementary schools and the mosques which were filled with the Islamic spirit. Thus the elementary schools grew in every town and village to attain high cultural standard for the Muslims. In this way the task of establishing elementary schools was accomplished with its academic programme concentrating on the teaching of the holy Qur'an, the knowledge of reading and writing and arithmetic. A separate house (as a building for school) was not the only place where knowledge could be imparted ; it was also extended to the mosque. Thus there were a number of elementary schools at various corners of the mosques. The interest of the people towards education and the Qur'anic studies was due to the following main factors :

(1) The very first verse of the Qur'an revealed upon the holy Prophet (p.b.u.h.) contains the exhortation for learning. Thus Allah says,

> Read : In the name of thy Lord who createth,
> Createth man from a clot.
> Read : And thy Lord is the Most Bounteous,
> Who teacheth by the pen,
> Teacheth man that which he knew not.

The holy Qur'an in many other verses also points out the importance of knowledge, its acquisition and the high position which the scholars occupy. Thus Allah says,

Are those who know equal with those who know not? Similarly it is said,

Allah will exalt those who believe among you, and those who have knowledge, to high ranks.

Again the Glorified Allah says,

...and say : My Lord ! Increase me in knowledge.

Further, it is said,

> As for these similitudes, We coin them for mankind,
> but none will grasp their meaning save the wise.

Such exhortations are also found in the *Hadith* where the people have been urged to acquire knowledge. Thus the Prophet said, "One who goes out in search of knowledge remains in the path of Allah till he returns."

Thus Islam had all along insisted upon the dissemination of knowledge without making any distinction between male and female education. In fact, it rendered the acquisition of knowledge a bounden duty for a Muslim man and a Muslim woman.

The Prophet had ordered to learn besides Arabic the foreign languages that reigned supreme during those days. Hence the Prophet asked Zayd b. Thabit, the scribe of revelations, to learn Hebrew, the language of the Jews, in the 4th century A.H. He said, "Learn the Jewish script for I, by Allah, have no faith in the Jews regarding their Book." According to another report, he said to him, "Letters from people are sent to me ; I do not like that any other person except you should read them. Can you, therefore, learn Hebrew script ?" Zayd replied, "yes." In this way we find that Islam has left the Muslims' intellectual faculty free and exhorted them to achieve knowledge so as to meditate and ponder over the universe.

Among the course of action that the Prophet had taken to give impetus to learning among the Muslims at the beginning of Islam was the incident in which the ransom of every educated prisoner from amongst the disbelievers who had been captivated after the battle of Badr was fixed as teaching the uneducated Muslims "reading" and "writing."

(2) The expansion of the boundaries of Islamic empire led to the establishment of various offices and government departments. It was thus compulsory for those who wished to serve the government offices to be well versed in reading and writing.

It is mentioned that after the advent of Islam 'Umar was the first to gather the children in the elementary school. Appointing 'Amir b. 'Abd Allah al-Khuza'i, he ordered him to keep the children occupied in attaining knowledge and fixed 'Amir's salary from government treasury (*Bayt al-Mal*). 'Umar, may Allah be pleased with him, directed that the dull students should be taught through writing on the tablet (*lawh*), while the intelligent ones should be taught orally, without making use of writing. 'Umar used to make them witnesses to prove matters liable to be forgotten with the passage of time. Among such matters may be mentioned the study of ethnology, species and tribes. On the students' demand to improve the teaching system, 'Umar ordered the teachers to take their classes from the morning prayer till the sun had come up fully and from the afternoon prayer to the *'Asr* prayer. Thereafter, the students were allowed to take rest for the remaining part of the day. After issuing this order, he proceeded to conquer Syria and stayed there for a month. Then he returned to Madinah where the people were feeling lonely without him. So they went out to meet him. The young pupils met him at the distance of a day's journey. That day happened to be Thursday. So the students spent the night and returned with him on Friday. This outing caused fatigue to them whereupon he introduced the legal rule of taking rest during these two days. This became a precedent (*Sunnah*) and he prayed for those who followed that practice and reprimanded those who stopped and discontinued this precedent.

Learning in the elementary schools continued to be on the same pattern as it was in 'Umar's time. During the Umayyad period there appeared some eminent scholars who graced the Muslim society. Well-known among them were: Al-Dabhak b. Muzahim (d. A.H. 105). Kumayt b. Yazid (d. A.H. 126) and 'Abd al-Hamid al-Katib (d. A.H. 132). As regards the famous scholars who wrote about the elementary schools the following may be mentioned : Ikhwan al-Safa , al-Ghazali, Ibn Juma'ah, Ibn Khaldun, Nasir al-Din al-Tusi, and Ibn Hajaral-Haythami.

Ahmad 'Abd al-Ghafur, after extracting the gist of what had been written by Ikhwan al-Safa' and others, critically examined and finally incorporated the result of his findings in his book entitled *Adab al-Mu'allimin.* This book is considered as the best account of the systems of education in the elementary schools and elsewhere. After Ikhwan al-Safa' came al-Qabisi who compiled a book regarding children's education and named it as *al-Ta'lim fi Ra'y al-Qabisi.* Since a large number of books and pamphlets have been composed on this subject, it is not possible to mention them all here.

The elementary schools, spreading all over Islamic territories, included in their curricula, the study of the holy Qur'an, its recitation, memorization, intonation (*tajwid*), Prophetic traditions, Islamic laws (*al-Ahkam al-Shar'iyah*), and the simple arithmetic and calligraphy.

Coming to the elementary schools in Hijaz during the half century, i.e. A.H. 1295-1345, in may be stated that this survey is based on intensive study of various original sources available on the subject. It is through these sources that the following information about the elementary schools of Hijaz during the above mentioned period had been acquired. We shall first of all give a statistical information about the elementary schools in the main cities of Hijaz. Thereafter a general survey will be made.

Elementary Schools in Makkah

In the first official report of the Ottoman Empire regarding the Hijaz State, issued in A.H. 1301, it has been shown that there had been in Makkah in 1301/1883-1884 thirty-three elementary schools with 1150 students. They were distributed in all localities of Makkah as under :

Zone/Locality	*No. of Elementary Schools*
Suq al-Layl	4
Al-Khararah	5
Al-Qashashiyah	3
Sha'b 'Amir	5
Al-Niqa	1
Al-Sulaymaniyah	1
Al-Misfalah wa Jiyad	1
Al-Shabikah	4
Harrat al-Bab	3
Al-Shamiyah	6
Grand Total	33

It appears that this number of elementary schools has been given in view of continuous yearly increase. Thus, according to the official report of the Ottoman Empire, the number of elementary schools at Makkah had increased to 43 in the year 1309/1891-1892.

In his report regarding the province of Hijaz in the year 1889/1300, the British consulate at Jeddah emphatically confirmed that the Makkans used to take a keen interest in education. He remarked that the special elementary schools established by the cultured group of this region received a hearty reception by the Makkans as well as other people of the Hijaz zone.

It appears that the progress in the increase of elementary schools at Makkah had been fairly slow since some of these schools had completely vanished while a few others appeared on the scene. This happened during the period under our study, i.e. between A.H. 1295 and 1344.

Special Elementary Schools to Teach Good Handwriting

Alongwith the elementary schools above-mentioned (i.e. *tajwid*), there were other schools specialized in teaching calligraphy, arithmetic, geometry, commerce and business. These elementary schools were sometimes known as *al-khitat* or *katatib al-khatt* (the schools of calligraphy). The important among them were named after the following scholars:

1. Al-Khalusi;
2. Al-Shaykh Muhammad Hilmi, situated at Bab al-Safa in the Masjid al-Haram;
3. Al-Shaykh 'Ali Kutbi, located outside Bab Ziyadah in the *haram* of Makkah;
4. Al-Shaykh Muhammad Marzuqi;
5. Al-Shaykh Mahmud Zuhdi;
6. Al-Shaykh Taj Farj Ghazawi, situated outside Bab Ziyadah;
7. Al-Shaykh Muhammad Farj Ghazawi—the school was located in his own house and its students were the sons of chiefs and noblemen of Makkah;

8. Al-Shaykh al-Farisi, located outside Bab al-Salam;
9. Al-Shaykh Muhammad Tahir 'Abd al-Qadir Kurdi;
10. Al-Shaykh Sulayman Ghazawi, located in his house at Harrat al-Bab;
11. Al-Shaykh Ibrahim Halwani, located at Bab Ziyadah, inside the *haram* of Makkah.

A few of these special elementary schools carried out their duties of teaching good handwriting to the students in some corners of the Masjid al-Haram, especially the area situated at Bab 'Ali and the regions adjacent to Bab Ziyadah inside the Masjid al-Haram. Other elementary schools were those which were located in the houses of the teachers themselves.

At Makkah there were special elementary schools for girls also where lady teachers were employed to teach. The subjects taught in these schools were similar to those taught to male students. These included reading and writing, recitation and memorization of the Qur'an, intonation (*tajwid*), arithmetic and basic principles of religious sciences and ethical behaviour.

Among these special elementary schools for girls were the following:

1. Lady Ashisa [?] Elementary School : It was founded in the beginning of the 14th century A.H. and was situated at al-Marvah.
2. Al-Shamiyah Girls' Elementary School : It was established in the beginning of the 14th century A.H. and was located at al-Shamiyah.
3. Al-Sawliyah Elementary School for Girls : Its foundation was laid in the year A.H 1340 and was situated at Harrat al-Bab near al-Sawliyah School. The school existed till the year 1383/1963 and the number of lady teachers at the time of its closure was four while the number of girl students was around 140. The girl students of this school were later shifted to the government schools.

Elementary Schools at Madinah

As for the elementary schools of Madinah in the period under study, it is mentioned in the annual report of Hijaz for the year 1301/1883 that there existed thirteen ordinary elementary schools, established by the Sultans 'Abd al-Hamid and Mahmud, and one special elementary school dedicated for teaching good handwriting only. At the time when Shaykh 'Ali b. Musa visited Madinah in the year 1303/1885, there were 24 elementary schools in which one was set apart for teaching the elementary Persian.

According to Ja'far Faqih's report about education in Madinah, at the end of 13th century/beginning of the 20th century there existed fourteen elementary schools. Six of these were located inside the Prophet's mosque while the remaining eight were outside. The schools inside the mosque were run by the following :

1. Al-Shaykh Mustafa b. Ahmad Faqih : The teaching was started in A.H. 1273. Later it was taken over by his brother Ibrahim.
2. Al-Shaykh Mustafa al-Zahar: The teaching was started in A.H. 1300. Then it was taken over by al-Shaykh Muhammad al-Tabi'i and thereafter by 'Abd al-Fattah Abu Khudayr.
3. Al-Shaykh Barahim al-Tarudi : The teaching in it commenced in the year A.H. 1300.
4. Al-Shaykh Bashir al-Maghribi : The teaching commenced in the year A.H. 1300.
5. Al-Shaykh Ahmad.
6. Al-Shaykh 'Ubayd al-Sinari and al-Shaykh al-Hafiz Hamdi Afandi who used to teach the good handwriting and Turkish and Persian languages.

The eight schools located outside the mosque at different places in Madinah were as follows :

1. Elementary school of al-Shaykh 'Abd al-Qadir Bishr, situated at al-Anbariya ;

2. Elementary school of al-Shaykh Hamid Shaykh, situated at Muradiya in al-Sib ;
3. Elementary school of Muhammad al-Ghati in al-Munakha;
4. Elementary school of al-Shaykh 'Abd al-Qadir al-Shani, located in the mosque of 'Ali b. Abi Talib (May Allah be pleased with him) :
5. Elementary school of al-Sharif al-Maghribi, situated in al-Mashariya.
6. Elementary school of Jalal Ilyas, located in al-Sabaq Mosque ;
7. Elementary school of al-Shaykh Muhammad Khalil, situated at Quba;
8. Elementary school of al-Shaykh Ishaq al-Turki in the Masjid al-Qiblatayn.

Muhammad Labib al-Batnuni has pointed out that during his visit to Madinah in 1327/1909 he saw seventeen schools where basic ordinary sciences were taught.

It is evident that during the period under study, the number of these schools in Madinah were more than this. It is also possible that the period when he visited Madinah was the time of the visit of *Hajj* pilgrims to the Prophet's mosque. The mention of very small number of elementary schools in Madinah leads us to believe that it was the vacation period when the students as well as the teachers had engaged themselves in serving the pilgrims of the mosque, as was the usual practice of the residents of Madinah who considered the religious seasons a great source of sustenance for them.

There existed a number of elementary schools of good handwriting in Madinah, the majority of them being located at the corners of the Prophet's mosque. But the source material available to us does not provide us with enough information with regard to these elementary schools and their numbers.

Alongside the elementary schools for male children there were special schools for girls, though they were limited in number. The education in these girls' schools was similar to that of the boys' schools. This included the teaching of the Qur'an, its recitation, memorization of some of its parts, and often, memorization of the whole of the Qur'an, depending on the girl's liking and her academic capabilities. Besides studying the holy Qur'an, the students also used to complete their education in reading, writing, learning rules of Prayer (*Salah*) and Fasting (*Sawm*), and arithmetic.

It is necessary to point out that sometimes girls were admitted in the boys' schools, provided their ages did not exceed eight years after which they were disallowed to continue their studies in these schools and had to join the schools meant for girls only.

Schools of Jeddah

According to the official report of the province of Hijaz, issued in 1305/1887-88 and 1306/1888-89 there were nine and ten officially registered elementary schools respectively in the city of Jeddah during this period. Through the report of Shaykh Muhammad Husayn Nasif we come to know that during his childhood there were several elementary schools at Jeddah some of which are as under :

1. School of al-Shaykh 'Abd al-Mun'im : al-Shaykh was associated to it in 1307/1889 ;
2. School of al-Shaykh Khalil Muhammad ;
3. School of al-Shaykh Muhammad al-Dasuqi ;
4. School of al-Shaykh 'Abd Allah Nasif.

Al-Shaykh Muhammad Nasif reports that there were a few special schools at Jeddah which were solely reserved for teaching good handwriting (*husn al-khatt*) to students ; the famous among them was the school of al-Shaykh Taha Ridwan which taught this art to the sons of the rich people and businessmen of Jeddah.

Ibrahim Rif'at, who visited the city of Jeddah in the year 1318/1901, reported that there were nine elementary schools in Jeddah. This, however, does not seem to be the exact figure ; perhaps the nine schools referred by him were the only ones he knew of. It is also probable that while recording this information he relied on the Annual Report of the Hijaz Province issued in 1305/1887-1888 for the number described by him tallies with the number referred to in the above report.

Muhammad 'Ali Maghribi reports that besides the boys' schools there were also special girls' schools. The most famous school was the school of Khadijah al-Shamiyah who was blind. The education in the girls' schools was not much different from that of the boys' schools.

Schools in Other Regions of Hijaz

The existence of elementary schools was not restricted to the main cities of Hijaz alone; rather, they were found throughout small towns and villages, located generally in the corners of the mosques.

According to the official report regarding Hijaz Province for the year A.H. 1306, there were four elementary schools at Taif. Ibrahim Rif'at reports that at the time when he visited the city of Wajh in the year 1318/1901 there was only one elementary school there. About this he says, "It was a small elementary school where I found no books whatsoever for teaching purposes. I, therefore, sent to it a copy of the Qur'an in separate parts and several independent parts of *"Amm"* and *"Tabarak,"* so that the holy Qur'an could be learnt by the children of the city. In his second trip in the year 1320/1903 he visited Yanbu and found that there was only one primary school there for learning.

Premises of Elementary Schools

Before the advent of Islam, the abode of elementary schools used to be the very house of the owner. But after the advent of Islam and spread of mosques everywhere, the "residence" did not remain the only place of learning. Instead, it was extended to other places also. Thus the monasteries and poor houses became the abode of many elementary schools. However, the teaching of small boys in the mosque was forbidden since children did not take care of the cleanliness of the mosque nor of its tranquillity. That is why when Imam Malik was asked to give his opinion about the permissibility of the establishment of an elementary school in the mosque, he remarked, "I do not consider it permissible because the children do not protect themselves from impurity." Similar reports are found in the books on *Hisbah.* Thus it is said, "The teaching of children in the mosque should not be considered proper, for there is a fear that these kids would blacken and smear its walls." But, despite this note of warning, it is affirmed that some of the school teachers adopted the corners of the mosques or some of its adjacent rooms as the premises of these schools, thus ignoring the consequences referred to in these recommendations.

In the elementary schools of Hijaz, the pupils used to sit on the ground covered usually with straw mats or carpets. Some of these schools later began to use stone benches, wooden desks (*dikak*) or long wooden benches on which more than two students used to sit in parallel rows in the house of the owner of the elementary school. The sons of the chiefs were accompanied by servants who brought earthen containers of drinking water for them. Muhammad 'Ali Maghribi describes an elementary school at Jeddah thus : "It was a room on the ground floor of one of the houses carpetted with straws (*khasaf*)."

Curricula and Method of Education

The course of study in the elementary schools of Hijaz began with acquainting the child firstly with unvowelled letters (*al-huruf al-hija'iyah*), then the letters with different vowels (*al-huruf al-muharrakah bi al-harakat al-mukhtalifah*), and thereafter the *abjadi* alphabet (*al-huruf al-ab jadiyah*) as given in well known *al-Qa'idah al-Baghdad-iyah.* In order to teach this, the teacher wrote three or four letters from amongst the unvowelled letters on the tablet (*lawh*) of the student. Each letter was written three times and had over it diacritical marks (*'alamat al-tashkil*) like *ba, bi, bu.* The student was required to read it several times till he learnt it by heart. After he memorised it, the teacher would write other letters according to the former order. This was repeated till the pupil learnt by heart all the letters alongwith diacritical marks.

Then came the stage of writing and formation of words. At this very time, the student was required to learn some of the short chapters (*surahs*) of the Qur'an. The first chapter with which the child started was the *Surat "al-Fatihah,"* followed by the *Surat "al-Nas."* The child continued to learn small verses/chapters by heart till he finished the last part *" 'Amma Yatasa'alun."* Then he went over to other chapters till he finished the Qur'an. His study of the Qur'an used to be in the descending order. Thus he commenced with Part 30 and ended with Part 1 of the Qur'an. This was in view of the fact that sometimes a student did not consider it sufficient to learn the Qur'an alone ; instead he wanted to memorise one or more chapters and often the whole of the Qur'an. This depended on the receptivity of the child and the financial capabilities of his father.

In the majority of the schools the students were required to acquire full proficiency in reading and writing and to learn such elementary mathematics as numerals, the rules of addition, subtraction, multiplication and division. This was in addition to the study of the Qur'an, its memorisation—either in full or in its parts—and intonation (*tajwid*). The education was imparted sometimes in groups and at times individually, depending on the capabilities of the teacher of the school. As for the teaching of good handwriting, there existed special schools for it. The students in these schools practised good handwriting until they got perfection. The students could join these schools only after completing the study of the holy Qur'an. Although it was not a rule, yet most of the schools included the subject of 'good handwriting' alongwith other subjects in their prescribed courses of study. This can be borne out from the statement of 'Umar 'Abd al-Jabbar who says, "My father got me admitted along with my brother in the school of Shaykh 'Abd Allah Hamduh before the 'discrimination of alphabets' as they say. When the number of students in the *Diwan al-Saman* became too large, the school was shifted from Bab Ziyadah to Bab al-Basitiyah and was housed in one of the mansions of a nobleman. Then al-Shaykh 'Abd Allah Hamduh introduced reforms in his school when he divided in into several class-rooms and suggested that mathematics and good handwriting should also be taught alongwith memorisation of the Qur'an and its intonation. Thus the popularity of the school of al-Shaykh 'Abd Allah Hamduh grew and its reputation increased especially when the guardians witnessed their sons' avaricious desire to learn the Qur'an and their substitution as leader (*imam*) of the *tarawih* (special prayers offered in Ramadan). Al-Shaykh 'Abd al-Quddus al-Ansari reports that besides this the children of the schools of Jeddah also used to learn the basic *fiqh.*

The owners of these schools were known to the residents of Hijaz as *al-faqih, al-mu'allim, al-ustadh* or *al-mulla,* while the students, called them by the name *Sayyiduna* (our Sir) or *Ustadhuna* (our Professor). These titles varied from one zone to another and from one city to another. The owner of the school himself took charge of teaching all the students of his school. At times some of the owners borrowed the services of other teachers also to assist them in teaching. Most often, the owner took the help of the best students of his school in teaching the beginners. On other occasions, he asked one of these brilliant students to look after the school in his absence, and at times he even asked them to do some of his private work. Usually the term *al-'Arif* (the Monitor) was applied to him.

The teacher of the elementary school was normally good at heart, though he was attributed with severity and roughness. The canes and wooden sticks used to be the instruments of punishment. It was not strange, therefore, that the students sometimes ran away from the elementary schools, abhorred their teachers and conspired against them. Consequently, they became indifferent towards their studies and preferred to run away to play instead of studying.

In order to open the elementary schools, the owners were not required to obtain the consent of the official authorities of Hijaz. No condition or special qualification was necessary for this purpose. Anybody having the knowledge and experience of reading and writing was permitted to open a school to educate the youngsters either in the corners of the mosque or in his own house. In the same manner, he was fully authorised to close down the school whenever he desired to do so. However, special attention was paid to the teachers of good handwriting (*mudarris al-khatt*) who was required to be fully proficient in this art so as to teach it to his students in the most correct and perfect manner.

Those who intended to make their children religiously cultured entrusted their children to some of the scholars engaged in teaching and delivering religious sermons in the mosques, and asked them to remain attached to them. But the number of such students was very small.

Al-Sarafa and al-Qalabah Ceremonies

When the student completed the study of the Qur'an, or its entire memorisation or some part of it, the guardian held a ceremony suited to the auspicious occasion. To celebrate it, the students, clad in clean clothes and headed by their teacher, went out from the school alongwith the student who had finished his studies. The whole party walked towards the house of the student, in a form of procession, chanting the songs and couplets suited to that particular occasion. They were received and welcomed at the gate of the house by the guardian or some other relative of the graduating child. They were then led into the house and were served with refreshments. Thereafter all of them listened some verses of the holy Qur'an from the child who had memorised it. Then they turned towards the dining table where sweets, prepared specially for this occasion, were served to them. In addition to this, the guardian of the child presented some precious gifts to the teacher alongwith new clothes. With this the ceremony ended and the party was given a hearty farewell.

Muhammad 'Ali Maghribi adds that similar ceremonies were held for girl students as well. Thus he says, "whenever a girl (in Jeddah) completed the chapter "*al-Duha,*" the *Sarafa* ceremony used to be held for her. In this ceremony, the *faqihah* (the female teacher) and the girl students, headed by the graduating girl, walked towards her house in such a manner that the graduating girl carried a tablet (*lawh*) over which was written the chapter "*al-Duha.*" The whole party, forming a procession, reached the house of the girl where the relatives, the friends and the neighbours, invited to witness the ceremony, received them. There the *faqihah* asked the girl to sit before the audience and recite the verses of the Qur'an. Complying with her order, the garduating girl read the verse with the help of the tablet. This was highly applauded and thrilling cries of joy arose. Thereafter the *halwah* (sweets) and *sukkar al-nabat* (sugar candies) were distributed. The *faqihah* stayed on to take her meals with the family of the graduating girl and did not leave the house till she received a handsome amount of money from the girl's mother, and other sums, accumulated through *nuqut* ceremony, from other family members. Very often she was given a full suit of clothes in recognition of the endeavours she had made in training the girl and bringing her to such high level of education. If the girl had completed the Part 30 the ceremony used to be bigger and was known as *al-Qalabah.* Thereafter, the girl was not supposed to stay in the house of the *faqihah* since she had to learn after it other sciences as well. These celebrations were just like awarding of degrees of modern schools because the boys and the girls were not awarded a degree after they had completed their education in the *kuttab.*

Paraphernalia of a Student in the Elementary School

Among the tools of a student in these schools, there used to be a tablet (*lawh*) on which the teacher wrote for his students the alphabet, the words, or the sentences taught by him. When the student got perfection in it, he used to clean the tablet at a place reserved for this purpose in the school. He cleaned it by a cleansing material, known as *mudar,* and by water. It was thus prepared for writing a new lesson over it by teacher. Alongside this tablet, the child had to have either a copy of the holy Qur'an or the Part (*al-Juz'*) thereof which he was studying. Usually, the students did not carry these tablets and the copies of the Qur'an to their homes. Instead, they were asked to leave them in the school lest they were lost or destroyed, especially when it was known that some of the schools did not have enough tablets and sufficient copies of the Qur'an to be distributed among their students. In such schools, the children used these articles by turns.

Expenses of Studies

The education in these schools was not free. The guardians of the students had to pay a fixed amount of money for educating their sons or daughters in the school. The historical literary sources do not supply us with ample information in this respect. However, after making a thorough investigation we could get the following information according to which the guardians had to pay the fees for their children studying in the schools of Hijaz.

Snouck-Hurgronje, who visited Makkah in the beginning of the 14th century A.H., reports that the guardians at the time of admission of their wards in the schools at Hijaz used to pay to the school-teacher a sum of money in the shape of Turkish currency equivalent to one fourth of a dollar, reaching sometimes to two dollars. He had also to pay some cents to the teacher on very Thursdays. Similarly, the guardian used to send to the school-teacher presents and gifts on the occasions of *'Id* and other religious ceremonies.

When the student completed two-third or half of the holy Qur'an, the father used to pay to the teacher an amount ranging between one and three dollars. When the student completed the holy Qur'an, the teacher used to receive from the father a rich reward which, in the case of wealthy people, reached sometimes to an amount equivalent to thirty dollars in addition to a suit of clothes or a *jubbah* (gown).

When al-Shaykh Hasan al-'Ibadi opened his school at Makkah in the year 1316/1898, he made the following regulations for his school according to which the guardian had to bear certain fixed expenses for his ward seeking admission in his school :

1. Initially the guardian should pay to the Shaykh two Majidis (two Turkish Riyals) at the time of admission.
2. On every Thursday, he should pay to the Shaykh one-fourth Majidi, i.e. five piastres (*qurush*), known as *al-Khamisiyah*. Out of these, one piastre was charged for the mat, one for the water and three for the Shaykh.

3. When the student completed the chapters *"al-Fath,"* and *"al-Duha,"* and the Parts *" `Amm"* or *"Tabarak"*, the guardian had to pay to the Shaykh three Majidis (three Turkish Riyals). Out of these, half Majidi was reserved for the monitor who carried out the duty of writing with colours on the tablet (*lawh*) during *Sarafa* ceremony, half for the cost of colours, and the remaining belonged to the Shaykh who was also provided with sweets and *batasah* to be distributed among the students.
4. When the student completed the whole Qur'an, the guardian had to pay to the Shaykh fifteen Majidis. Out of these, two Majidis were reserved for the monitor while the rest were used by the Shaykh to provide sufficient quantity of sweets and coloured *batasah* for distribution among all the students of the school.
5. When the guardian arranged for his child the *Qalabah* ceremony, or gave in this connection a feast, the people other than himself were to throw coins on the tablet (*lawh*).
6. The guardian was required to pay respects to the Shaykh on different occasions. For instance, at the end of the month of Ramadan, he had to send the presents (*'Idi*) regularly.

Shaykh Muhammad Nasif in his report states that the guardian of the student in the schools of Jeddah used to pay to the school—teacher two or three Turkish piastres which was called *Khamisiyah* since it was paid on every Thursday. The amount used to be paid according to the financial position of the students' guardian.

Describing the schools of Madinah, Ja'far Faqih reports that the staff-members of the six elementary schools, located in the Prophet's Mosque, received their official salaries from the treasury of the Ottoman Empire at the rate of two hundred 'Uthmani coins for the Shaykh and one hundred 'Uthmani piastres for the monitor. As regards other elementary schools of Madinah, their staff-members received their salaries from the guardians of the students. The average amount per month paid by a father to the school—teacher as a tution fee of his son used to be one Majidi Riyal for the Shaykh and more than half of this amount for the monitor.

Working Hours and Holidays

Teaching in the elementary schools started early in the morning and continued till before the *Zuhr* prayer. Thereafter, the students came back to their houses to take their luncheon and rest for about an hour. Then they returned again to attend to their studies till the call (*adhan*) of *'Asr* prayer. In some schools the students continued their studies till the call of the *Maghrib* prayer. There used to be holidays on the afternoon of Thursday and full Friday, the two *'ids,* and religious and official occasions.

After the establishment of the Kingdom of Saudi Arabia these schools gradually disappeared as most of the students got themselves admitted in the government schools opened by the Kingdom in each region of the country. In these schools, immediate steps were taken to adopt modern methodology in education but on purely Islamic pattern. This made the demand of other types of elementary schools unnecessary, especially when the Kingdom itself took the responsibility in this respect and opened a large number of schools in every town and village, appointed teachers and made education free for all. Moreover, it awarded scholarships to the students encouraging them to take admission in these schools.

6

The Traditional Texts Used in the Persian Madrasahs

SEYYED HOSSAIN NASR

Abudl-Latif Tibawi's scholarship has made available a great deal of detailed knowledge of the curriculum and texts used in the programmes of various *madrasahs* in the Arab world. Many studies have also been devoted to the *madrasash* of Muslim India and the transformations they underwent during the past century. But much less attention has been paid to the detailed programme of the Persian *madrasah,* which in fact reflect more than the *madrasah* of many other areas the full spectrum of transmitted (*naqli*) and intellectual (*aqli*) sciences taught in the Muslim universities when they were in the full flower of their activity in the Abbassid and even later periods.

In Persia and certain adjoining areas such as Iraq, Afghanistan and some of the republics which now lie within the Soviet Union, until two or three generations ago there were many *madrasahs* in which not only law and theology but also all the other disciplines included in the traditional curriculum, ranging from medicine to astronomy, were still taught. It is only during the last century that even in this area some of the subjects have been discontinued, while others have been changed or modified and new books of instruction introduced for their teaching.

Nearly forty years ago the Persian scholar and statesman Seyyed Hasan Taqizadeh, who had himself received his early education in one of the *madrasahs* and who was much interested in the Islamic sciences, asked one of the leading Islamic scholars of the day, Muhammad Tahir Tabarsi, known as Mriza Tahir Tunikabuni, to write a treatise in which the works studied in the *madrasahs* would be described and made known to posterity before this knowledge became forgotten. Mirza Tahir, who was one of the leading traditional philosophers of Persia during the past century, set about this task and composed a treatise, which has been published only recently after a long period of neglect. It remains one of the most authoritative and complete works on the subject, reflecting the practice of Persian *madrasahs* for the several centuries which preceded the composition of the treatise in 1938.

According to Mirza Tahir, the texts used in various sciences in the *madrasahs* of Persia and adjacent regions were as follows:

THE TRANSMITTED (NAQLIYYAH) SCIENCES

I. The Science of Morphology (sarf)

1. *sarf-i-mir:* A short treatise in Persian on the subject by Mir Sayyid Sharif Jurjani, who lived in the 8th/ 14th century.

2. *Tasirf-i-zanjani* with commentary : The text was written by 'Izz al-Din Ibrahim Zanjani, who lived in the 7th/13th century, and commented by Sa'd al-Din Mas'udibn 'Umar Taftazani (8th/14th century).

3. *Sharh-i-nizam*: The text of this work is the *Shafiyah* of Jamal al-Din Abu Umar, known as Ibn Hajib Al Maliki (7th/13th century), while the commentary is by Nizam al-Din Hasan Nayshaburi, whose commentary is favoured over the numerous other commentaries written upon this celebrated work.

In older days, students also made use of the *marah al-Arwah* of Ahmad ibn 'Ali ibn Mas'ud, but this work lost its popularity and gradually was dropped from the list of the main texts to be studied.

II. The Sicence of Syntax (grammar) (nahw)

1. The *'Awamil* of Jurjani: The work of he 5th/11th century scholar, 'Abd al Qahir Jurjani, upon which many commentaries have been written, but it is the text itself which had remained popular throughout the centuries.

2. The *'Awamil* of Mulla Muhsin : Although some consider this work to be by Mulla Muhsin Fayd Kashani, the celebrated student of Mulla Sadra, most likely it is by Mulla Muhsin Muhammad ibn Tahir Qazwini, who lived in the late Safavid period and who also wrote a commentary upon the *Alfiyyah* of Ibn Malik.

3. The *Samadiyyah* : This celebrated treatise is by Shaykh Baha al-Din Amili and was written for his nephew 'Abd al-Samad. Numerous commentaries have been written upon it, of which the most famous are the major and minor commentaries by Sayyid 'Ali Khan, who was his contemporary.

4. The *Unmudhaj* : This is a summary by the famous 6th/ 12th century grammarian Jarallah Abu'l Qasim al Zamakhshari of his own extensive grammar, which is one of the peaks of grammatical studies of Arabic.

5. The *Kafiyah* : This is another of the important grammatical works of Ibn Hajib, upon which numerous commentaries have been composed in Arabic and Persian, including those of Sayyid Sharif Jurjani and Sayyid Rukn al-Din Astrabadi, who was a student of Nasir al-Din Tusi.

6. The *Alfiyyah*: This popular work by the 7th/ 13th century Andalusian grammarian, Ibn Malik, contains a thousand verses in which the principles of *nahw* are outlined. Of the numerous commentaries written upon it, that of Jalal al-Din al-Suyuti is the most popular in Persia.

7. The *Mughani al-labib*: A work by Jamal al-Din ibn Yusuf known as Ibn Hisham, who lived in the 8th/ 14th century. There are several well-known commentators of this work, including Muhammad ibn Abi Bakr al Damamini and Jalal al-Din al-Suyuti.

III. The Literary Sciences (Rhetoric (ma'ani wa bayan)) and the Art of Metaphors (badi)

1. Talkhis i miftah

The most popular work in this field has been the summary made by Jalal al-Din 'Abd al-Rahman Qazwini (8th/14th century) of the *Miftah al-ulum* of Siraj al-Din Yusuf al Sakkaki (7th/13th century), whose third section is devoted to the literary sciences. This summary is usually studied along with the two commentaries of Sa'd al-Din Taftazani, the long (*Mutawwal*) and the short (*Mukhtasar*).

2. Dala'il al-ijaz

This work by th 5th/11th century scholar, 'Abd al-Qahir Jurjani, has become popular only during the past century or two.

3. Asrar al balaghah

Another fairly short work by Jurjani.

IV. The Principles of Jurisprudence (Usul al fiqh)

1. Dhariah

This famous work is by 'Ali ibn Abi Ahmad Husayn, known as Sayyid Murtada as well as 'Alam al-Huda (5th/11th century).

2. 'Iddat al usul

One of the most respected works on *usul,* by the famous 5th/ 11th century Shiite scholar Shaykh al-Taifah Muhammad ibn 'Ali al Tusi, usually studied with the commentary of Mulla Khalil ibn Ghazi Qazwini.

3. Minhaj al wusul ila ilm al usul

By the 7th/13th century scholar, Najm al-Din Abul-Qasim, known as Muhaqqiq-i Hilli.

4. Minhaj al-wusul ila ilm al-usul

By the well-known 'Allamah Hilli (7th/13th), upon which Miqdad ibn 'Abdallah al-Suyuri al-Hilli has written a commentary.

5. Tahdhib al-usul

Another well-known work on the subject by 'Allamah Hilli.

6. Ma'alim al-din

This work by Hasan ibn Shaykh Zayn al-Din, known as

Shahid-i Thani (10th/16th century), is very popular and has been commented upon by numerous authors.

7. Zubdat al-usul

This is one of the best known religious works of Shaykh Baha al-Din 'Amili, upon which his own student, Jawad ibn Sa'dallah al-Baghdadi as well as Mawla Salih ibn Ahmad Sarawi have written widely studied commentaries.

8. The Kitab al-wafiyah

This short but masterly treatise is by Mulla 'Abdallah ibn Hajj Muhammad Tuni Bushrawi Khurasani (11th/17th century). Several of the outstanding scholars of the past three centuries, including Sayyid al-Sanad Bahr al-Ulum have written commentaries upon it.

9. The Qawanin

By the 13th/19th century jurisprudent Mirza Abu'l-Qasim ibn Muhammad Gilani.

10. The Fusul fiilm al-usul

This very popular work of Muhammad Husayn ibn 'Abd al-Rahim Tihrani Razi (13th/19th century) gained almost immediate acceptance after its composition.

11. The Fara'id al-usul

Also known as Raasa'il this work was composed a little over a century ago by Shaykh Murtada ibn Ahmad Amin Ansari.

Most of these works belong to the later centuries of Islamic history. There are also several other works in *usul* which were written earlier and were popular before the composition of these later works and which have continued to be studied, but not to the same extent as earlier. Some of these works are the *Mustasfi* of Ghazzali, the *Ahkam fi usul al-ahkam* of Sayf al-Din Amidi (7th/13th century), the *Mukhtasar al-usul* of his student, Ibn Hajib, upon which many commentaries have been written, the *Minjaj al-wusul ila ilm al-usul* by Qadi Nasir al-Din Baydawi (7th/13 century), the *Mahsul* of Fakhr al-Din Razi (6th/12th century), and its summary by Siraj al-Din Urmawi (7th/13th century) and the *jam al-jawami* of Taj al-Din al Subki al-Shafi'i (8th/14th century).

V. Jurisprudence (Fiqh)

Among the Shiites, the main sources of *Hadith,* which includes the sayings of both the Prophet and the Imams, and which serves after the Holy Qura'an as the fountainhead for the injunctions of the *Shari'ah,* consists of four books which are as follows :

1. The Kafi

The *Kitab al-kafi* comprised of both *usul* (principles) and *furu* (branches) by Muhammad ibn Ya'qub al Kulayni (4th/ 10th century), which is the most authoritative of all these sources. Numerous commentaries have been written on this work, especially upon the *usul,* including those of Mir Damad (10th/16th century), Mulla Sadra—his being one of the most important works of Islamic philosophy—Rafi al-Din Muhammad Tabatabai (11th/17th century) and Mulla Muhammad Bauir Majlisi (11th/17th century).

2. The Man *la yahduruhu l-faquih* of Ibn Babuyah, known as Shaykh-i- Sauq, upon which Mulla Muhammad Taqi Majlisi (11th/ 17th century) wrote two commentaries, one in Persian and the other in Arabic.

3. The Tahdhib

A major authoritative source by Shaykh al-Taifah Muhammad al- Tusi (5th/11th century).

4. Thc Istibsar

A second work of authority by Muhammad al-Tusi.

As for works on jurisprudence itself and its basis in the Quran and *Hadith,* numerous works have been written by both Sunni and Shiite authorities, of which thc following became particularly popular during the past few centuries when Persia became predominantly Shiite :

1. Wasa'il al shi'ah ila ahkam al Shari'ah

By Muhammad ibn Hasan, known as Shaykh Hurr-i-Amili (11th/17th century).

2. The Wafi

The *Kitab al -wafi,* by Mulla Muhsin Fayd Kashani (11th/17th century), is concerned mostly with both the traditions upon which *fiqh* is based and the injunctions themselves.

3. The Bihar al anwar

This voluminous religious encyclopaedia by Muhammad Baqir Majlisi includes nearly every branch of the religious sciences from sacred history to jurisprudence. All parts of this work have been and still are popular in *madrasahs* throughout Persia.

4. The Nihayah

By Muhammad al-Tusi with numerous commentaries by *mujtahids* of nearly every generation.

5. The Mabsut

Also by Muhammad al-Tusi and commented upon by numerous *mujtahids* over the ages.

6. The Sharayi al islam

By Muhaqqiq-i Hilli and usually studied along with its summary called the *Mukhtasar-i nafi.*

7. Masalik al afham ila fahm sharayi al istam

By Shaykh Zayn al Din, known as Shahid-i Thani.

8. Madarik al ahkam

By Shams al Din Muhammad ibn 'Ali Amili (10th/16th century). Many commentaries have been written upon this work, the most famous being the *jawahir al-kalam* of Muhammad Hasan Najafi (13th/19th century).

9. The Irshad al-adhhan fi ahkam al-iman

By Hasan ibn Yusuf ibn Mutahhar al-Hilli. Several well

known commentaries have been written upon it, such as the *Ghayat al-murad of* Jamal al-Din Makki, known as Shahid-i Awwal (8th/ 14th century), and *Majma al fa'idah wa'l-burhan* of Ahmad ibn Muhammad Muqaddas-i Ardibili (10th/ 16th century).

10. The Qawa'id-al ahkam

Also by Muhaqqi-i Hilli, Several important commentaries have been written upon it, such as the *Idah al qawa id* by the author's son, *Kanz, al-fawa* id by his nephew Sayyid 'Amid al Din, *Tami al-maqasid fi sharh al-qawa 'id* by Muhaqqiq-i Thani Nur al-Din 'Ali ibn 'Abd al-Ali Karaki 910th/16th century), *Kashf al litham 'an mu' dalat qawa'id al-ahkam* by Baha al-Din Muhammad Isfahani known as Fadil-i Hindi (12th/18th century), and *Miftah al-karamah fi sharh qawa'id al allakmah* by Sayyid Jawad 'Amili (12th/ 18th century).

11. Lum'a-yi dimashqiyyah

By Shahid-i Awwal with commentaries by Shahid-i Thani

During the last century, the *Makasib* and *Taharat* of Shayih Murtada Ansari, dealing with specific aspects of *fiqh* have also become very popular and have been commented upon by some of the most celebrated *mujtahids* of his era, such as Mulla Muhammad Kazim Khurasani and Sayyid Muhammad Kazim Yazdi.

VI. The Sciences of Hadith and its History (ilm-i dirayah

1. *Risalat al-bidayah fiilm al-dirayah*

By Shahid i Thani.

2. The Wajizah

By Shaykh Baha al Din Amili.

3. Rawashih al-samawiyyah

By the great philosopher and founder of the school of Isfahan, Mir Damad, who before composing his commentary upon the *Kafi*, wrote the *Rawashih* on the science of *Hadith.*

4. Nuzhat al-nazar fi sharh nukhbat al-fikar

Both the text and the commentary are by Hafiz Shihab al-Din

Asqalani (9th/15th century). The work has many other commentaries which, however, have not become popular in Persia.

5. The Alfiyyah

By Jalal al-Din Abu Bakr al-Suyuti (9th/15th century).

VII. The Quranic Sciences (tafsir)

This is the crown of all the Islamic sicences and possesses many branches. As far as the science of the recitation of the Quran (*qira'ah wa tajwid)* is concerned, the popular treatises in Persia have been the *qasidah, Hirz al-amani wa wajh al-tahani,* of Abu Muhammad Qasim al-Shatibi (6th/12th century), among the many commentaries upon which are the *Siraj al-gari*, of Ibn Qasih (8th/14th century), which is the best known, and the *Muqaddimah* of Muhammad ibn Muhammad al-Jazari (9th.15th century).

As for Quranic commentaries both those composed by Sunni scholars and Shiite ones are studied, the most popular being the following:

1. The *Tafsir* of 'Ali ibn Ibrahim Qummi (4th/10th century)

2. The Majma al-bayan

By Abu 'Ali Fadl ibn Hasan Tabarsi (6th/12th century), summarized by the author himself as *Majma al-jawami.*

3. Rawh al jinan wa ruh al-janan

By Abul-Futuh Razi (6th/12th century), a vast Persian commentary which is also a masterpiece of Persian literature.

4. Tafsir i safi

By Mulla Muhsin Fayd Kashani, a commentary which is at once gnostic and theological.

5. The Tafsir of Tabari

The celebrated commentary by the 4th/10th century author Muhammad ibn Jarir al-Tabari.

6. The Tafsir al-kabir

One of the most extensive of all Quranic commentaries, by the 6th/12 century theologian Fakhr al Din Razi.

7. The Kashshaf

By Jarallah al-Zamakhshari (6th/12th century). Upon it numerous commentaries have been written.

8. Tafsir anwar al-tanzil wa asrar al-ta'wil

By Qadi Nasir al-Din al-Baydawi. Many commentaries have been written upon this work.

9. Kanz al-irfan

By Miqdad ibn 'Abdallah Hilli (8th/14th century), dealing mostly with the Quranic basis of Shariite injunctions.

10. Zubdat al-bayan

By Ahmad ibn Muhammad (Muqaddas-i Ardibili), also dealing with the Quranic foundation of Shariite injunctions (*ahkam*).

THE INTELLECTUAL (AQLIYYAH) SCIENCES

I. Logic (mantiq)

1. Risala yi kubra

A short treatise in Persian by Sayyid Sharif Jurzani.

2. The Hashiyah of Mulla 'Abdallah

This is one of the most popular works on logic and consists of glosses upon the *Tahdhib al mantiq* of TAftazani by Mulla 'Abdallah Yazdi 9th/15th century). The work has two parts, the first on logic and the second on theology (*kalam*). The first part alone became widely popular while the second part is studied only among the religious students of Kurdistan.

3. Sharh-i shamsiyyah

The text of the *Shamsiyyah* is by Najm al-Din Dabiran Katibi Qazwini (7th/13th century), while the commentary is by Qutb al-Din Razi (8th/14th century), and is one of the most popular works on logic.

4. Sharh-i matali al-anwar

The text of *Matali al-anwar* is by Siraj al-Din Urmawi (7th/13th century), while the best known commentary is by Sayyid Sharif Jurzani.

5. Sharh-i man zumah

Both the text and commentary are by the great Qajar philosopher and sage, Hajji Mulla Hadi Sabziwari (13th/19th century). The work includes a complete cycle of traditional philosophy starting with logic and ending with eschatology and finally prophetology and ethics.

6. Sharh-i isharat

The celebrated *al-Isharat wa'l-tanbihat* of Ibn Sia (4th/5th/10th-11th century)with the commentaries of Fakhr al-Din Razi, Tusi and Qutb al-Din Razi has been over the centuries one of the mainstays of the programmers of study in various branches of philosophy including logic.

7. Jawhar al-nadid fi sharh mantiq al-tajrid

The *Tajrid* is Nasir al-Din Tusi's main theological work, but the first part is devoted to logic. With the commentary of his student 'Allamah Hasan ibn Yusuf ibn al-Mutahhar al-Hilli, this section on logic became known as a separate work and gained popularity during the past century.

8. al-Basa ir al-nasiriyyah

The work by the 7th/12th century philosopher Zayn al-Din 'Umar ibn Sahlan Sawaji was neglected until Muhammad 'Abduh wrote a commentary upon it and began to teach it at al-Azhar University in Cairo. It then gained popularity not only among Egyptian students but among Persian ones as well.

9. The logic of the Hikmat al ishraq

The whole of this masterpiece of *ishraqi* theosophy by the founder of this school, Shaykh al-ishraq Shihab al-Din Suhrawardi (6th/12 century), is extremely popular in Persia and is usually studied with the commentary of Qutb al-Din Shirazi and the glosses of Mulla

Sadra. The logic, which is a departure from Peripatetic logic, is usually studied by students after they study the usual works on formal logic based upon the *Organon* and the modifications made upon it by the Islamic logicians.

10. The logic of the Shifa

Because of its inaccessibility and difficult style, the logic of the *Shifa* of Ibn Sina has never become a popular work. But being the most thorough and extensive treatment of formal logic in Islamic philosophy, it could not escape the attention of the most advanced students of the subject, who usually studied it with the glosses of Mulla Sadra, Sayyid Ahmad 'Alawi' and several others of the later *hakims* of Persia.

II. The Philosophical and Theological Sciences (falsafah and kalam)

1. Sharh-i hidayah

The text of this celebrated work is by the 7th/13th century philosopher Athir al-Din Abhari and consists of three parts : logic, natural philosophy and metaphysics. The section on logic was commented upon by the 9th/ 15th century philosopher and Sufi Shams al-Din Fanari, but while this commentary has always been popular in Turkey, Syria and Iraq it has never become widely accepted in Persia. There are, however, numerous commentaries of fame on the last two sections, those of Husayn ibn Mu'in al-Din Mibudi Yazdi and Mulla Sadra being extremely well-known in Persia, Afghanistan and the Indian sub-continent.

2. The Tajrid

This work of Nasir al-Din Tusi is the main text for Shiite Kalam and is usually studied with the following commentaries:

(a) That of 'Allamah Hasan ibn Yusuf al Hilli;

(b) The *Tasdid al qawa id fi sharh tajrid al aqaid of* the 8th/14th century theologian Shams al-Din Ahmad Isfahani, to which Mir Sayyid Sharif Jurjani has written-important glosses.

(c) The very popular commentary of the 9th/15th century scientist, philosopher and theologian, 'Ala al-Din Qushchi, which is famous throughout the Islamic world and upon which over four hundred scholars have written glosses, including Dawani and Khafri.

(d) The *Shawariq al-ilham fi sharh tajrid al-kalam* by 'Abd al-Razzaq Lahiji (11th/17th century), which although incomplete is widely read and considered on e of the most important commentaries upon the Tajrid.

3. Sharh-i isharat

As already mentioned in the section on logic, the whole of the Isharat of Ibn Sina, not only logic but also natural philosophy and metaphysics, as commented upon by Fakhr al-Din Razi, Tusi and Qutb al-Din Razi, has been over the centuries and continues to be one of the basic texts of Islamic philosophy in Persia.

4. The Hikmat al-ishraq

The *Kikmat al-ishraq* of Suhrawardi along with the commentary of Qutb al-Din Shirazi and the glosses of Mulla Sadra constitutes the central work of the *ishraqi* school and is studied by everyone who wishes to master the doctrines of this school.

5. The Sharh-i manzumah

The already mentioned work of Sabziwari is as popular in the field of philosophy as it is in logic, and since the last century it has come to be taught in nearly all the *madrasahs* where philosophy forms part of the curriculum.

6. The Asfar al-arba'ah

The major opus of Mulla Sadra consists of four journey *(safar)* and deals respectively with metaphysics, natural philosophy, theodicy, and psychology and eschatology. This vast work is considered the most advanced treatise on philosophy in Persia and is studied only after the student has mastered all the other branches and schools of the 'intellectual' and even 'transmitted' sciences. Many commentaries have been written upon it, including those of the 13th/19th century students of Mulla Sadra's school, Mulla 'Ali Nuri, Hajji Mulla Hadi Sabziwari and Mulla 'Ali Zunuzi.

Several other works of Mulla Sadra such as al *mabda wa l-maad, al Shawahid al-rububiyyah, al-mashair, al-Arshiyyah, Mafatih al-ghayb* and *Asrar al-ayat* have also been popular among students of *madrasahs* since the beginning of the 13th/19th century when the teachings of Mulla Sadra were revived throughout Persia.

III. Sufism and Gnosis (tasawwuf and irfan)

1. The Kitab al tamhid fi sharh qawa id al-tawhid

Also called *Tawhid al qawaid,* this important treatise on the Sufism of the school of Ibn 'Arabi by Sain al-Din ibn Turkah (9th/15th century), deals with the two poles of all Sufi doctrine, the transcendent unity of being (*wahdat al-wujud*) and the universal man (*al-insan al-kamil.*) It has always been very popular as a treatise on gnosis (*irfan)* and has been commented upon by several masters including Aqa Muhammad Rida Qumasha.

2. Sharh i fusus al-hikam

The text of this most celebrated of all works on the doctrines of Sufism is by Muhyi al-Din ibn 'Arabi and numerous commentaries have been written upon it. As far as Persia is concerned, the most popular commentaries over the centuries have been those of Daud Qaysari (8th/14th century) upon which Aqa Muhammad Rida Qumsha has written extensive glosses; 'Abd al-Razaaq Kashani (8th/14th century); Abd al-Rahman Jami (9th/15th century), and Bali Afandi (10th 16th century). But these commentaries are nearly all based on that of Mu'ayyid al-Din Jandi which, however, has never become popular itself.

3. Sharh-i miftah al-ghayb

The text of this advanced work on Sufi doctrine is by Sadr al-Din al-Qumyawi (7th/13th century), the foremost expositor of Ibn 'Arabi in the East, and the commentary by Shams al-Din Hamzah Fanari, who has been already mentioned.

IV. Medicine (tibb)

1. Sharh-i nafisi

The text of this popular medical treatise is the *Mujaz* by Ala al-

Din Ali ibn Abi l-Hazm Qarashi (7th/13th century), which is itself an epitome of the *Canan* of Ibn Sina. The most famous commentary which has been printed with the *Mujaz* is by Nafis ibn 'Iward Kismani (9th/15th century). There are other commentaries upon the *Mujaz,* such as those of Jamal al Din Aqsara and Sadid al Din Kaziruni, which however, have never reached the fame of *Sharh-i nafisi.*

2. Shorh-i asbab

The text of this work is the *Asbab wa alamat of* Najib al-Din Samarqandi, the well-known 7th/13th century physician and pharmacopist and the commentary by the same Nafis ibn Iwad Kirmani mentioned above.

3. The Qanain (Canon)

This magnum opus of Ibn Sina, consisting of five books, is the most important medical work in Islamic medicine. It is usually studied in Persia with the commentaries of Fakhr al-Din Razi, Qutb al-Din al Misri, Ala al-Din Qarashi and Muhammad ibn Mahmud Amuli. But the most thorough and respected commentary is that of Qutb al-Din Shirazi which stands as a major medical work of its own.

4. Fusul-i Buqrat

Many of the works of Hippocrates have been popular among medical students, perhaps the foremost being the *Fusul,* which, in Persia, is usually studied with the commentaries of 'Abd al-Rahman ibn 'Ali (known as Ibn Abi Sadiq), Ibn Quff and 'Ala al-Din Qarashi.

V. The Mathematical Sciences (riyadiyyat)

One: Geometry

The students of geometry relied most of all upon the *Elements (usul)* of Euclid in the translation, recensions and commentaries of Hajjaj ibn Matar, Hunayn ibn Ishaq, Thabit ibn Qurrah and Abu 'Uthman al Dimashqi until the 7th/13th century. At that time, with the appearance of the *Tahrir* of *Nasir* al-Din Tusi, this work became the main text for the study of geometry along with the glosses of Mir Sayyid Sharif Jurzani. This in tun was translated into Persian and commented upon by Mulla Mahdi Naraqi (12th/18th century). Actually the section on geometry in the *Durrat al-taj* of Qutb al-Din Shirazi is also a Persian version of Nasir al-Din's recension.

Two: Arithmetic *(hisab)*

In the older days, the *Shamsiyyat al hisab* of Nizam al-Din Hasan ibn Muhammad Nayshaburi (7th/13th century), and the *Miftah al hisab* of Ghiyath al Din Jamshid Kashan were the most common works, but in the Safavid period they were replaced to some extent by the *khulasat al-hisab* of Shaykh Baha al-Din 'Amili (11th/17th century) with the commentary of his student, Jawad ibn Sa'dallah Kazimayni. In the Qajar period, Mu'tamid al-Dawlah Farhad Mirza wrote another important commentary upon it which also became popular.

Three: Astronomy (hay'at)

1. Risala yi farsi dar hay'at

The text is by the already mentioned 'Ala al-Din Qushchi and it is usually accompanied by the commentary of Muslih al Din Lari (11th/17th century).

2. Sharh-i mulakhkhas

The *Mulakhkhas* is by Mahmud Chaghmini (8th/14th century) and is commented by Musa ibn Mahmud, known as Qadizada-yi Rumi (9th/15th century), who composed it for Ulugh Beg. 'Abd al-Ali Birjandi and Mir Sayyid Sharif Jurzani have written glosses upon the commentary, which are usually studied with the text and the commentary, while many other existing glosses have been forgotten.

3. The Tadhkirah

This is the celebrated work of Nasir al-Din Tusi upon which many commentaries have been written, the most popular being that of Birjandi.

4. The Almagest

Since the early Islamic period, the *Almagest* of Ptolemy was popular in the Arabic translation of Hajjaj ibn Matar,, Ishaq ibn

Hunayn and Thabit ibn Qurrah. Later it was studied in the recension of Nasir al-Din Tusi with the commentaries of Nizam al-Din Nayshaburi and 'Abd al-'Ali Birjandi.

But before studying the *Almagest,* several other works were studied which stood between the *Elements* and the *Almagest* and which for this reason were called the 'intermediate' works (*mutawassitat)* They include:

(a) The *Spherics* of Theodosius.
(b) *On the Moving Sphere of* Autolycus.
(c) The *Spherics* of Menelaus.
(d) The *Optics* of Euclid.
(e) The *Data* of Euclid.
(f) The *Phenomena* of Euclid.

All of these works have been studied in the recension of Nasir al Din Tusi.

Four: Other Branches of the Mathematical Science

An important branch of these sciences, which always attracted the interest of students, was the science of the astrolabe, in which many works exist, such as the *Kitab al-usturlab of* 'Abd al-Rahman Sufi, whose *Suwar al-kawakib* has also always been popular; the *Istiab fil-amal bil-usturlab* of Biruni; the *Bist bab dar fann-i usturlab* of Tusi, upon which 'Abd al-'Ali Birjandi has written a commentary; and two treatises by Shaykh Baha al-Din 'Amili, one in Arabic called *Safihah* and the other in Persian entitled *Tuhfa yi hatami*

The description of the texts used in the *madrasahs* of Persian and adjacent areas until a couple of generations ago is an indication of the breadth of Islamic education when it was full alive and embraced all the intellectual disciplines. It is true that this *madrasah* system did not come to terms with the modern scientific disciplines in the same way that it did with the Graeco-Hellenistic ones, but the fault lies much more with the educational authorities who sought to establish separate educational systems than with the *madrasahs* themselves. Today, there is educational havoc nearly everywhere throughout the Islamic world, with contending and often contradictory educational systems vying of the souls and hearts of the new generation.

The *madrasah* system, as reflected in the breadth of the programme outlined above and as seen in the classical period when this system was at the height of its vigour, is not only the precious repository of the traditional Islamic sciences, but also the model which any total educational system claiming to be integrated within the various modes of Islamic culture, be in Persian, Arabic or Turkish, must follow in many basic ways. There is still a great deal that all contemporary Muslim educationalists can learn from the *madrasahs*, and these venerable institutions are of much greater import to the future educational life of various Islamic countries than the modern educationalists who are enamoured with the rapidly changing pedagogical theories of the West are willing of admit.

7

Educational Development in Turkey

SYED MAJID RAZA JAFFREY

The degree of progress made by a country emerging from a primitive to the more complicated economy of today, based on industry and mechanised agriculture, can be measured to some extent by the degree of literacy and especially of technical education among the population. All the countries of the Middle East are aiming at greater industrialisation, at the development of their raw material resources and at its processing, as far as possible, by themselves. They seek to import machinery and capital goods to this end. But not all of them take as yet very seriously the problem that is arising in the wake of these importations and developments, namely the training of the professional staff and of the skilled mechanics to run such equipment and undertakings such as hydro-electric plants, chemical industries or agricultural combine harvesters. The tendency in all these countries, including Turkey, the Arab lands and Persia, has been in the early stages of its renaissance, to produce in the schools and colleges potential members of the free professions. If they are doctors and teachers, they fit into the new economy. But unfortunately too many lawyers and journalists are produced to enable them all to find work. Consequently the ranks of the political agitators with a grievance and an ability to rouse the mobs of the principal towns are unduly swollen. But Turkey's reaction to this new situation is somewhat different from the others.

Until the middle of the nineteenth century the only schools that existed for the mass of the people were the religious ones—called Madressahs, run by Mullahs who only taught pupils to recite the Koran by heart in Arabic. Yet in the sixteenth century Turkey had the most powerful army in Europe and Western Asia, with the best equipment of the day. The economic advance of Western Europe which failed to influence Turkey, coupled with the Capitulations which gave privileges to importers of foreign goods, effectively killed all technical progress in Turkey in the nineteenth century. But at the time of the Tanzimat reforms in the middle of the nineteenth century an attempt was made to establish some secondary schools with a liberal education. This was encouraged by Sultan Abdul Mejid, in 1859 an Imperial decree ordered general and compulsory education, which, however, became largely a dead letter. Nevertheless, the Liberal Grand Vizier, Midhat Pasha, founded with State help industrial schools in Istanbul and the Balkan Provinces to teach boys various crafts. On the other hand, under the shelter of these Capitulations, British, American, French and, later, German schools were started. The famous Robert College at Istanbul and the American University at Beirut arose out of this movement. But unfortunately the results were not entirely satisfactory. Being foreign, they were to some extent suspected by the Government, as having political motives. The Moslem population patronised them only to a small extent. But the Christian minorities sent their children there in large numbers. Most of the younger generation of the more well-to-do Armenians, Greeks and Bulgars at the turn of the century had been to one of these foreign colleges, and this still further separated the Moslem from the Christian population of the Empire and increased the educational disparity. In the darkness of the reaction that accompanied the rule of Abdul Hamid II after 1876, nearly all education except that protected by the Capitulations was suppressed. Yet in spite of the reaction the Sultan realised that Turkey could not survive in the world without some education, especially technical, so he allowed Hassan Fehmi Pasha with private funds to found a Civil Engineering School at Istanbul in 1883, which later became the Istanbul Technical University.

But it was not till the Young Turk Revolution of 1908 that a real attempt was made to start primary education on a popular scale. Even then, however, decrees by the Government, supported by Parliament, ordering compulsory education became virtually a dead letter because, on account of high military expenditure connected with the Revolution and foreign complications arising from it, no money was available from the Treasury. So the responsibility of finding money for education was thrown entirely on the provinces, which meant that in practice virtually nothing was done.

The First World War showed how hopelessly backward Turkey was in general education and technical equipment, and the continuing wars from 1911 to 1922 made all technical progress impossible. At last, after the National Revolution in the 1920's a real start could be made. It is safe to say that not more than 10% of the population of Turkey could read or write in 1925, while the only section of the population where probably 40 to 50% were literate namely the Christians, had either succumbed in the war or had left the country. The Republic found itseif with a population of which 80% were living in villages, and there were about 3,000 primary schools and about 5,000 teachers. By 1935, twelve years after the foundation of the Republic, the number of primary schools was not more than 5,000 and the teachers not more than 7,000. So the prospect seemed grim.

But, as so often in Turkey, the hour brings forth the man and the idea to meet the situation. Led by the Ataturk himself and the Director of Education, Bey Hakki Tongush, a plan was drawn up to secure teachers. The first thing to do of course, was to get Turkey free from the Arabic alphabet, at least so the founders thought, and not without reason. So the Latin alphabet was introduced, partly for the sake of simplicity and partly to facilitate Western and European ideas. Then came the next difficulty. The primary schools could be built in the villages, given time. Most of the village elders were interested in Education and were ready to get the schools built. But there were no teachers there. The few teachers training schools that had been founded during the early days of the Revolution in the principal towns turned out young men who did not want to go back to the villages. The trouble, more or less common to all Middle Eastern states, was the idea that Education must lead to head-work in offices in the towns and that life in villages was beneath one's dignity. But the Turks showed by what happened in the 1930's that they had a way of solving this difficulty. Instead of training a young teacher in the towns and thus giving him the chance to acquire snobbish ideas about his superiority to his fellow citizens in the village to which he came, he was in future to be trained in 'village institutes' scattered about all over the face of Anatolia. Not only was the young teacher to have no taste of the comfort of the towns but he was to be trained under conditions of Spartan severity. The village institutes for training primary teacher were in remote regions and only had the bare necessities of life. The whole training was arranged so as to make the young man or woman learn that not only were they teachers but also leaders and pioneers of new ideas in the development of rural life. They were taught to dig irrigation canals, take the initiative in building a tractor station and repair shop, and help the village elder in any movement that aimed at raising the standard of life of the village.

The courses at the village institute were for six years, and covered not only the teaching of the three R's with geography and history but also practical work of carpentery and blacksmith, gardener and farmer work while the girls were taught housework, needlework, hygiene and cooking. The danger in these institutes is that the curriculum is so wide and the young teachers are supposed to cover such a large ground on so many subjects that it is impossible for them to master them all. It is probable that there is a good deal of superficial knowledge among many that issue from these institutes to take on the mastership of village schools up and down Anatolia. Yet there is no doubt that the main objective of the Ataturk and his colleagues has been attained. A start has been made and primary schools are now covering the greater part of the country. Improvement in the quality of teaching will doubtless come later. Meanwhile the numerical results are impressive. If in 1935 there were 7,000 teachers, after some years of village institutes these had risen to 35,000. This showed itself in the figures for primary school children. In 1945 out of about 3,000,000 children eligible to attend school, 1,026,410, actually attended. In 1949 this had risen to 1,700,000. By 1951 the figure was found about 2,000,000. About 1,000,000 children still do not receive primary education, either through lack of a school in the village where they live or lack of a teacher, or due to the remoteness of their home. The difficulty about building schools, however, is being got over. The peasants, whose responsibility it is to build the schools, are now getting Government grants for this, which formerly was not the case. As regards shortage of teachers, pending further recruits from the institutes, headmasters are appointed to cover a group of four or five schools and supervise instructors who are not fully qualified. It may be said, therefore, that two-thirds of Turkey's children are now receiving primary education, and the gap is closing. It can roughly be said that of the total population 70% are still illiterate in the village, but probably not more than 20% or so in the towns. It may be guessed, therefore, that perhaps 60% of the population of Turkey is literate. The only other country in the Middle East which has anything comparable to this is the Arab Republic of Syria, where the French did great pioneer work in the last half-century. But Turkey achieved this result by her own efforts after the Revolution, and her primary education today forms a basis on which her higher and technical education can definitely be built.

But all this has not been without some opposition and obstruction from the reactionary elements in the remoter parts of Anatolia. A graphic account of the sort of difficulties experienced by a young teacher in one of the poorest parts of Anatolia near the Tus Gol is given in a book published recently in English translation. The book created a sensation at the time, but is in some degree exaggerated. It undoubtedly shows, however, that the Ankara Government and the progressive forces in modern Turkey have even now to meet the hostility of secret societies based on the suppressed Dervish Orders, who still hanker after reviving the regime of the old Sharia religious law.

In order to pave the way for some form of specialisation, so that a pupil leaving the primary school can acquire some knowledge of a trade, there have been started over a wide area vocational courses for boys and girls who have finished their primary education after thirteen years of age. This is designed to assist the education of those who for one reason or another are unable to go to higher Educational institutions. The establishment of scholarships and bursarships gives assistance to the more promising pupils from the primary schools, but they are not sufficiently generous yet to give all children a chance, and those whose parents need their help at home must have recourse to the vocational courses in the villages. There are commercial courses given by some instructors in a local business on book-keeping, accounts and typewriting. There is a garden and farming class, giving a boy or girl some knowledge of horticulture or agriculture. There is a course of carpentery and metal-work, and for girls domestic courses in sewing, cooking and hygiene. The numbers of these schools, called 'Sanat Okulu' (technical schools), has increased from 28 in 1942 to 284 in 1949. The instructors move about, and it is hoped in time to cover all the 40,000 villages of Turkey. They give the opportunity for boys to become efficient artisans and for girls good housewives.

Next in the Educational ladder come the secondary schools. These are divided into Lycees based on the French system, giving a general Education which will lead to higher Education and the University. Secondly, there are middle schools which are designed for those who do not intend to go to higher Education but to proceed to work. They can enter business as clerical workers, and the lower grades of the civil service, railway administration and become foremen in industry. There were over 500 Lycees and middle schools in the country with over 100,000 pupils in 1945, and the number has increased since then.

Those who are able and wish to go to higher education can then enter the Technical Institutes ('Sanat Institutu'). There are a number of these schools for engineering, building and construction, woodwork and civil engineering. There are about 10,000 pupils in 78 of these institutes who take a five-year course, if they pass their examinations, they can then enter the professions as engineers or architects, without going to the University or to the higher technical institutes. The candidates for these technical institutes are taken by preference from the villages and small towns, so as to make technical education as widely spread geographically as possible. Every facility is provided for the students, and they are under an obligation when they leave the institute to work for the Government for one and a half time the period of their education. This kind of work is generally with the Ministry of Works or the State railways. After this period they can go to private employment if they wish. It is interesting to note that in the last ten years the number of students who have entered the technical institutes have greatly increased, while the number of those who enter the Lycees for general Education remains about the same. The desire for technical Education has become more and more popular.

Finally, there are the highest educational institutions in the country the Universities of Istanbul and Ankara and the Technical University of Istanbul. The first two are for those who seek careers in a profession, the higher civil service and as business executives. These two Universities are of long standing, and their standard is comparable to the Universities in Western Europe. There are a number of French, German, British and American professors and lecturers, especially now since the American-founded Robert College has been merged into the education system of Turkey. The third University, the Technical University of Istanbul, prepares engineers with theoretical and practical training, and also technicians to act as assistants. This University probably turns out annually as many trained engineers as the country can absorb in its present stage of economic development. There have been attempts to start another one at Ankara which has been unsuccessful, and that Institution has now been merged into Ankara University as its engineering faculty. The one weakness that has shown itself in connection with higher technical education in Turkey has been that there is insufficient opportunity for practical experience in workshops. This is largely due to the still backward industrial state of the country, so that the chance of sending the student for a period of practical work to the bench is often not afforded. This tends to foster a weakness which is found in all middle Eastern countries, where students when they reach a certain standard do not want to 'dirty their hands.' This tends to make them theorists and planners only. Yet it can be said that this danger is less common in Turkey than in other Eastern states, though it does exist there, too.

As Turkey is predominantly an agricultural country, the need for specialised education in this basic industry is all-important. In 1884 the only agricultural school in Turkey was at Halkaly near Istanbul. But in 1933 the Agricultural institute was founded at Ankara. This is now the only centre of higher agricultural education in the country and is affiliated to Ankara University. Recently there has been started also Agricultural technical schools in the provinces. There are seven of them, and they take the sons of peasants on a two-year course and send them back to the villages better farmers. This is good work. But in the higher grade of agricultural research and education matters are not so satisfactory. There are several able men in charge of the Agricultural Institute at Ankara who are mostly German trained. But there educational work is largely theoretical and there is no demonstration farm attached. In fact, these kinds of farm are not yet well-developed in Turkey, and until this is done agricultural education will tend to be too theoretical.

Education is the fourth item in the national budget in regard to the amount of expenditure. In 1945 it was 8% of the total. In 1953 it was 10% and reached 34,888, 6000 Turkish liras. It came next after the expenditure on defence, public works and industrial investment.

The year upto 1960 show further progress in the directions indicated above. Since 1951 the figure for the children attending the Ilk Okolu (Primary schools) rose from roughly two to three millions.

In nine years one million more children attended primary schools. There were in 1960 forty-two teachers training institutions and three hundred and fifty thousand teachers were teaching in the primary schools.

8

Perspectives in Education

DR. ABDUL HAQ ANSARI

In this paper we will restrict ourselves to the content of education, particularly that aspect of the content which concerns ideas that constitute particular sciences and disciplines and ideas that form the general perspective which shapes the development of particular sciences.

Education in an Islamic setting in our age has three dimensions. The first concerns the content of education which consists primarily of ideas, although it also includes work and experimentation. The second concerns the method of education and involves preparation of text books, training of teachers, and building of habits and character on the part of the students. Methods of research in various disciplines may also be mentioned in this context. The third dimension of education is its organisation and management. It involves the division of education into lower, middle and higher categories and into disciplines and subjects. Instruction in traditional disciplines, such as the studies of the Qur'an, *Hadith, Kalam* and *Fiqh,* and the education of women and children may be placed in this category.

From the point of view of ideas, education at the lower levels in an Islamic setting is not a problem, for the ideas that are to be imparted to the students at this level, may be partly derived from our own traditional resources, and partly taken over from modern text books with little or no modification. The preparation of text books, or the training of teachers for this level is not a difficult job. It only needs faith and determination, and can be taken up any time.

But at the middle level of education where the student is initiated into various disciplines, the Muslim educationist encounters a real problem which becomes more serious on the higher levels of education. He faces here a problem regarding the concepts and theories of particular disciplines as well as the general perspective in which they are worked out. Of course, the nature and gravity of the problem varies according to the discipline concerned. If it is a matter of natural sciences, for instance, the problem is not so much of particular ideas, as it is of the general view of the nature and the logic of science concerned whereas in the case of social sciences, the problem is not confined only to the questions of general perspective on man and society, but also concerns many of the concepts and theories in these disciplines, because they have more or less a direct bearing on the various ideas and ideals of Islam. And if it is the case of philosophical disciplines, which enquire into the questions of knowledge and truth, values and ideals, the conception of God and the world, the nature of man and his destiny, in short, into the questions of general perspective the Muslim educationist is confronted with a problem of the greatest magnitude. He cannot reject a part of the modern perspective and accept the other. He can select a few ideas, but that would not form a perspective. He must have his own perspective, and he must have it spelled out and formulated in a manner that can be used in reviewing the literature in various disciplines, before he can write text book for his students.

During the last hundred years various efforts have been made in different parts of the Islamic world, and they have done a great service. But so far as the reorientation of education on Islamic lines is concerned they have not gone beyond a particular limit. In traditional *madrasas,* the highest point of our achievement is that we have added to the curriculum some European languages, and and a few modern subjects, and given a new look to the teaching of the old subjects. But there has been no modernisation of the perspective. Consequently what we have is a discordant juxtaposition of modern and traditional ideas. On the other hand, in the new-styled schools and colleges, the effort of Islamic orientation of education does not go beyond the primary level. What we teach in our institutions in the middle or higher levels is not at all different from what is taught in western institutions.

The reason is neither the lack of determination, nor the paucity of resources. The reason is the absence of a perspective, which may guide the educationist as well as the scholar and the researcher in various fields. What is more deplorable is that many of us are not even conscious of the importance of the perspective; and the proof of this lack of consciousness is that we never think of a concerted effort to work out our own perspective. Indeed, there has been no conscious planning for it. We do not fully realize that all talk of the Islamic transformation of education, or the preparation of text books and training of teachers for middle and higher education before we have a transformation of the perspective, is idle.

One might say that it is not true that we don't have a perspective. Yes, we do have it, but we have it at the level of faith. We don't have it translated in terms of a general theory or philosophy which may help us review ideas of the modern sciences, and which may guide intellectual pursuits and inspire research. Some may turn for a perspective to that literature which the intellectual leaders of Islamic movements in various countries have brought out during the last fifty years. Remarkable though this literature is in many respects, it is mostly concerned with issues in the social, political and economic fields, and in these fields too it is more interested in practical problems. Contemporary Islamic thought has so far shown little interest in the issues of general perspective.

One might think that this is an incidental phenomenon. But actually it is not an accident; it has deeper roots in our history and tradition. After the western domination of the Islamic world in the nineteenth century, Muslim thinking turned away from the outside world and centred on its own problems. As there were no problems of general perspective among the Muslims, naturally Islamic thought did not get interested in it. It was diverted to practical problems in society and politics. At the same time thought in the West was passing through a period of disillusionment from theology and was looking for the essence of religion in moral and social concerns.

This trend of the western thought took the movement of Islamic thinking further away from the philosophical questions of the perspective. This tendency was welcome to many sections of the Muslim scholars who have always looked down on philosophy and theology with suspicion and contempt.

There is another reason why Islamic thought in recent years has been confined largely to social fields. It has been a common belief among Muslim intellectual leaders that the distinction of Islam as a religion lies in its concern with society. Islam is essentially a *Shari'ah.* They have been working on the assumption that if the social concern of Islam embodied in the *Shari'ah* is sufficiently elaborated in modern idiom, the world at large will be convinced of the truth of Islam, and the *Ummah* will regain confidence in its own future. Muslims will then be urged to struggle for the Islamic transformation of society and for the restoration of power and glory to Islam. This is the common premise of the strategy which the present movements in Islam working for the Islamic revolution have adopted. But their experience in the past few years has led many people in these movements to the realization that their understanding of the problems of the community, particularly the working of the mind of the western educated ruling class, has been rather superficial. The perspective with which this class looks at things, is different from the Islamic perspective which has not been presented to them in terms they know. There is a big gap between the perspective ruling class and that of the revolutionaries. Some in the Islamic movements have also come to ask whether the socio-political approach to Islam in contemporary Islamic literature is very much sound. They wonder if the stress should not now be laid on the basic questions of the Islamic perspective.

This leads us to ask how Islamic perspective differs from the western perspective. The major premise of the western perspective is that all our beliefs and ideas, aspirations and institutions are our own creations; they have developed through a long process of history. Similarly, all our perceptions of reality and truth, goodness and beauty are the products of history. There are, of course, various understandings of the historical process. Some believe that it is dialectical, others think that it is evolutionary, and still others have given their own differing formulations. But all of them agree on the human origin and the historicity of all the forms of ideas and institutions.

Religion, they believe, is a human creation. If there is reality outside the historical process, as religions believe, it works in and through history. God or the Divine is immanent in the world. He inspires rather than reveals. Beliefs are human responses and aspirations, and what is called sacred literature is a record of all kinds of fallible human interpretations and experiences, sanctified through ritual over a period of history. There is nothing absolute in history; every thing is relative and is subject to change and transformation.

A Muslim reader of a western work on Islam often comes across a ruthless application of the historical method and disposes it off by attributing it to the religious bias of its author. It is, of course, true that most of the earlier works on Islam were produced under a strong religious bias, but many of the recent works are largely inspired by the historical view of knowledge we are talking of. The same view is also applied on a far-greater scale to the study of Christianity. There was a time when it was practised by the critics of Christianity. Now, it is used by a growing number of faithful scholars and theologians. As a result we have a vast literature on the history of different books of the Old and the New Testaments, on the life of Christ, on the development of Christian beliefs, rituals and worship, values and institutions. The method has also been applied to the study of Judaism, and various other religions, primitive, classical or modern.

Most of the modern literature on Islam by Muslim authors is completely unaware of the historical approach. If it never goes beyond the boundaries of society and touches the issues of general perspective the views that it chooses to criticise, are the old-fashioned materialism, dialectical historicism, and biological evolution. None of these theories is essential to the historical approach, which is primarily a method though it has some important philosophical pre-suppositions. It is on account of these pre-suppositions that the need for the Islamic perspective becomes imperative.

The first problem in the development of an Islamic perspective is the problem of revelation. Contemporary Jewish and Christian theologians understand revelation in the sense of inspiration or the extraordinary quickening of the human spirit, with the clear implication that the content of revelation is essentially human and fallible. They are forced to take this line and interpret the word of God in the Bible in this light because of the modern criticism on the Bible. Our belief regarding the word of God in the Qur'an is that it is a speech articulated by God himself revealed to the Prophet through an infallible way and preserved in the form that we have it now without the admixture of any element contributed by the Prophet or any other human being. It is, in other words, metahistorical.

Jewish and Christian writers treat the word of God in the Qur'an as they treat the word of God in the Bible. They argue their case from two sides. They study the content of the Qur'an in its historical background, and try to show, to their satisfaction, that almost all the important Qur'anic ideas are taken from Christian and Jewish sources, and that the rest are devised from the pre-Islamic Arabian Society. They also argue on the authority of the history of the text of the Qur'an as they have constructed it. Literature on the former aspect is quite considerable, on the latter comparatively meagre.

Muslim scholars have looked down upon this literature with contempt and refused to take note of it, even though it determined the attitude of a great number of men and women in the world and still exercises quite a considerable influence on our own educated people. I believe, this is high time when we give up the attitude of ignoring this literature and proceed to subject it to a thorough criticism. Criticism,however, should not be our end. We should rather come out with a positive account of the history of the

Qura'nic text, taking into consideration all the relevant modern research into the origin and development of Arabic language and script.

We should also make thorough studies of the various aspects of the Qur'an. There are verses in the Qur'an which refer to the natural phenomena, and there are statements on historical events and personalities. There are also remarks on the books of the Jews and the Christian—the Torah, the Psalms and the Gospel, and comments on their beliefs and practices. On all these subjects there are numerous observations in commentaries on the Qur'an and there are also independent studies. However, we need fresh efforts on these subjects that take into account modern historical method as well as the critical literature on the Qur'an and the Bible.

Our old literature on the *i'jaz* of the Qur'an and its divine authorship is outmoded. We have to produce a new literature on the Quranic *i'jaz*.

The second subject that should be taken up with utmost seriousness is research on Islamic values and a comprehensive statement of the entire value-system. There is no work on the subject in any Islamic language. There are only a few elementary works on the ethics of the Qur'an and the other aspects of the system are almost untouched. The traditional literature on Islamic Jurisprudence is concerned with the method of finding out the right *hukm* for a new act or event. With the notable exception of Abu Ishaq al-Shatabi (d. 790 A.H.) in Spain, and Waliy Allah (d. 1276 A.H.) in India none of the jurisprudents have taken up an investigation into the ends (*maqasid*) of the *Shari'ah* and the relation of the *maqasid* with *ahkam*, or to use the terminology of ethics, the relation of the good and the right. Waliy Allah's work is of a general philosophical nature, whereas Shatabi's work is more factual and analytical. But both the studies are far from fulfilling our requirements.

What we need is a comprehensive formulation of the structure of Islamic values and its dynamics. We have to know how far various priorities have been actually fixed by the Qur'an and the Sunnah, and how far they have been left to individuals and societies in various periods and circumstances to define themselves. How is the relation between ends and priorities on the one hand, and changes in technology, Industry and population, on the other, visualised ? We need to know what is *absolute* and what is *relative* in the Islamic values.

Recent works on Islamic society, polity and economy touch on one or the other aspect of Islamic values. They are helpful so far as they go. But in order to have a comprehensive view of the system one has to investigate the structure and the dynamics of the *Shari'ah* as a whole. This is necessary not just for a theoretical understanding of the Islamic values, but also to carry further the work on various aspects of Islamic Society. It is my feeling that the work on Islamic Society based upon the jurisprudential principles laid down centuries ago, has attained the highest level. A further breakthrough in the work needs a fresh enquiry into the structure of the *Shari'ah* and the system of Islamic values.

Another dimension of the work on Islamic values is philosophical. The system has to be viewed in the context of Islamic views on the questions of reality, truth, and the nature of man and his destiny. Without this, the *Shari'ah* as a whole or a part of it, cannot be fully justified.

The work on Islamic values is also important from the point of view of establishing the rationality of fundamental Islamic beliefs in God and the hereafter. For beliefs in metaphysical truths are to an extent value statements. Consequently, they are to be justified to that extent in terms of values.

The third problem that I want to mention here, concerns the Islamic view of the history of religion. The Qur'an is interested in the subject in order to show how God has been working in guiding the destinies of the peoples known to the Arabs, and show he has acted, and would act, to various responses which people have made or would make to God's message and its bearers. What role various statements of this type have played in the success of the Prophet's mission in Arabia can hardly be over emphasised. Similarly, the success of the efforts for Islamic revival in our age will be determined to a considerable extent by the formulation of the Qur'anic perspective on the history of religion by taking into consideration all that has been made known regarding the religions the Qur'an mentions and those that it does not.

In this connection it is necessary to point out the difference between an Islamic view of history in general and of the history of religion in particular. The Qur'an is directly concerned with the latter. But this does not mean that we cannot have or should not have an Islamic view of history. In fact, we can and we should have an Islamic view of history. And that is one of the important tasks which scholars should take up. But here I am particularly underlining the work on the history of religion, or the study of the Divine scheme for the guidance of humanity.

There are a number of problems besides those I have mentioned which are equally important for the development of the Islamic perspective. These concern the nature and the destiny of man, the concept of God, and the place of reason and experience *vis-a-vis* revelation in the religious formation of the perspective. If I have chosen three problems or three areas of research for specific mention here, the reason is there is no sufficient realization of their importance and urgency.

In view of all that I have said I strongly propose the establishment of an Institute of Fundamental Research in Islam. The Institute should take up the study of and research into the various problems of the Islamic perspective, and should come out with formulations that guide the work of Muslim educationists, scholars, and leaders in their respective fields. The details of the programme for such an Institute would not be difficult to work out if this international Conference realizes the importance and the urgency of the task. It is, of course, true that the transformation of the basic perspective is not the job of one Institute. But the Institute will certainly be a big step towards the realization of our goal.

9

Muslim Approach to Education

MOHAMMED PEER

Viewed from the perspective of development, the educational backwardness of Indian Muslims is not merely a problem of the Muslim community but of the entire nation. It is, therefore, imperative that steps are taken to ameliorate the condition of backwardness in their own interest in particular and the larger interest of the society in general. But before this can be achieved, it is necessary to study the problem in depth with a view to assess its magnitude and identify the factors responsible for it.

Education has always been an indispensable instrument for socio-economic development. The useful and constructive role of education is widely acknowledged. It is against the bcakground of the pivotal role of education the present study is visualised. The development and ali round progress of a country depends upon the creation, harnessing and utilisation of skills and energies of all sections of society irrespective of caste, class, religion and sex. The backwardness of any segment of a society is not only a problem of that segment but also a drag on the overall development of the country. It is a widely acknowledged fact that the level of education among the Indian Muslims is low as compared to that of other communities. As a matter of fact the educational level of the Indian Muslims is even inferior to the most backward sections among the Hindus.

Generally, two explanations have been advanced to account for the educational backwardness of the Indian Muslims. One explanation hinges on the fact that the Muslims are slow in taking advantage of the vast educational developments witnessed by the country because of their rigid and dogmatic attitude. The second explanation puts the blame on the society at large, and holds that their backwardness is due to the discrimination practised against them by the non-Muslims in the fields of education and employment.

In the present paper an attempt has been made to examine the rationale of the explanation, that the Muslims in India have neglected modern education, lest it should undermine their religious faith. In this context it is rewarding and more useful to unravel the connection between Islamic religion and education from historical and theological perspectives. It is also necessary to portray the historical account of the educational situation of the Muslim countries and examine whether Qur'anic injunctions or the commandments of Prophet Muhammad enjoin upon the Muslims to refrain from the pursuit of secular education. In the light of the foregoing, it is possible to assess whether Islamic religion has impaired the educational advancement of the Muslims in India.

If we look at the history of the Muslim countries, we find that education throughout the Muslim world was absolutely informal and it was imparted in institutions like *maktabs* and *madrasahs.* It was the religious men who administered and managed the affairs of education. When a child attained the age of four years, four months and four days, he was admitted to *maktabs* by performing a formal ceremony called *bismillahkhani,* where he received the elementary knowledge of religion which was required to say his daily prayers (and devotions).

Against this background, it is important that we examine the injunctions of the holy Qur'an and the commandments of Prophet Muhammad about the pursuit of religious and secular education.

Accordingly, it would be of considerable interest to make a careful examination of the following issues:

1. Does the Qur'an require the Muslims merely to say the prayers, i.e. *namaz,* as a preparation for the next world and exhort them to withdraw from worldy pursuits?
2. Did the Prophet preach to his followers that they acquire only religious education?

3. Has the tendency of resistance towards the acquisition of secular knowledge been present ever since the beginning of Islam or did it originate later?

With regard to the first issue, it is obvious even to a casual reader that the importance of education has been repeatedly emphasised in the Qur'an. As a matter of fact, education has been prescribed as compulsory for every man and woman in Islam.

The Qur'an recognises that the empirical attitude is an indispensable stage in the spiritual life of humanity, attaches equal importance to all the regions of human experience as yielding knowledge of the ultimate Reality which reveals its symbols both within and without. The aphorism attributed to the Prophet declares that knowledge is twofold: knowledge of religion and knowledge of bodies. The Qur'an stresses the need for both religious and secular education. There is nothing in the Qur'anic injunctions which is opposed to the pursuit of secular education; on the contrary, all evidence seems to support it. On the other hand, if the Muslims emphasised only the religious education and failed to stick to the Qur'anic exhortations, it is not correct to hold religion responsible for the dismal state of education of the Indian Muslims. Iqbal underscores the same point when he remarks:

> If he does not take the initiative, if he does not evolve the inner richness of his being, if he ceases to feel the inward push of advancing life, then the spirit within him hardens into stone and he is reduced to the level of dead matter. But his life and the onward march of his spirit depends on the establishment of connections with the reality that confronts him. It is knowledge that establishes these connections, and knowledge is sense perception elaborated by understanding.

Time and again Prophet Muhammad preached to his followers to seek *ilm* (knowledge). The Prophet has imposed upon every Muslim, man or woman, a duty to seek knowledge (acquire education) and consider no suffering or sacrifice too great in its fulfillment. He has declared good education and training of children, sons as well as daughters, as the best gift a father can give. Even though an *ummi* (unlettered), he exhorted the Muslims to seek *'ilm* even if they had to go as far as distant China. *'Ilm* here means scientific studies which were quite advanced in China in those days. The Prophet might have in mind scientific and modern knowledge when he asked his followers to seek *'ilm* in China. It has been reported that in the Battle of Badr against the Quraysh, led by the Prophet himself, enemies were captured and the Prophet, instead of penalising them, asked the literate among them that each one of them should teach twelve Muslims. This again shows that the Prophet was not opposed to the acquisition of knowledge even from the unbelievers. He also advised his followers to acquire knowledge and learning from everyone and from everywhere, as if knowledge and learning were the lost property of the faithful. The two maxims of Prophet Muhammad which greatly exercised the minds of Muslims and which are often quoted by Muslim theologians are : "a fragment of knowledge is worth more than a hundred prayers" and scholar's ink is as precious as the martyr's blood." These sayings clearly reveal that the Prophet accorded the highest value to education and exhorted his followers to acquire education by all reasonable means. We may, therefore, conclude that neither the Qur'an nor the *Ahadith* enjoin upon the Muslims to refrain from acquiring modern education.

It is a well-known fact that during the Dark Ages in Europe, the Greek and the Roman heritage was preserved in the Hellenistic world, which was preponderantly Muslim. In this context, it may be useful to look at the history of Muslim countries in understanding the system of education prevalent during these days.

From about the eighth century, the Muslim savants not only freely received knowledge from different countries, but they even contributed to the enrichment of science and medicine. It is for this reason that the period between the eighth and twelfth centuries is described as the 'Renaissance' by Mez.

The contribution of the Muslims in different fields of knowledge has had a decisive role not only in the Renaissance of Europe in the twelfth century, but also in the Industrial Revolution in later times. In this context Prof. Hitti has rightly remarked, "they [the Muslims] laid the basis of that canon of knowledge which lay at the bottom of modern European renaissance." He also asserted, "no people in the Middle Ages contributed to human progress so much as did the Arabs."

A similar view has been expressed by Briffault, according to whom "Science is the most momentous contribution of Arab civilization to the modern world; but its fruits were slow in ripening. Not until long after Moorish culture had sunk back into darkness did the giant which it had given birth to rise in this might. It was not science only which brought Europe back to life. Other and manifold influences from the civilization of Islam communicated its first glow to European life." Alfred Guillaume has underscored the same point when he observed: "Had the Arabs been barbarians like the Mongols...., the Renaissance in Europe might well have been delayed more than one century."

Thus, from the middle of the eighth upto the early part of the twelfth century, the Arabic-speaking people made tremendous advances in the various branches of knowledge. It has been argued by Levy, Arnold and Guillaume, and Iqbal, that scientific knowledge and specially medical sciences had reached a very high level of development in those days as testified by the works of great Muslim physicians like Abu Bakr al-Razi (the famous Rhazes of the Western world), Abu 'Ali ibn Sina (Avicenna of the Western world) and 'Ali Ibn 'Abbas.

Thus it is very clear that in the heyday of Islam the Muslims did not eschew or neglect the pursuit of secular knowledge. On the contrary, they made significant contributions to the advancement in various branches of scientific knowledge. The scientific achievements of the Muslims of this period, namely the ninth, tenth, and the eleventh centuries, had reached a stage which can only be compared to the period of Renaissance in Europe. However, because of certain factors, this golden age of Islam was followed by a dark age beginning from the twelfth century and lasting right upto the early nineteenth century. One of the important factors was the role of the orthodox *'Ulama'* of the period, who opposed the learning and teaching of Greek philosophy, for it generated heresy and scepticism among the Muslims who learnt it. Since the teachings of Aristotle and other Greek philosophers on the eternity of the universe, the world hereafter, etc., were at variance with the teachings of Islam, it was thought best to avoid them. Thus a conflict arose between those who upheld freedom in academic matters and freedom of knowledge, and those who upheld the orthodox view. It was a struggle between the orthodox *'Ulama'* on the one hand and the free thinkers, on the other. However, by about the twelfth century a stage was reached when the orthodox view prevailed and a period of decline and stagnation set in which was very pronounced in the field of education and it lasted until the modern times. Throughout this century, from the twelfth to the nineteenth, Muslim school and college education remained backward. Certain fixed syllabi were taught throughout the Islamic world with a theological bias. Again, this period hardly produced any great scientists or intellectuals who could be compared to those who lived in the earlier centuries and to whom modern civilization owes so much in the realm of scientific advancement. Thus, it was the dogmatism of the *'Ulama'* of the later middle ages which came in the way of scientific and intellectual progress of the Muslims. It was only from the nineteenth century onwards that liberal Muslim thinkers and educationists revolted against the orthodox and obscurantist attitude of the *'Ulama'* and today most of the Muslim countries have given up the traditional system of education and taken to modern methods of education.

During the later part of the nineteenth century, Muslims realised their mistakes and learnt to adapt themselves to the changing requirements of the time. This is apparent from the fact that the non-Arabic speaking Muslims of the world, for instance, the Turks, the Afghans and so forth, realised that the Arabic language was meaningless for them, except, of course, for religious purposes. Most of the Muslims regarded education as a preparation for life. By keeping this in mind, emphasis was placed on teaching technical, scientific and other secular subjects in most of the Muslim countries.

According to Lefton S. Stavrianes, today the Muslims from Afghanistan to the banks of Nile use the common slogan, "our future depends on our schools." Prof. Lerner, in his study of social change in the tradition bound Islamic society, has also reported the educational development of six Middle Eastern countries. The study conducted by Lerner in Turkey, Lebanon, Egypt, Syria, Jordan and Iran, shows the changes that have taken place in these Islamic societies. He has also reported the transformations that have taken place in the traditional scheme of education in these countries. Against this background, it would be very useful to analyse the various measures taken in Muslim countries for secular educational advancement.

Let us now briefly review the kind of education imparted in schools and colleges and the measures taken to spread modern education in Islamic countries.

Afghanistan, which is a predominantly Muslim country, has taken various measures to spread modern education. It has thoroughly modified the teaching and recruiting methods and launched a vigorous campaign against illiteracy. In order to meet the new challenges, many secondary, technical and teacher training institutions have been started in the country. In 1950, the Afghan Institute of Technology was founded in Kabul and it produced a number of electronic engineers, mining and automobile technicians. To meet the rising demand for teachnical for technical education, both the Government and the private individuals are starting technical institutions.

Iran has played a most pivotal role in the development of education in the post-oil era. Unlike other Muslim countries, a number of secondary schools, engineering colleges and universities have been started, but these institutions suffered from want of qualified teaching staff. However, arrangements have been made for recruiting qualified teachers from other countries and sending Iranian students for higher education abroad. So today, Iran has given the green signal for technical education. The most important fact to note is that, all children aged eleven to thirteen will henceforth spend fifty per cent of their time on manual work at work benches in city schools and at school farms in villages. Each village school will have its own fields for cultivation and experimentation and special watering system for gardening. Each city school will have its workshop complete with tools and equipment.

The impact of the West is even more marked in Lebanon, which is the most modern Arab land today. It has the highest proportion of people living in cities, and almost seventy per cent of the total population is literate. It has moved farthest away from Arab Muslim traditionalism. In Lebanon, educators are busy revising the school textbooks using scientific norms, and are now administering psychological tests to teacher trainees in order to select better qualified teachers and provide vocational guidance for young people. Even though the government has taken up the responsibility of education since independence, private institutions are still the mainstay especially at the secondary and university levels. Primary and secondary schools have proliferated within a short span of time in Lebanon. In 1966-67 there were four universities, and in all these four universities much emphasis is placed on technical education. The medium of instruction in the American University of Beirut is English, in the Jesuit University of Joseph is French. Thus educational standards in Lebanon are the highest in any Arab State and literacy is estimated at eighty-eight per cent for those over fourteen years of age.

Turkey is no longer a traditional society owing to its close contact with Europe. Turkey has followed an urbanizing pattern. There is a revolutionary shift from the antique Arabic orthography of the Ataturk regime to a simpler Western script to facilitate modern education. Kemal Ataturk in his fifteen years of rule from 1923 until his death in November, 1938, introduced a series of reforms to root out ignorance and fanaticism and modernize his country. In 1924, he established a unified secular system of education and closed all the *madrasahs* which were imparting religious education. In 1928, he instructed that instruction would not be imparted through the medium of Arabic and Persian in elementary schools. In 1933, he abolished the Faculty of Divinity in the University of Istanbul.

On account of the liberal educational policy, the percentage of illiterates among those aged seven and over has fallen from 79.6 per cent in 1935 to 65.4 per cent in 1950 and further down to 52.3 in 1966. All the state schools are co-educational and education is made available to all the people. The educational system is highly centralised, curricula, text-books and the appointment of teachers being controlled by the State. A curious flaw in the system is that the methods of imparting instruction in the primary schools are based on German and Australian practice, the middle schools are run on French lines, and the technical schools follow the Belgian pattern.

Rural education has also received much attention. In rural schools the syllabus is set depending upon the requirements of the day. The students spend half of their time in practical work particularly from secondary schools. Boys receive education in agricultural techniques, building and carpentry, and for girls training is imparted in housekeeping, first aid and child care. In this way, Turkey has taken various measures for the development of education.

After half a century of continuous contact with the British, Egypt struggled hard to transform the traditional scheme of education. President Nasser shaped a new image of Egyptian society during his rule. While commenting upon the educational advancement of the country Prof. Lerner says: "Literacy is their tool, mobility their method and participant life their goal." Education has been made compulsory for all people since 1993.

It is important to note that the educational system in Yemen was very backward till 1962. There were absolutely no schools for girls. However, after 1962, due to financial assistance offered by Egypt, Kuwait, Bulgaria, USSR, and the Peoples Republic of China, Yemen gave top priority to all levels of education, viz., primary, secondary and technical.

Jordan once considered an ancient Islamic land, has become a modern nation today. The rapid growth of schools in towns is one of the signs of the rapid spread of education. Even in the sacred land of Islam, viz., Saudi Arabia, the Islamic Foundation for Science, Technology and Development has drawn up an action plan to promote modern education, science and technology in Islamic states. The major Islamic countries of South East Asia, viz., Malaysia, Singapore and Indonesia, also experienced the cultural reform on the Western model. In singapore Muslims have greater concern for Western education. Indonesia, Malaysia and other Islamic countries of South East Asia have given much attention to Western education.

The demand for the rapid expansion and modernization of education at all levels from primary to higher, including scientific and technological training in Gulf countries, viz., Bahrain, Kuwait, Qatar, Abu Dhabi and Dubai has increased in the post-oil era. The traditional educational system which remained prevalent among the local and village communities of these states until the introduction of the modern system was a one-man enterprise. Education in these countries was imparted through the institutions of traditional learning like *maktabs* and *madrasahs. Maktabs* were primary schools where fundamentals or elements of education were imparted. They were also termed as the Qur'an teaching schools, where necessary portions of the Qur'an were taught by heart for their daily prayers. Generally, the *Imam*, the prayer leader, used to impart instructions in *maktabs* and *madrasahs* and he was usually called as *miyanji* or *mawlawi.* The final stage of education was memorizing the Qur'an. The traditional education was exclusively a male domain with the exception of a few girls from the elite families, for whom special arrangements were made at home for teaching elementary reading and writing. The teaching of the Qur'an was primarily for religious purpose, knowledge of writing and basic arithmetic was considered useful for keeping records and accounts of pearl trade and simple commercial transactions.

It is significant to note that by the beginning of the twentieth century, both Kuwait and Bahrain had accomplished some limited socio-economic progress due to their increased sea borne trade. They strongly felt the necessity of transforming the traditional scheme of education which was imparted in *maktabs* and *madrasahs* as they thought that the traditional education would not suffice to cater to the requirements of the society. Towards the end of the nineteenth century certain Christian missionaries had established a primary school for boys in Bahrain, which was followed by the opening of community schools of Iranians and Indians. Several well-to-do Bahrain families took the initiative of sending the boys to these non-Arab schools.

The first Arab school of this region Madrasah al-Mubarakiyah was established in Kuwait in 1911 with a modified syllabus and poorly trained teachers (mostly trained in Iraq). The basic contents of teaching at that early stage remained very much like those of the traditional educational system, but in course of time the syllabus was thoroughly revised by keeping in mind the requirements of the time. In 1919, a similar school was started in Bahrain. From 1950, the modern type of education was started even in Qatar and the constituents of the present day United Arab Emirates.

After the consolidation of primary education for boys in Kuwait and Bahrain they took the initiative of extending the same privilege for girls. Bahrain took an earlier initiative by opening a girls' school in 1928 nine years after establishing the boys' school. In Kuwait, however, it was delayed until 1937, almost twenty-six years after the beginning of its first boys' school. In Qatar, there was only a one year interval between the opening of boys' and girls' schools, the former having been established in 1956 and the latter in 1957. In the United Arab Emirates, modern primary education for boys began in 1953. During the initial years it was organized and financed by the State of Kuwait. The most significant achievement came in the late 1930s, when Bahrain and Kuwait extended secondary educational facilities to both boys and girls. The United Arab Emirates had a late entry into this phase of education; the first boys' secondary school was opened in Abu Dhabi in 1968.

The process of modernization of the educational system which began at a very modest level in Kuwait in 1911 and in Bahrain in 1919 gained momentum in the 1930s. The emergence of oil economy put up further demands for rapid expansion and growth of education leading to the establishment of many new colleges and universities. Thus, during the 1960s and '70s the progress of education throughout the Gulf region gained unprecedented speed. In 1966, a University was started in Kuwait with a combined faculty of Arts and Science. By the end of 1970, courses in other subjects like Medicine and Engineering were started. In 1970, a University College in Bahrain was established which has already been merged into the Gulf University. In most of the Gulf countries the universities and the colleges have come up rapidly.

The pattern of modernization and growth of education in both Qatar and the United Arab Emirates in proportion to their populations are almost the same as in Kuwait. The pace of current progress in Bahrain, however, has slowed down due to the decline in oil revenues and restricted financial resources.

In the traditional social set up, girls' education throughout the Gulf region was socially discouraged. The society as a whole was reluctant to open the doors of schools to the females even at a modest level until almost half a century ago. This is apparent from the fact that in 1930 when the Government of Bahrain extended educational facilities for girls, even the general public vehemently opposed the stance taken by the Government. The post-oil modernization and its direct impact on all walks of life caused a basic change in social attitudes, including education of girls.

Once the traditional barriers against women's education were lifted and demands of the newly emerging modernized socio-economic organization for equal opportunities for women came to the surface, the sex ratio in higher education changed drastically.

Although the proportion of girl students at both primary and secondary levels remained lower than that of the boys, at the higher educational stage the proportion of girls increased. For instance, the latest figures of enrolment in Kuwait University show 55 per cent girls as against 45 per cent boys studying in the constituent faculties of the University. The higher ratio of female students in the University education in Kuwait has been consistent ever since the University was established in 1966. In Bahrain University College the enrolment of girls is much higher : it is almost five to one. A similar pattern of higher number of female students is also prevalent in both Qatar and the United Arab Emirates. There are two factors responsible for the higher proportion of female students in the Gulf region:

(a) a considerable number of male students are studying abroad in England, the United States and Egypt. Thus their percentage decreases in colleges and universities in their native countries;

(b) because of better employment avenues, most of the boys enter into services after completing secondary school education.

However, it must be said that a large number of girls are seeking employment every year after completing their primary and secondary education. The female students who continue their higher education are either those who look for better job positions or those who consider that a University degree will provide them with a better status in society.

In Bahrain, 82 per cent of the school-age population were enrolled in the schools, followed by 79.91 per cent in Qatar, 72 per cent in Lebanon, 70.78 per cent in Jordan, 64.36 per cent in Kuwait and 62.77 per cent in Cyprus. In Iraq, Turkey, UAR, Syria and Algeria, 59.17, 56.38, 54.94, 56.36, 56.39 per cent respectively of the school-age population were enrolled in schools. However, in Libya, Iran, Morocco and Pakistan only 45.37, 41.17, 38.80 and 32.40 per cent respectively were enrolled in schools. Only in Chad, Mali, Mauritania, Saudi Arabia, Southern Yemen and Spanish Sahara the enrolment of children of school-age population was less than 30 per cent in 1965-66.

It is obvious from the foregoing analysis that neither the Qur'an nor the *ahadith* enjoin upon the Muslims to refrain from secular education; indeed all evidence seem to point to the contrary. This is evident from the fact that during the heyday of Islam, Muslims did not eschew or neglect the pursuit of secular knowledge; on the contrary, they made significant contributions to the advancement in various branches of knowledge. It was only during the middle ages the Muslims were backward in education because of the influence of the dogmatic attitude of the *'Ulama'*. However, towards the middle of the nineteenth century the Muslims in other Islamic countries realized their mistakes and thoroughly modified the contents and the system of education imparted in schools and colleges.

If we trace the history of education among the Indian Muslims, we find that they have not remained backward at all times and everywhere. The Indian Muslims in the pre-colonial era have played an important part in educational development. After the establishment of Muslim rule in India, the rulers since the reign of Mahmud of Ghaznah (999-1030) contributed large funds and constructed innumerable *madrasahs* for the dissemination of knowledge. It is significant to note that, contrary to common belief, even secular subjects were included in the course of instruction. To train the students in secular sciences, distinguished scholars were invited from different parts of the world. Thus Muslims during the medieval India, particualrly during the Mughal period, made significant contributions in the fields of science, architecture, painting, and music, and these contributions were both extensive and of a high standard, although, as anywhere else, a religious bias was prevalent in the context of education. It was only during the early British rule that the Muslims were antagonistic towards receiving English education because of their pride in the bygone superiority, fear of the Christian missionaries, fear of their children mingling with the commoners, anti-*firangi* propaganda of the *'Ulama'* coupled with the discriminatory attitude of the British. However, after the revolt of 1857, because of the untiring efforts of many social reformers in convincing the Muslims to accept the system of education introduced by the British, their educational position has improved. It is observed that the Muslims were comparable to the Hindus in literacy and education during the period 1881-1931. It was only after 1931, particularly in the post-independence period that their educational status began to decline.

It is clear from the foregoing analysis that religion has never impaired the educational advancement of Muslims either in India or elsewhere in the world. The data show that the Muslims in Islamic countries are changing the content of education according to the requirement of society and not sticking merely to the acquisition of religious knowledge. Even in India, the Muslims were not backward at all times and everywhere, on the contrary they themselves have made remarkable contributions for the enrichment of knowledge. Their educational backwardness is of recent origin. In the light of these facts it is necessary to look elsewhere for the real causes of the educational backwardness of the Indian Muslims.

10

Muslim Education in India

Y. B. MATHUR

A negative attitude of Muslim in learning English and the positive of Hindus, made much of a difference. This conservation vs. Liberalism was a distinct mark, which basically contradicted the respective ideologies of Islam and Hinduism.

It is well-known that when the British first assumed the sovereignty of the Eastern Provinces of the Mughal Emperor of Delhi, the Muslims, in spite of many vicissitudes of fortune, still enjoyed power and wealth. The treaty of August 12, 1765, by which Shah 'Alam, the last of the Mughals, entrusted the collection of revenue of Bengal, Bihar and Orissa to the East India Company, made no alteration in the political condition of the Muslims. Until the time of Lord Cornwallis the Muslim law continued to be the law of the land and the judicial and executive appointments remained in the hands of the Muslims.

The Muslim community received the first shock from the Permanent Settlement. It elevated the Hindu collectors, who till that time had held unimportant posts, to the position of land-holders, gave them a proprietary right in the soil, and allowed them to accumulate wealth which would have gone to the Muslims under their own rule. The resumption laws fell heavily on the Muslims and deprived many of the learned classes in Bihar and Bengal of decent living. The annexation of the Oudh and the Mutiny had a similar effect on the Muslims of Delhi and Lucknow. These persons were quite naturally unfriendly to the Britishers.

The government's firm determination to carry out a system of English education proved unfavourable to the Muslims and a great boon to the Hindus. The latter, who had been for ages under the

Muslim rule, had no dislike to learn the language of their new rulers. As they had learnt Persian and Urdu under the Muslims, so they were willing to learn English under the British. But this was not so with the Muslims. They objected to study English because they said they feared English education would undermine their religion. This objection did not, however, contain the whole truth. In reality, it was based on a far more serious consideration. According to the Muslim law, as expounded by Sunnis of the *old* school, it was not lawful to learn English or the language of any other non-Muslim people except for the purpose of answering letters, or of combating the religious arguments of those people. Learning a foreign language for any other purpose was not allowed.

Such an attitude towards learning the English language weakened the position of the Muslims, and gradually they began to lose all important offices. They now possessed little influence, and that too in their capacity as government servants. The abolition of the Muslim law offices on the introduction of the Penal Code deprived the Muslims of almost all the respectable appointments and greatly checked vernacular education.

From the first establishment of the Mughal rule in India till 1837, Persian continued to be the official language. The conquest of India by the Mughals had been achieved by men belonging to different races and speaking a variety of tongues, but the Persian language was considered sufficient for administrative purposes not only by the Mughal masters but also by their successors who were in power till 1837.

The contact of the Muslims with the Hindus gave birth to the composite language which is known as Urdu. It was spoken by the Muslims all over India, with the exception of the deltaic districts of Eastern Bengal. From the Punjab as far down as Bhagalpur in the Lieutenant Governorship of Bengal, Urdu, more or less pure, was not only the vernacular of the Muslims but also of the majority of the Hindus. In 1837 an order was promulgated that office work should in future be done either in English or in the provincial dialects. The language of the people of each province and the character in which it was originally intended to be written were fixed upon as the most convenient and practicable substitutes for the Persian. This plan succeeded in those provinces where the language was not Urdu or Hindustani. Hence the Tamil, the Telugu, the Marathi, the Gujarati and the Bengali languages superseded Persian without much difficulty in Madras, Bombay, Gujarat and Bengal. In Bihar, the North-Western Provinces and the Punjab, where the language of the people had for several centuries been Urdu, this attempt not only caused great discontent both among the Hindus and the Muslims, but ended in absolute failure. The British Government wished to introduce the Hindi-Kaithi, written in the stiff archaic Nagri character, as the official language of these parts. But the change proposed was based upon a misapprehension and the attempt consequently failed signally. Urdu written in the Persian character was substituted for Persian in Bihar, the North-Western Provinces and the Punjab. The substitution of the vernacular dialects and the vernacular character for Persian in other provinces resulted in throwing out of employment a considerable body of Muslim subordinate officers who were totally dependent for their subsistence upon the pay of the Government.

The actual impoverishment of the Muslim middle class dates from this epoch. English educated Hindu youths, trained for the most part in missionary institutions, from which the Muslims naturally stood aloof, now poured into every Government office and completely shut out the Muslims. A few unimportant offices remained in the hands of the Muslims, but day by day their number decreased. This led Dr. Hunter to observe that "there is now scarcely hope for any post above the rank of porter, messenger, filler of ink-pots, and mender of pens." The Muslims, who in the time of Lord Cornwallis were holding 75% government jobs, no longer occupied the front rank among the Indian communities.

While this radical change was introduced in the administrative policy of the country by making it necessary on all aspirants for office under Government to know the language of the rulers, no order was passed to make English education compulsory. On the contrary, till 1864 the Muslims were fed with the hope that their own classics were the *sine qua non* for Government employment or for entering the legal profession. The orders of the Government permitting candidates for the offices of *munsif* and pleader to take their examinations either in English or Urdu remained in force till 1864. A year or two later, however, a sudden change was introduced. It changed the previous orders and declared that in future examinations for higher grade posts of pleaders and *munsifs* would be conducted only in English. This measure placed the Muslims under a complete disadvantage. For them the British system of education was a failure because they were unable to participate in the material advantages which the government education had conferred on the Hindus. The statistics available for the years 1860-61 to 1866 and 1871 proves the lamentable deficiency in the education of the Muslims who were not very long ago the most powerful rulers of India.

The special obstacles which hindered the education and social progress of the Muslims were very often discussed by the Government of India. In 1871 the Government issued a Resolution on the state of Muslim education and made it clear that the main drawback in their advancement was owing to their inability or unwillingness to take advantage of the Government system of education. Noting with regret that so large and important a class as the Muslims should stand aloof from the new educational system, and thus lose the advantages, both material and social, which the other people of India enjoyed, the Earl of Mayo took steps to remove their disabilities. He decided to give systematic encouragement and recognition to the classical and vernacular languages of the Muslims in Government schools and colleges, appoint qualified Muslim teachers in English schools, assist the Muslims by financial grants to enable them to open schools of their own, and encourage the creation of a vernacular literature for the Muslims. The whole subject was commended to the attention of the Local Governments and of the three universities of India.

The reports which were received from the local governments showed that wherever the ordinary vernacular of a province was Hindustani or Urdu, written in the Persian character, or, again, where the Muslims used a form of the provincial or district dialect, there the Muslims occupied proper positions in the primary and secondary schools founded or aided by the Government. But where, on the other hand, they spoke a language different from that of the majority of the population, or expressed in a different character, the special arrangements necessary to meet these circumstances had not always been carried out, with the inevitable result that the claims of the Muslim community were disregarded. The obstacles which kept the Muslim students apart from the ordinary school system naturally grew stronger as the higher standards of education were reached. With a strictly limited grant for educational purposes, it was not possible to maintain a double educational agency. Consequently, it was in high schools, the colleges and the universities that the absence or backwardness of Muslims was most conspicuous. The reports all agreed that the existing system of education had not attracted them to the higher ranges of the educational course, or induced them to persevere up to the point at which studies impress real culture and fit young men for successes in the services and the open professions.

The reports of the local governments were reviewed at length by the Education Commission in 1883. It laid much greater stress on the educational than on the social or historical difficulties that contributed to the backwardness of the Muslims and debated the causes which kept them aloof from receiving higher education. While some members of the Commission were of the opinion that the absence of instruction in the tenets of their faith, and still more the injurious effects of the English education in creating a disbelief in religion, were the main obstacles, others—a small minority—thought that religion had little to do with this question. Some contended that the system of education prevailing in government school and colleges corrupted the morals and manners of the students. The small proportion of Muslim teachers in government institutions ; the unwillingness of government educational offices to accept the advice and co-operation of the Muslims; numerous minor faults in the departmental system; the comparatively small progress in real learning made by the students in government schools; the practice among the well-to-do Muslims of educating their children at home; the indolence and imprudence too common among them; their hereditary love of the profession of arms; the absence of the friendly contact between Muslims and the Englishmen; the unwillingness felt by the upper class to associate with the lower; the general poverty among the Muslims; the coldness of government towards them; the use in government schools of books whose tone was hostile or scornful towards Islam—these and a variety of other causes were put forward at different times by members of the Muslim community to account for the scant appreciation which English education had received at their hands. But the Commission concluded that while all these factors must have combined in driving the Muslims away from English education, "a candid Muhammadan would probably admit that the most powerful factors are to be found in pride of race, a memory of by-gone superiority, religious fears, and a not unnatural attachment to the learning of Islam."

Apart from social and historical difficulties, there were educational difficulties also in promoting education of the Muslims. First, whereas the object of the young Hindu was to obtain an education which would fit him for an official or a professional career, a young Muslims was not allowed to turn his thoughts to secular instruction until he had passed some years in going through a course of sacred learning because for him "the teaching of mosque must precede the lessons of the school." The Muslim boy, therefore, entered school later than the Hindu. Secondly, he very often left school at an early age. The Muslim parents were usually poorer than the Hindu parents in a corresponding social position. A Muslim boy could not therefore receive thorough education. Thirdly, the Muslim parents often chose for their sons while at school an education which would secure for them an honoured place among the learned of his own community, rather than one which would command a success in the modern professions or in official life. The years which a young Hindu spent in learning English and Mathematics in a public school, the young Muslim devoted in a *madrasah* in learning Arabic, Islamic jurisprudence and theology. These were the three principal causes which retarded the prosperity of the Muslims.

It now remains to examine the Commission's recommendations about the Muslims. The Commission treated the Muslim claims not merely with justice but with generosity to give them special assistance in view of their backward condition. The proposals of the Commission covered the whole field of education and, indeed, went beyond it into the domain of public life and employment. The following were its recommendations:

(i) Indigenous schools for Muslims should be liberally encouraged to add purely secular subjects to their curriculum.

(ii) In public primary schools for Muslims, special standards should be prescribed.

(iii) Higher English education for Muslims both in schools and in colleges should be encouraged.

(iv) A graduated chain of scholarships leading from the primary school through all intermediate stages up to the B.A. degree, and also a system of free scholarships in schools under public management should be established for the exclusive benefit of the Muslims.

(v) The benefits of Muslim educational endowments should be reserved for Muslims and applied to the promotion of English education among them.

(vi) Special provision should be made to increase the number of Muslim teachers and Muslim inspecting officers.

(vii) Employment should be offered to the Muslims in public offices by the local governments.

The recommendations of the Commission did not escape criticism. There were three main objections. First, it was not in the interest of the Muslims that they should be offered special facilities for learning Hindustani and Persian, instead of the vernacular of the country in which they were to be employed. (This objection, so far as it related to Persian, seemed to spring from a misapprehension. Persian was not to supersede the vernacular but to take the place of Sanskrit which was taught as a second language to Hindu boys in high schools.) Secondly, it was still less in the interest of the Muslims to establish special schools for their benefit. The spirit of exclusiveness or 'separatism' had been the worst foe of the Muslims, and it was a duty incumbent on the government to repress and discourage rather than to foster it. Muslim boys could not begin too early to learn the lessons of tolerance and emulation in association with those amid whom their lives were to be spent. Lastly, it was unfair to other sections of the community to establish scholarships for the special benefit of Muslims, while they were also allowed to compete on equal terms for the government scholarships that were open to all. There was danger that sympathy with the Muslims might result in unfairness to other classes. The Education Commission in their "leaning towards generosity seemed to have overstepped the limits of justice."

In commenting upon the Report of the Education Commission, the Government of India, while explaining its policy said :

> It is only by frankly placing themselves in line with the Hindus, and taking full advantage of the Government system of high and especially of English education, that the Muhammadans can hope fairly to hold their own in respect of the better description of State appointments.....The object of the Commission is to attract Muhammadan scholars by giving adequate prominence to those subjects to which their parents attach importance, and to hold out special inducements to a backward class ; but ...due regard is everywhere to be paid to local circumstances, and care must be taken to avoid unnecessary widening of the line between Muhammadans and other classes of the community.

This policy of the Government of India showed good results. The number of Muslim students increased from 114,816 in 1871-72 to 261,887 in 1881-82. The educational progress in the four years following the Commission's report showed that the number and percentage of students attending the school went up considerably. In primary schools, the percentage of the Muslim students was higher than that of the other communities in India. But in the higher stages of instruction, the proportion of Muslim students rapidly declined. Still, judged by the position in 1881-82, a striking advance was recorded. From 1881-82 to 1885-86, great progress was made in the education of all classes, but that of the Muslim community was exceptionally rapid. The number of Muslims in Arts colleges increased from 197, or 3.5 per cent of the total number of students, to 330 or 4.4 per cent. In colleges giving instruction in law, medicine and engineering, the number increased from 73 to 132, and the percentage from 4.3 to 5.1. In secondary schools, the proportion of Muslim students increased from 9.3 to 13.5 per cent.

The Commission's proposals and the objections taken to them were discussed in the Resolution of the Government of India of July, 1888. This Resolution thus described the principles upon which the education of Muslims should be encouraged by the State:

> As to the principles upon which the education of Muhammadans should be encouraged by the State, His Excellency in Council need say little here, for they appear to be understood by all Administrations, and with general consent accepted by the people,—by none more openly than by the leading Muhammadans of India. The State has only to apply its education apparatus and aid, so as they may best adjust themselves to existing languages and habits of thought among all classes of the people without diverging from its set mark and final purpose—the better diffusion and advancement of real knowledge in India. His Excellency in Council is anxious that the attainment of this object shall in no class of the population be hindered by differences of language or of custom; and with this view the Government of India is very willing that the entire body of Muhammadan (as of Hindu) classic literature shall be admitted and take rank among the higher subjects of secular study; and that the languages shall form an important part of the examinations for university degrees. In short, His Excellency in Council is prepared to listen favourably to any well-considered proposal for modifying or extending in these directions the existing educational system. One measure to which the Resolution of 1871 particularly adverted was the development of a vernacular literature for Muhammadans. His Excellency in Council would be slow to believe that such a literature still needed creation. To this suggestion Local Governments attach differing degrees of importance or practicability; and, on the whole, His Excellency in Council sees reason to believe that we must be cautious in attempting to proceed in this direction much beyond the point we have reached already. It is most desirable to frame a series of high class textbooks, to encourage the printing and publication of valuable

> Muhammadan works, and to offer prizes either for good translations of foreign works or for original studies. But in regard to the patronage of what may properly be called literature, the exercise of it must necessarily be restricted by the pressing demands of general education upon our finance, and by the difficulty of making a fair selection, or of distributing any money available with due discrimination and indubitable advantage.

The Resolution concluded as follows :

> His Excellency in Council has now reviewed rapidly the general measures which have been taken, or are being taken, for the encouragement of education among Muhammadans. The papers before him, received from all parts or British India, show that the Earl of Mayo's Resolution has succeeded in its main purpose of drawing the attention of all Administrations to needs and obligations which before had perhaps not everywhere been adequately realized. These needs and obligations may now be entrusted with confidence to the care of Local Governments. The Supreme Government has satisfied itself that the principles upon which Muhammadan education should be supported or subsidized are clearly understood; while the conditions and rate of progress in this as in all branches of public instruction, the range of its operations, and all other practical details depend chiefly in each province upon local circumstances, administrative skill and financial resources.

The Report of the Commission and the Resolution of the Government of India which was issued in 1885 gave a considerable impetus to Muslim education. Under the patronage of men like Sir Salar Jang and other illustrious princes and nobles, and of such English gentlemen as Lord Stanley, Earl Lytton, Sir William Muir and Sir John Strachey, great pressure was put on the Muslims to receive education. But much of the good done was through the efforts of the Muslims themselves, of whom Maulvi Sayyid Ahmad Khan, whose life was devoted to the cause of liberal education, was the most distinguished leader. Many of the drawbacks which existed in 1870 had now been removed.

From 1886 to 1897, i.e., in a period of 12 years, the total number of Muslim students rose from 754,036 to 966,632, but generally speaking the Muslim education did not advance beyond the primary stage. A comparison of Muslim students, male and female, with general population during the period 1897-1902 showed that on the whole the comparison was unfavourable to the Muslim community. Only 60 *per mille* of Muslim males were literate against 102 *per mille* on the general population. This backwardness of Muslim education was due in a great measure to the traditions and character of the people, and the special efforts made by the government could only have been successful if the Muslim parents had showed willingness to impart secular education to their children. The influential classes in several provinces showed appreciation of this situation and an earnest desire to improve it.

Speaking as President of the Muhammadan Educational Conference in December 1900, Nawab 'Imad al-Mulk Sayyid Husain Bilgrami said:

> We usually take it for granted that everyone is alive to the benefits of education, that at any rate every literate parent is convinced of the duty he owes to his children of giving them a sound education, but in practice the majority of literate Muhammadans are accustomed to feel satisfied that they have discharged their duty in an effective manner when they have put their children under a village pedagogue at the door, or sent them to the nearest school. They think they have made an end of the matter, their consciences are satisfied and they give themselves no further concern about it. The result is that in the majority of cases the children grow up in ignorance and are perhaps led into evil ways, for which the parents are primarily responsible. They are responsible because they have not taken the trouble to find out what sort of education is wanted for their children and how it is to be obtained.

Observations similar in tenor were made by His Highness the Agha Khan who was President of the Muhammadan Educational Conference which was held at Delhi at the time of the Coronation Darbar. The following quotation is of special interest:

And now gentlemen, let us direct our attention to a question with which your conference is intimately concerned, namely, how have the Indian Muslims taken advantage of the chances which Providence has placed in their way ? We must all acknowledge with shame and regret that so far we have failed. Throughout the whole length and breadth of India, how many national schools are there in existence which educate Muslim boys and girls in their faith and at the same time in modern secular state ? Is there even one to every hundred that our nation needs and which we should have established had we been like any other healthy people ? There are, indeed, a certain number of old-fashioned *matabs* and *madrasahs* which continue to give parrot-like teaching of the Qu'ran, but even in these places no attempt is made either to improve the morals of the boys or to bring before them the eternal truths of the faith. As a rule, prayers are but rarely repeated, and when said, not one per cent of the boys understand what they say and why.

From now onwards there was a remarkable awakening in the Muslim community to the advantages of modern education. The steady efforts made by the government to ameliorate their lot as well as the attitude of the leaders of their community towards education was more and more favourable. During the nine years, *i.e.,* from 1904 to 1913, the number of Muslim students increased by approximately 50% and stood at nearly a million and a half. In primary education, the number of Muslims had gone up a little as compared to children of all races and creeds in India, but as regards higher education they still lagged behind and had much lee-way to make up before they could reach the educational level of the Hindus. Various measures were, therefore, taken between 1913 and 1922 to encourage Muslim education. Chief among these were the appointment of special Muslim inspectors, the employment of Muslim teachers, establishment of new Muslim schools in suitable localities and the reservation of scholarships for Muslim children. Similar steps were taken for the development of Muslim education in Bihar, Orissa, Madras, Bombay, Bengal, U.P., Sind and the Frontier.

But the progress made by Muslims in the field of technical

education was not yet satisfactory. In 1913, the President of the All India Muslim Education conference commented upon this state of affairs in the following words:

> Thirty years ago the cry of the Indian Muslims used to be the cry of despondency, that in the matter of English education we have allowed ourselves to lag behind. Thirty or forty years hence I am afraid the burden of our cry would be that we have fallen behind all other communities in the peaceful avocations of manufacture, commerce and industry.

In 1927-28, the percentage of literacy amongst the Muslims in the various provinces of India was as follows: Bombay, 9.6; Madras 7.8; Punjab 4.6; U.P. 3.2, and N.W. Frontier 2.0. These figures show that the Muslims of Bombay stood first in the field of education. But even now they were worse than the advanced classes of the Hindu community because their percentage of literacy at this time was 16.1. Mrs. R.S. Husain tells us that in India at that time all the doors to wealth, health and wisdom were denied to Muslims on the plea of inefficiency. Some newspapers owned by Muslims admitted this fact. The late lady Shams al-Huda often used to say that the Muslim public abused her husband because he gave certain high posts to Hindus ignoring Muslim claims, but they failed to see their own fault. The Muslim applicants were really unfit for the posts.

It is an irony of fate that the Hindus, who were bound by their *shastras* to treat women like slaves and cattle and to get their daughters married before they were hardly out of their girlhood, were as a matter of fact quite liberal in sending their children to modern schools. They were trying to get laws passed against child-marriage and raising the age of consent to sixteen years. They were also devising means to popularize widow-marriage heedless of their *pandits* who quoted *shastras* saying, "Not only should a woman refrain from marrying a second time but she should do penance by living only on fruits etc., after her husband's death." On the other hand, while Islam allowed every freedom to women so much so that a woman could not be given in marriage without her consent or free-will, thus indirectly prohibiting child-marriages, many people were giving away their daughters in marriage without their consent. Many a time a bride bitterly bewailed her fate on being compelled to marry a bridegroom whom she knew to be a drunkard or an old man of sixty, but the marriage celebrations proceeded despite her silent protest. Respectable families of Muslims took pride in preventing widow-marriages whether the widow was a girl of thirteen or a child of seven. In such a state of affairs, therefore, it was not surprising that in 1927-28 "not one out of two hundred girls even knew their alphabet." Much was, therefore, yet to be done to improve the standard of education amongst the Muslims.

11

Reorganisation of Madrasah Education

SAYD SHAHABUDDIN

The Jashn-i-Darul-'Ulum, Deoband, provides an appropriate opportunity for the Muslim community of India to consider various aspects of religious and theological instruction.

Need for Islamic Education

There is no doubt that in order to maintain the Islamic identity of the community against the pressures of westernisation, the onrush towards modernisation, the growing tide of atheism and the overwhelming influence of a non-Islamic environment, the Muslim society needs institutions of various grades and at various levels for preserving Islamic values and transmitting Islamic principles to the coming generations.

One of the directive principles of the Constitution of India is to provide compulsory primary education up to the age of 14, though at the same time it grants the right to religious, linguistic and cultural minorities to establish and administer educational institutions of their choice. The fact is that most Muslim children receive and increasingly more and more shall receive instruction in general schools, established by the State, where not only religious education but even ethical or moral instruction is not available and where available, it largely reflects the Hindu ethos to an extent unacceptable to other religious communities. There is also a tendency, particularly in urban areas, for children to join schools at a very young age at pre-primary levels, thus limiting the possibility of religious or moral instruction at home or in special institutions before joining the common educational stream. The net result is that most Muslim children do not have the basic knowledge of

Islam and when they grow up, many of them cannot even read the Holy Quran or perform the basic tenets of their faith.

Analysis of Requirements

To my mind, the requirement of the Muslim community can be analysed into three categories. The first requirement is that all Muslim adults should have basic knowledge of the principles of Islam, should be conversant with the fundamental dogmas and rituals, should imbibe the moral and ethical values associated with their faith, should be able to recite the Quran and follow its meaning in their mother-tongue and should have some preliminary notions about the application of the principles of Islamic jurisprudence to the daily life, so that they can distinguish between the enjoined and the forbidden. The second requirement is that the community should have sufficient number of religious teachers for the religious schools, of *Khatibs* and *Muazzins* for their mosques and of *Muftis* and *Qadis* to administer their personal law. The third requirement is that the community should produce scholars in various branches of Islamic learning so that they can participate in the propagation of the faith, rebut and refute the calumnies broadcast by hostile elements and keep the torch of learning alive and transmit Islamic values and traditions to the coming generations.

Islamic Content in Minority Educational Institutions

Most of the minority institutions unfortunately have not fulfilled the expectations of the community or justified the reason for their existence. The motivating force behind the establishment of these institutions has become material profit and to some extent expansion of employment opportunity for some of the unemployed graduates among the kith and kin. Emphasis should have been on the content of education so that the primary purpose behind the constitutional right, i.e., preservation of religion, language and culture, should have been served. But the emphasis has been on management and control, on appointment and dismissal of teachers. And admission has been un-restricted on the principle of the more, the merrier. The result is that while enjoying constitutional protection as minority institutions, they are no different in syllabus or atmosphere than the general institutions. Only by striving towards an Islamic content and an Islamic environment can the minority institutions established by the Muslims or in the name of the Muslim community serve a useful purpose, in meeting the first requirement. I would strongly urge that such educational institutions should include a course in Islamic Studies at the primary level, outside and in addition to the normal syllabus prescribed by the State. Similarly, at the secondary level, Islamic Studies should be offered as an additional subject for those children who show interest and promise and at the college level, also, there should be regular classes—optional though they may be—punctuated by weekly study circles and occasional seminars and syndicate studies on various elements of Islamic way of life. Secondly, the Muslims should concentrate on opening *maktabs* where the Muslim children could spend one year learning to read the Holy Quran, to say prayers and gaining general knowledge about Islam and the Holy Prophet. Muslim kindergarten could have a syllabus with an Islamic bias. These could feed both the normal primary schools or the *Madrasah Ibtidaiya.*

The other two requirements can be met only by institutions like Nadwat-ul-'Ulama and Dar-ul-'Ulum. Unfortunately, there is a wide divergence among the hundreds of such institutions spread throughout the length and breadth of the country not only in syllabus and standard but even in their nomenclature. There is no all-India authority to prescribe a uniform syllabus or consider necessary revisions thereof from time to time. There is no All-India authority to establish common standards of achievement and evaluation.

Uniform Nomenclature

Speaking of nomenclature, a one-room institution or a one-man show boldly advertises itself as a Dar-ul-Ulum in order to gain the sympathies of gullible Muslims, as if they were on par with Deoband or Nadwah. Notwithstanding the existence of religious sects, it should be possible for the Muslim community to enforce through social pressure that the term *Madrasah Ibtidaiya* should be used for institutions at a primary level whose product may be termed as *'Mawlvi';* that institutions at the secondary level should be termed as *Madrasah Thanawiyah* whose product may be designated *'Alim'* ; that a theological institution comparable to an undergraduate college should be termed *'Jami'ah'* and its product may be called *'Fazil';* and, that, an institution offering facilities for post-graduate instruction and research in theology and associated subjects may be termed as Dar-ul-Ulum and the degree it offers may be termed *'Kamil'* as equivalent to M.A.

Syllabus for Islamic Education

Without claiming any competence to prescribe a model and a syllabus for *madrasahs* I feel that these institutions should be residential as far as possible and should, on one hand, offer instruction in Arabic language, *Tafsir, Hadith, Fiqh* and Islamic philosophy and logic. On the other, they also should offer courses in Islamic and Indian history, geography, general science, politics, civics and economics, arithmetic and geometry, and in Hindi, Urdu (or the mother tongue) and English. The *Mawlvis* and *'Alims* coming out of these institutions would thus be in a position to understand the spirit of the time and to serve as leaders of the community.

At the college level the medium of instruction should be Arabic as far as possible and apart from Arabic itself, *Tafsir, Hadith* and *Fiqh* should be compulsory, apart from courses in current affairs and/or Islamic history, political, social and cultural. Such institutions should also offer correspondence and refresher courses for Muslim laity who may be interested in advancing their knowledge of Islam.

At the post-graduate level specialisation should be possible in either of the four disciplines, namely, Arabic literature. *Tafsir, hadith* or *Fiqh.* In addition, it should be possible for the schools to offer certificate courses in *Hifz* and *Qira't.*

Islamic and General Education : Parallel Streams should meet at various Terminal Points

The assumption behind the scheme outlined above is that the system of Islamic instruction should run parallel to the national system of education so that at every stage it should be possible to exchange students between the two streams, e.g., a product of an ordinary primary school should be in a position to join a *Madrasah*

Thanawiyah or a product of a *Madrasah Thanawiyah* should be in a position to join a college or the product of a college, after getting his B.A., should be in a position to join *Dar-ul-Ulum* for specialisation and *vice versa.*

There is no doubt in my mind that the proposed system demands not only streamlining of the present structure, organisation and management of religious institutions but above all dedication to the cause of Islamic education in a spirit of sacrifice and mutual tolerance among various sects as well as among various existing centres of religious instruction. Shall our Ulema rise to the occasion and above the barriers of sectarianism?

Organisation

Every district in India should have its Council of Islamic Education affiliating all the *Madrasahs* topped by a state level Council and a National Council. The District Councils should meet every year, while the State Councils should hold a conference every two years and there should be a National Conference every five years.

Similarly, there should be annual meetings, at the state and national levels, of teachers of Arabic, *Tafsir, Hadith* and *Fiqh* for cross-fertilisation of ideas and for considering suggestions for improvement in the syllabi and the method of teaching.

Financing by Voluntary Donations

The existence of thousands of Madrasahs all over the country is a living testimony to the spirit of charity which Islam has inculcated among the faithful. Most of these institutions of Islamic education are supported by voluntary donations. Of course, the manner of collection leaves much to be desired. Particularly the utilisation of students for door-to-door collection should be avoided. If the proliferation of institutions can be avoided after careful assessment of the needs of the community, it should be possible to rationalise the method of collection and to evolve a formula for the distribution of the collection among various institutions. Undoubtedly the Deoband experiment continues to be relevant. Our religious institutions must be financed by the combined effort of the community and they should not in any way depend upon the financial aid or assistance from the State. No doubt there are Madrasahs in various parts of the country which are financed by the State for historical reasons. But very few ever achieve an environment conducive to the inculcation of Islamic values. Like all *'sarkari'* institutions, they become dens of corruption, wastage and inefficiency. The teachers spend less time teaching and more time in pleasing the educational authorities, and thus cornering a share of the State patronage. The distinction between legitimate and illegitimate income disappears. My view is that *'sarkari' madrasahs* should gradually be transformed into *'azad' madrasahs,* though I am conscious of the fact that the trend is very much in the opposite direction.

Employment Opportunity

Finally, a word about employment opportunities. If a uniform syllabus and a common examination is prescribed, effort should be made to affiliate all Madrasahs and Jamiahs to one or two Dar-ul-Ulums, so that the *'sanads'* awarded at the completion of education at the *Ibtidaiyah* level (*Mahir*) or at the secondary level (*Alim*) or at the college level (*Fazil*) or at the post-graduate level (*Kamil*) are all awarded in the name of the Dar-ul-Ulum and thus carry national recognition and weightage. In appointing teachers in various *Maktabs* and *Madrasahs* and *Khatibs* and *Moazzins* for the various mosques or *Qadis* and *Muftis* for various *Imarat-i-Shari'ah* or in selecting the personnel for missionary activities or for research these *'sanads'* would be taken into account. Such standardisation would undoubtedly raise not only the level of teaching but also the general religious level of the Muslim community and, at the same time, create a national leadership—rooted in the life of the community and yet aware of the wider world, to whom the community could turn when, individually or collectively it needs some disinterested guidance. Islamic values can be transmitted to the future only through Islamic education, well-organised and responsive to the needs of the community. This is the essential message of Dar-ul-'Ulum, Deoband, which has acted as a pioneer in this field. But today we also need unification and standardisation.

12

An Educational and Sociological Perspective

M.M.M. MAHROOF

The educational and social pursuits of the Muslims during the period 1780 to 1901 have already been discussed by the present writer across the pages of this Journal. This article attempts to present the important educational reforms and rise of Muslim middle class in the period between 1902 and 1914.

The Mechanism of the State

This period covers the regimes of two Governors, Sir Joseph West Ridgeway (1895—1903) and Sir Robert Chalmers (1913—1916), and those of Sir Henry Blake (1903—1907) and Sir Henry McCallum (1907—1913). Ceylon being a Crown Colony, the Governor was usually a senior member of the Colonial Service or a man distinguished in military or constabulary services. The Governor had under him an Executive Council and was answerable to Legislative Council which also constituted opposition members. The Executive Council and the Legislative Council (almost entirely European) comprised senior officers of the Crown service, including legal and technical branches. The Governor with the phalanx of the Executive Council and the official members of the Legislative Council behind him could effectively run the government. The Civil Servants, well paid and well looked after "by comparison with both the Ceylonese and with many of their compatriots at home," were, perhaps, expected "where necessary to stand up for the interests of the villagers against those of white planters or native headmen." These well-meaning attitudes were not always appreciated at home. Nevertheless, the British bureaucracy had two permanent opponents in the shape of white planters (and merchants) and the indigenous middle class.

The white trading and planting class, obviously, looked upon itself as a catalyst of economic progress and desired to be recognized. Harry Creasy, in 1910, proposing a resolution stated :

> ... this meeting of the General European Community respectfully begs to express its regret at the decision of the Secretary for the Colonies to reduce the number of European representation in the Legislative Council of Ceylon from 3 to 2 and prays that the decision may be rescinded....

He also said :

> We mark every type of prosperity. Among the private population, we see the cooly who used to eat his rice and curry from a palm leaf now taking it from a plate with a knife and fork and spoon. We see the native who lived in a hut and slept on mat now living in a brick built and tiled house and sleeping on a bed, like "master." Going higher up, we see men who used to drive a hackery and bull now driving their carriages. We see the private citizen who was content with a one-horse chaise now blooming into a carriage and pair. We see motor cars and all modern luxuries all around us and we see new houses going up in every direction.

Creasy, himself a leading businessman, was emphasizing on the economic improvement of those times, though some of his illustrative examples verge on the hyperbole. Those were the years in which Ceylon saw the first car (1902) and the first aeroplane (1911). The burgeoning of the plantation sector was signalled by the formation of the Ceylon Agricultural Society, and the Low Country Products Association to which infrastructure was extended. In 1909, the railway was introduced in Jaela, Negombo, Ratnapura. Motor mail and telegraphic services were set up. Associations like the Law Society of Ceylon and Engineering Association for Ceylon were formed in 1903 and 1905 respectively.

However, the interests of the European trading class were not neglected. The seconder of Creasy's resolution, Rev. H. Highfield, the principal of a leading missionary school, made out a case for the ruling class when he said,

> I stand here among you and I represent an interest that is of distinct importance to the land—I mean its modern educational interests. I have a great deal to do with the educating of the youth of Ceylon. It seems to me that it is desirable that men in my position should in some way be able to influence the election of one European, who would feel that he did not represent capital, that he did not even represent the interests of his fellow-countrymen alone but was sent to the Legislative Council in order that he might occupy a free but a very important position in being able to understand the desires of the other communities perhaps better than a good many of his fellow-countrymen could do so and so to join them in important moments at times.

The Ceylonese middle class, of course, could not be sidelined. It was not, certainly, a social grouping arranged in neat layers but consisted of an amorphous but active mass of individuals ranging from the salaried classes of teachers, government servants, professionals like lawyers, doctors, land-owners, big and small, and businessmen of various categories. Astutely exploiting all the opportunities for material advancement, this was particularly true of the business community, the middle class exercised more political influence for itself, its forum being the Legislative Council. That a knowledge of English and English education ran like a golden thread through the over weening stance of the Cylonese middle class was a notion specially favoured by most Europeans in Ceylon. Dr. Llewelyn Thomas, at the same meeting alluded to above, expressed view in very clear terms:

> Where do all the men… who are on the Government and merchants' offices and in all places where English is required? Where did they all get their education and knowledge? In Christian schools founded and run by European money. We

have educated the people of this country for the last sixty or seventy or eighty years and up to a pitch that they are now fit to sit in the Legislative Council. That is what the Christian schools and colleges have done. For doing all that the European representation is to be reduced. I cannot imagine anything so absolutely foolish as that.

The British educational social and economic interests in Ceylon emanated from an uneasy triangle of forces, viz., the British bureaucracy, the white interests and the Cylonese middle class.

The Muslim Configuration

By the beginning of this century, the "kasbah system" of the Muslims underwent a critical phase. The non-viability of a closed economic system based upon an urban precinct, or a village area together with such disparities as the migration from one's town precinct or village and setting up households in plantation areas, the sudden affluence of individuals, the growing influence of English, are some of the eroding factors which are quite discernible. Let us look first at the census report of 1901 and 1906.

TABLE I

Race Distribution of Population in Census Yr. 1901 and in 1906

Race	*1901*	*%*	*1906*	*%*
Europeans	6300	.01	6484	.01
Burghers	23482	.06	24588	.06
Sinhalese	2330807	65.3	2547355	64.1
Tamils	951740	26.6	1127978	28 .4
Moors	228034	6.3	237221	5 .9
Malays	11902	.03	12003	.03
Others	13689	.03	13063	.03
All Races	3565954	100	3901471	100

Source: Registrar-General, *Vital Statistics 1903* (E. F. Hopkins), p. 0/2, Table B ; Registrar-General, *Vital Statistics 1906* (P. Arunachalam), p. 0/3, Table B. 1906 is the mid-year for the period under review. Burghers is the term used for the descendants of the Dutch in Sri Lanka.

The Muslims of Ceylon during the period under review constituted between 6% and 6.5% of the total population. Though they lived throughout the length and breadth of the country, substantial concentrations were found in and around Colombo (the capital) and the eastern sea-board (primary concentrations) and the western sea-board and the central hill country (secondary concentrations).

An index to the communities' health is afforded by the birth and death rates. They relate to the positive and negative factors which affect the people, which include the effect of food, clothing, housing and their availability or otherwise.

TABLE II

Birth and Death Rates among Different Races, 1903 and 1906

Race	*B.R. (1903)*	*D.R. (1903)*	*Dif.*	*B.R. (1906)*	*D.R. (1906)*	*Dif.*
All Races	40.0	25.9	14.10	35.7	34.3	1.4
Europeans	27.7	21.7	6.0	22.5	23.1	-0.6
Burghers	30.8	23.9	4.9	34.9	24.9	10.0
Sinhalese	44.4	24.4	20.0	38.7	34.6	4.1
Tamils	30.9	29.1	1.8	29.2	34.1	-4.9
Moors	39.9	29.8	10.1	36.9	34.2	2.7
Malays	26.8	25.9	0.9	36.2	38.6	-2.4
Others	16.3	26.5	-10.2	20.5	33.9	-13.4

The birth and death statistics of the different communities in Ceylon show a variety of patterns. According to Table 6.2, 1906 opens the lid of troubles and tribulations and is marked by a heavy incidence of malaria — a very distressing and debilitating disease. (This year is given here for control purposes.) In the year 1903 the death rate is fairly stable, the range approximating to 8 only. The death rate among the Moors was the highest, a part cause being the insanitary surroundings induced by the declining "kasbah system" as well as the pressure on space. A shift of value-systems by which the traditional Unani medicine was replaced by Western allopathy (because the Muslims still look askance at allopathic practitioners) was yet another causative factor. The birth rate was more variable in 1903 among the different communities, the range being 28. The Moor birth rates were fairly high. In spite of medical deficiencies, the Moors remained unaffected by the calamaties of the year 1906. A more pertinent index of medical well-being is afforded by the number of deaths of women at child-birth.

TABLE III

Deaths of Women at Parturition (to 1000 births)

Races	*1903*	*1906*
All Races	14.5	16.9
Europeans	—	—
Burghers	13.6	3.5
Sinhalese	16.0	19.1
Tamils	9.6	11.5
Moors	14.8	13.3
Malays	12.4	23.0
Others	18.4	3.8

Source : Vital Statistics 1903, p. F 12 ; *Vital Statistics 1906,* p. 0/15.

The figures for the Moors resemble all races but for the Malays it is less. (The figures in the control year 1906 is exceptional.) Whatever the statistical consequences of the parturition death figures might be, they have the societal consequence that high figures usually fuel medical reformism and attempt at amelioration of social hygiene. The following figures relate to Colombo, the capital city, where the "kasbah system" was particularly strong.

TABLE IV

Birth, Death Rates for Each Race in the Town of Colombo

Race	*B.R.1903*	*B.R.1906*	*D.R.1906*	*D.R.1906*
All Races	21.8	27.3	34.8	39.8
Europeans	30.7	27.5	33.6	35.4
Burghers	29.9	36.4	28.0	29.5
Sinhalese	27.9	34.9	38.2	43.8
Tamils	11.1	14.6	34.2	41.4
Moors	18.6	23.5	31.1	32.6
Malays	19.0	32.0	31.4	33.8
Others	10.9	14.2	33.0	40.0

Source : Vital Statistics 1903, p. F14 ; *Vital Statistics 1906,* p. 0/18. The rates are for mille.

According to Table IV, the birth rates appear to vary according to the rate of affluence of the communities, thus setting at naught Castro's contention (in his *Geography of Hunger*) that the birth rate varies in inverse proportion to the addition of protein supplement to the diet. The birth rate of the Moors (of Colombo) is fairly low and reaches a moderately high rate. The death rates do not vary for the communities and are stable at approximately mid-thirty (per mille).

In brief, the "kasbah system" whether in Colombo, or frequently elsewhere, was markedly healthier than "free-living" situations. But it was the unusual circumstance that attracted the outside observer. The Assistant Government Agent (i.e., the seniormost government officer) for Matara wrote in 1905.

> [Small pox] attacked with special virulence the Moorish inhabitants who are numerous in this neighbourhood. Their houses consist for the most part of small, dark, dirty and window-less rooms built around one or more courtyards and there is usually a through communication from house to house. The Mohammedan has, as is well-known, a strong objection

> to any intrusion of the authorities upon his domestic privacy……

Other observers were more realistic in realizing that the Muslims' life-style was not without its excellences. The Medical Officer of Health of Colombo Municipality wrote in 1906,

> Mohammedans are for the most part a grave, courteous people amongst whom it is a pleasure to work ; but they are intensively conservative and sternly resent the encroachment upon their domestic privacy which modern sanitary measures entail.
>
> A number of representations were, I believe, made to Government against the intrusion by the male Inspectors of the Department in the exercise of their duty and as a result Government called for a report and suggested the desirability of employing a female Inspector for this work. The [Colombo Municipal] Council agreed to this and Mrs. Salgado was appointed and commenced work on February 19, 1906. Her services have been of great value in the detection of cases of infectious disease and insanitary conditions generally in the Mohammedan quarters.

The value-system of the Muslims did not remain unaffected in the process of modernization of society as a result of the educational reforms set in motion by the government and the consequential response by the people of the country.

Ruling Ideas in Education

It is possible to trace out the various strands of the government's policy during the years under review. These were, roughly, a strengthening of the educational machinery, the quest for basic education for all, an interest in primary teaching and teaching methodology, and the espousal of an all-English education. Behind these were the emerging "public school syndrome" and the greater activity of the assisted schools which were under the control of various missions and communities.

Governor West Ridgeway, who had well-balanced views on education, set up a Board of Education over which the Director of Public Instruction presided. The idea of basic education for all was stressed by the Committee on Elementary Education which reported in 1905 (Sessional Paper XXVIII of 1905). Its views were neatly summarised in the *Administrative Report of the Director of Public Instruction* for the year 1905 in the following terms:

> (1) that it is desirable that the male population as a whole should receive elementary education; (2) in place where schools exist attendance should be made compulsory in Aided Schools as well as Government Schools; (3) a conscience clause should be adopted as a guarantee that religious instruction is not given to those who disapprove of it ; (4) in all parts of the Island (i.e. Ceylon) where the population is sufficiently dense the establishment of schools for boys should be made compulsory and that improved local organizations should be introduced for the purpose; (5) this organisation should take the form of District School Committees and Divisional School Committees ; (6) it is not possible at present to meet the cost by new local rate or cess; (7) the payment of salaries in Government schools and grants-in-aid schools should continue to be met from general revenue; (8) the local funds now devoted to the construction and maintenance of school buildings should be augmented by handing over to the District School Committees a portion of tax now levied locally as road tax.

The outcome of the exercise was passing of the Town Schools Ordinance (Ord. No. 5 of 1906) and the Rural Schools Ordinance (Ord. No. 8 of 1907). The Town Schools Ordinance was to be applied to Municipal and Local Board Towns as well as "townlets" coming under the Small Towns Sanitary Ordinance of 1892 regarding compulsory "vernacular" education. The Rural Schools Ordinance catered for vernacular education in planting and rural districts. "These two Ordinances provided for the compulsory education of children between the ages of six and twelve years except in the case of girls of Muslim and Tamil parentage, where the age limit for compulsory education was set between six and ten years."

The two ordinances ran into rough weather from the first. Apart from the intrinsic intransigence of the Muslims, which will be discussed later, there were other factors like the practical impossibility of building sufficient schools, the lack of financial capacity of District School Committees and the sheer impracticability of forcing poor parents to send their children without the existence of an income support system. The concept of a regularly organised school for every child, it appeared, was not practicable at all. Earlier, Van Cuylenburg who had reported on the educational system of the Madras Presidency had advocated a kind of "bare-foot" school system which he had found there. He wrote,

> "Sessional schools," a sort of peripatetic training agency, is worked exclusively among teachers of village primary schools. . . The schools taught by these men have no exact parallel in any class of schools aided by us. They can only be likened to Mohammedan verandah schools and to those efforts at school-keeping of the village guru which are to be seen in occasional operation even amongst us in the countryside. It seemed to me that these "indigenous schools," as they are called in India, is a special anxiety of the Department and no trouble was spared to induce these proprietory teachers to come under the Department system. Training actually served as a bait to draw these men and their schools into the Department net. . . and considering the success with which the presence of trained teachers has enabled the Department in Madras to introduce the latest reforms in teaching and organisation into their schools, the establishment of at least one central training college for men and women teachers in our Colony [i.e. Ceylon] is a step which should not, I think, be any longer delayed. If we are content ourselves with the view that the mere ability to read and write do a little ciphering is all that need be comprised in education, then our system cannot be cavilled at but if in the light of modern advancement, education is to be based on the cultivation and development of the powers of observation and reasoning, then we must admit that the machinery available to us for this purpose is utterly unsuited and utterly deficient.

The idea of such training or the induction of village schools into the mainstream of education was not envisaged by the government. The rationale for the government's enacting the Town and Rural Schools Ordinances was poised between two stools — a mere sop to the middle class and, as an alternative, a creation of the demi-educated, who would be free from the customary obedience which they rendered to the middle-class (which was, more or less, a state of mind) and yet be without the technical expertise and the organizational ability to force concession from the government.

The position of English was sound, for it had powerful forces working on its behalf. A knowledge of English had distinct uses. The obstinacy on the part of British bureaucracy which required the indigenous people to talk to it in English was one crucial factor. Another was the development of schools by Christian missionaries that manifested a "public school syndrome" which inevitably required an in-depth study of English language and literature, a boarding-school ethic, a fondness of games like cricket, introduction of perfect and "fagging" system, an obsession with Graeco-Latin culture and a Mitfordian sense of class distinction.

The classification of English schools as elementary and secondary was first made in the Education Code for 1908. Regulations Nos. 29 and 30 dealt with this issue. Reg. 29 (1) stated that English schools were to be of two types : elementary and secondary. In each school the work of the five lower standards was to follow either Schedule A or Schedule B. Reg. 29 (2) laid down that elementary schools were those in which the work did not include more than the range of work covered by Schedules A and B of the Code, together with Drawing and Vernacular Literature. Reg. 29(3) said that secondary English schools were those in which the range of work included a fairly reasonable number of subjects specified in Schedule C of the Education Code and in which a fairly good number of pupils were prepared for any of the following examinations:

(i) The Cambridge Junior and Senior Local examinations ;

(ii) The examination in Arts and Science of the London University;

(iii) The First in Arts Examination of an Indian University.

The syllabus for English Language and Literature for senior students consisted of texts of Shakespeare, Milton, Scott and Matthew Arnold. But what was noticeably striking was a serious concern for the peccadilloes of English grammar. One examining syndicate, referring to English Grammar of Form III, observed :

> Three quarters of the papers were good and only one was below standard. All the more elementary questions were well answered. About half the boys could not manage the analysis of a complex sentence. A good many were unable to punctuate properly the set passage, the majority omitting the necessary inverted commas or inserting them wrongly. . . .

What the evaluating system demanded of the students was, it may be concluded, grammatical accuracy, and precise expressions. Such a technical grammatical competence was aimed at and therefore inculcated in the pupils as an educational objective. Another examining body had declared earlier referring to Royal College, Colombo (the principal secondary government school in Ceylon),

> I was very much pleased with the work done in English grammar. There were signs of intelligent and thoughtful teaching in all the Forms. Parsing was well done. The weakest points were found in those questions which depended on the ability to write English. The analysis was generally good but it was very untidily written and the relationship of different clauses was not clearly expressed . . . . *The King Alfred Readers* are excellent books but many years experience has taught me that Reader IV in any good series is usually quite difficult enough for all but the oldest and most talented boys I think too that the poems should be changed from time to time and that the same subjects should not be offered for examination in two consecutive years.

TABLE V

Percentage of Literacy According to Religion in Census 1901 and 1911

Religion	*Males*	*Females*	*Males*	*Females*
	1901		*1911*	
Christian	55.2	30.0	60.3	38.8
Buddhist	34.9	5.2	41.8	9.1
Muslim	34.4	3.3	36.2	3.2
Hindu	25.9	2.5	29.6	4.0

Source : U. D. I. Sirisena, "Promotion of Literacy," *Education in Ceylon—A Centenary Volume,* Pt. II (Colombo, 1969), p. 530.

In spite of infirmities' constraints the figures show a little progress as regards Muslim males and a decline as regards Muslim females. A more pertinent index is the number of school-going Muslim children. The following table indicates the situation in 1906 (the mid-year for the period under review).

TABLE VI

Government English and Vernacular Schools (Average Attendance) 1906

Provinces		*Total Attendance*	*Attendance*	
			Moor	*Malay*
Western	Province	20124	130	11
Central	"	6986	321	40
Northern	"	72	106	—
Southern	"	7879	449	1
Eastern	"	175	183	—
North-Western	"	4530	32	1
North-Central	"	1191	4	—
Uva	"	1017	41	10
Sabaragamuwa	"	5532	46	3
Total		47506	1312	66

Source: J. Harvard, *Administrative Report of Director of Public Instruction for 1906,* p. A 32. Average attendance means "average daily attendance for twelve months preceding the month fixed for examination."

The amount of money that was spent by government on the education of the Ceylonese, mostly middle class people, was considerable.

Response of the Muslims

The educational efforts of the government have a little effect on the Muslim community. The Table V is suggestive.

TABLE VII

Grant-in-Aid English, Anglo-Vernacular and Vernacular Schools (Average Attendance 1906)

Province		*Total Attendance*	*Attendance*	
			Moor	*Malay*
Western	Province	41212	1049	185
Central	"	8356	685	245
Northern	"	20733	234	10
Southern	"	14410	184	58
Eastern	"	8703	568	23
North-Western	"	5993	58	64
North-Central	"	341	16	17
Uva	"	1370	52	39
Sabaragamuw	"	1563	40	1
Total		102681	2886	632

Source : J. Harvard, *Administrative Report of Director of Public Instruction for 1906,* p. A32.

The total attendance at grant-in-aid schools (in essence, private schools run by missionaries and communities) is more than double when compared with that of government schools. This is true of Moor attendance, too. In the case of Malays, the ratio of attendance at private schools to those of government schools is nearly 10 : 1. Though the percentage of the Muslim population, i.e., the Moors and the Malays, of the total population of Ceylon ranged between 6% and 7%, the Muslim school population was perhaps less than half. Of the total attendance at government schools, the ratio of Muslim attendance comes to 2.9% while it is a little higher, i.e. 3.42% in respect of grant in-aid schools.

Within the respective provinces, there were significant variations. Government schools were popular among the Muslims in the Central Province, the centre of the tea planting industry, where there was scope for the entrepreneurial activities of the Muslims. But the province having the highest rate of attendance was the Southern Province, where the Muslim entrepreneurship was traditionally strong and crafts like jewellery selling and lapidary were being built up. Surprisingly, the Western Province having within it Colombo (the capital, the seat of government and commercial centre—all combined) and a considerable Muslim population ranks only fourth in rate of attendance. Others low in ranking are the North-Western, the North-Central, Uva and Sabaragamuwa Provinces, themselves economically under-developed regions lacking infrastructure.

The statistics as regards the aided school is rather different. The rate of Muslim attendance is highest in the Western Province. The existence of properly organized Muslim aided schools would partly explain it. The Central Province maintains its rate. And expectedly, the North-Western, the North-Central, the Uva and the Sabaragamuwa Provinces show low ratings. The Eastern Province, where there was a heavy concentration of Muslims, shows a high rate indicating an indigenous tradition of Tamil and Arabic studies.

One of the reasons for the low figures for Muslim education was the scarcity of Muslim educational organisations. The table below is suggestive.

TABLE VIII

Educational Financing 1906

Managed Schools —	*No. of Schools*	*Nominal Attendance*	*Average Attendance*
Total Managed Schools	1661	162931	99655
Muhammadan "	7	825	440

Muhammadan managed schools were only 0.42% of total managed schools a hopelessly low figure. The management of Muslim schools was largely undertaken by eager amateurs driven by their religious and social zeal and financed by a few of the committed rich among the Muslims. Not unexpectedly, they did not exhibit the kind of organisational maturity and expertise of the missionary bodies. The rate of average attendance of Muslim schools vis-a-vis average attendance of total managed schools shows a similar figure 0.44%.

Educational financing (i.e. the sums of money given by the government to aided schools) is unsatisfactory.

TABLE IX

Grants Made in 1906

Missions	*No. of Schools*	*Amount of Grant*
Grants-in-Aid English Schools		
Total Missions	178	Rs. 115884.25
Grants-in-Aid Anglo-Vernacular Schools		
Total Missions	71	Rs. 17717.50
Muhammadan	nil	nil
Grants-in-Aid Vernacular Schools		
Total Missions	1432	Rs. 321183.84
Muhammadan	4	Rs. 770.00
Grants-in-Aid English, Anglo-Vernacular and Vernacular Schools		
Total Missions	1641	Rs. 454785 59
Muhammadan	7	Rs. 930.00

Source : J. Harvard, *Administrative Report of Director of Public Instruction for 1906,* p. A38.

In order to raise the low educational standards among Muslims Siddi Lebbe, a lawyer and educationist, launched a two point scheme, one was relating to the establishment of schools for Muslims where Arabic and Islam may be taught in addition to usual syllabus of government schools, and the other was, again, the establishment of a well-maintained grant-in-aid school in Colombo (which was later to become famous as Colombo Zahira College). While the latter was admirably successful, the former ran into difficulties from its inception. The underlying reasons were stated in the Administrative Report of the Department of Public Instruction for 1906.

> The number of Mohammedan children at Government schools was 1383 and [in that of] grant-in-aid schools [was] 3613 giving a total of 4996 -- an increase of 103 on the numbers in 1905. The number of Mohammedans receiving instruction is still only 1 in 48.
>
> In the larger towns there is a demand for English education for boys among the shop-keeping class of the Mohammedan population; at the same time there is considerable unwillingness to allow the boys to remain at school for any considerable number of years. The parents have a natural and well-grounded apprehension that if the boys remain too long at school they will become unfitted for the ordinary life of the native shop-keepers. The wants of this class would very well be met by Anglo-Vernacular schools working under Schedule E of the Code but starting English at a lower standard than that prescribed in the Schedule. There is no reason why the Schedule should not be allowed to be worked with a certain amount of elasticity as regards this point in cases where the circumstances render it necessary. Mohammedan custom prescribes that education whould begin with a period of the Koran and Arabic teaching which necessarily causes the period of beginning the ordinary venacular education to be deferred. The result is that boys in the lower standards in a Mohammedan Tamil school are older than boys in the same standards in an ordinary Tamil school. Such boys if the school is worked under a Schedule for Anglo-Vernacular Schools may very well be allowed to begin English in a lower standard that is prescribed by the Schedule.

The Report then proceeded to give statistics of special "Mohamedan" schools.

Name of School	*No. of Boys*	*No. of Girls*
New Moor St (Colombo) Girls School	—	71
Alutagama Boys School	29	—
Katukele Mixed School	42	60
Galle " "	76	44
Matara " "	49	31
Weligama " "	51	23
Tangalla " "	40	22
Galbokka " "	85	28
Total	372	279

It is difficult to resist the conclusion that, to significant sectors of the Muslim community, the educational efforts of the government or private bodies (other than the acquisition of English language as a discipline) was mainly an irrelevant exercise. They could acquire the necessary rudiments, as for instance an ability to read Arabic, to read and write Tamil, and to do mental arithmetic, through the Qur'an school. Apparently, Siddi Lebbe did not address his mind to the possibility of strengthening the Qur'an school and even training them on the lines suggested by Van Cuylenburg (which has been discussed above). Neither did the government, though the Department of Public Instruction maintained statistics of all unaided schools.

The Societal Structure among the Muslims

The societal structure among the Muslims of the period under review was quite different from that of other communities living in Ceylon. Centred around the mosque, it was based on the "kasbah system" which at that time was undergoing a change due to external forces. In any typical Muslim locality, the organisational layers would consist of the elite, the sub-elites, the professionals (as, for instance, the masons, the book-keepers), the artisans, and the fringe of socially recognized mendicants like the *faqirs*. These layers would vary depending on the locus. It is possible to classify the societal organisation of the Muslims schematically as follows:

(a) The Town Moot (*oor kootam* system); (b) South West village; (c) South West village variant; (d) *Madige* village; (e) *Madige* village variant; (f) *Kudi* village.

The oldest type is the Town Moot. They were found in the oldest urban settlements of the Muslims, mainly in towns like Colombo and Galle. The most recent were the *madige* village variant found in the underdeveloped provinces of North-Central, North-Western Provinces, etc. The *kudi* or tribal type village found exclusively in the Eastern Province had a strong matrilineal slant. The Table X lists schematically the main features.

TABLE X

(Principal Societal Structures)

---

1. *Town Moot* Oorkootam *system*

(a) *Locality*

Principal towns

(b) *Elites*

Principal traders (Chief trustees of mosques)

(c) *Sub-elites*

Other large-scale traders

2. *South-West village*

(a) *Locality*

Western and Southern Provinces

(b) *Elites*

Traditional *madicham* (mosque trustee) family

(c) *Sub-elites*

Cadet branch of *madicham* family 'arrivistes'

3. *South-West village variant*

(a) *Locality*

Parts of North-Western Province and Mannar district of Northern Province

(b) *Elites*

Principal land-owning family (*marikars*) often Colombo-resident)

(c) *Sub-elites*

Other land-owning families (usually resident in locality)

4. Madige *village*

(a) *Locality*

Central Province

(b) *Elites*

Principal land-owning family with feudalistic connections

(c) *Sub-elites*

Arriviste land-owning families

5. Madige *village variant*

(a) *Locality*

Uva, Sabaragamuwa provinces

(b) *Elites*

Principal trading (or land-owning) family

(c) *Sub-elites*

Other trading or landed families.

6. Kudi *Village*

(a) *Locality*

Eastern Province

(b) *Eiites*

Chief of principal *kudi (podiyar,* i.e. great land-owner)

(c) *Sub-elites*

Other *podiyars*

The elites used their traditional base as a rationale of their authority. Position and authority was transferred from father to son. Generally, such an authority was never challenged, as junior members of the immediate family and members of the cadet family found it expedient to recognise the authority of their senior relative. As the scope of capital accumulation was limited, arrivistes were rare, As a means of social enforcement, the elites who were most frequently trustees of mosques, took the mosque functionaries into confidence. Social recalcitrants were, in the ultimate act, refused the services of *imam* and *khatib* at functions like weddings, circumcisions, and, rarely, funerals. Generally, the possibility of such coercion being enforced was sufficient to ensure social conformity. In the long run, however, the elites could be challenged by the sub-elites who could become elites in their turn. This was possible by capital accumulation and social welfare activities in consequence.

That another possibility existed was shown by the educational activities of the government and private bodies. A knowledge of English was often needed for this process. There were the government servants ranging from senior law officers and administrative officers to peace officers which included village headmen and police officers. There were teachers who certainly did not possess power yet had at least persuasive influence. There were the more affluent traders who quite frequently had at least a nodding acquaintance with English. Above all, there was the political establishment of the Muslims, ranging all the way from the Muslim member of the Ceylon Legislative Council, the members of the Municipal Councils to members of village bodies. In addition, Muslim professionals were also coming on the scene. A certain amount of ex-officio recognition of elite status was given by the government's conferring "status honours."

By virtue of their acquired status in the society the sub-elites were a potential threat to the traditional elites and were capable of replacing them. In order to influence and exercise their power, the sub-elites made inroads upon mosques and controlled their administration.

Mosques were stepping stones for their success, so to say. The functionaries of the mosques, for instance, the *imams* and *khatibs,* tended to carry out requests of the trustees; and over the town or village moots which enforced social sanctions, it was the trustees who presided. Sometimes the sub-elites became the trustees and managers of *madrasahs* or Arabic colleges which trained '*Ulama.* Generally, the sub-elites mediated between the British or the local bureaucracy and the ordinary Muslim, by way of writing or reading official letters and accompanying him in interviews with state officials. In the circumstances, the ordinary Muslim did not feel in the "dead-letter status" of the Town Schools and Rural Schools Ordinances any serious deprivation.

However, the economic strength and the social position of the traditional elites inevitably brought them into the English-knowing spheres, either directly or indirectly. One potent cause was the accepted doctrine that the scope of Islamic law in Ceylon was limited. The result of this doctrine was put in a nutshell when Garvin, Senior Puisne Justice (of the Ceylon Supreme Court), stated that the "whole immense body of Mohammedan law is not law in Ceylon" and that "the branch of law known as Wakf was not introduced into Ceylon and did not become part of the customary law of the Ceylon Muslims."

Besides, the usual business transactions had to be carried out according to secular English. Land had to be bought, sold, leased and mortgaged; movable property had to be bought and sold; questions of land tenure, trespass had to be finalised; and wills and deeds had to be drawn up. English law in the form of Civil Procedure Code (consolidated by Ordinance No. 2 of 1889), Wills Ordinance (No. 21 of 1844), Entail and Settlement Ordinance (No. 11 of 1876), Prescription Ordinance (No. 22 of 1871), Prevention of Frauds Ordinance (No. 7 of 1840), and Execution of Deeds Ordinance (No. 17 of 1852) had become an established part of the legal landscape. The more affluent the Muslim elites and the sub-elites (the operative part of the Muslim middle class) became, the more amenable to English thinking they became.

The Muslim middle class, however, had no intention of becoming pale versions of Englishmen. The type of "assimilisme" found in certain countries of the Maghreb does not appear to have had any attraction for the Muslims of Ceylon. The vestiges of the "kasbah system" prevented any such developments taking place. Nevertheless, the comfortable life-style of the elites and sub-elites, comprising large houses, many servants and horse carriages, induced a hankering for the simple joys and the congregational life of the pristine "kasbah system." The remedial measures which the elites and the sub-elites took (perhaps unconsciously) were an increasing concern with the fabric of Islamic life, namely, the mosques and Arabic colleges, and steps to reorganise their management and extend their efforts. Another was a more extended interest in the Islamic world. But the most obvious was the resistance and rejection of all official attempts (or proto-attempts) to induce changes in Muslims' mode of behaviour, food or even dress. The last was a "cause celebre" which became famous as the fez controversy of 1905.

From the time of his entry into Ceylon in 1883 as an exile, Ahmad 'Urabi Pasha, the Egyptian patriot, had advocated the fez (or the tarboosh) to be adopted as the accepted headgear of the Muslim middle class in Ceylon. Since the educated Muslim, in the beginning of this century, adopted the British three-piece suit as his walking out costume, the fez remained the sole signal of his religion and race.

The fez controversy began when the first Muslim graduate and first Muslim advocate (the Ceylon equivalent of barrister) took oath on 7th October 1904 as advocate of the Supreme Court, wearing the fez. He practised in this headgear for seven months. However, during this period, the then Chief Justice, Sir Charles Layard was away in England. When he returned matters came to a head. On 2nd May 1905, Sir Charles required the advocate either to remove his fez or his shoes as a mark of respect. Being unable to comply with this request, the advocate withdrew. A group of leading Muslims decided to see Sir Charles, who agreed on the condition that the deputation should be a private one. In the course of the ensuing discussions, Sir Charles suggested that the advocate should submit a statement to the Supreme Court so that it could be decided formally. However, the Supreme Court after considering this statement minuted that the advocate should not come to court wearing the fez.

The group of influential Muslims decided on a series of actions. Thirty-nine meetings were held throughout Ceylon and the thirty-nine delegates were present at a mass meeting in Colombo (described by the *Times of Ceylon,* a national paper, in its issue of 1st January 1906 as a "monster meeting"). The meeting passed a unanimous resolution requesting the King-Emperor to rescind the minute. However, the authorities in Ceylon decided themselves to act. The Supreme Court made another minute on 16th March 1906 under which the fez was allowed.

Other questions were no such open and shut cases. Questions of Muslim reformism were mainly ventilated through the "little magazine." One such magazine, the *Muslim Guardian,* carrying articles in English and Tamil, was published from 1901 to 1908. Its editor and publisher, I. L. M. Abdul Aziz, was a well-known man of letters and came close to being an official spokesman of Muslim elites and sub-elites. In the pages of his journal, largely written by him, he espoused such causes as the need for registration of Muslim marriages and divorces officially ; the prevention of wasteful ceremonies in connection with Muslim marriages ; and the establishment of a Muslim Religious Council consisting of laymen and *'Ulamu'*.

Abdul Aziz was particularly keen on assessing events occurring in the world of Islam: "Through the columns of the *Muslim Guardian* he invited and encouraged donations for the Hedjaz Railway, intended to connect Damascus with Madhina [*sic.*]; as a result the fortunes of the Railway were followed with fervour and its completion in 1908 was celebrated enthusiastically in Colombo." Among the articles he wrote in his *Muslim Guardian* were those on Habib Allah Khan, king of Afganistan, Khedive `Abbas Hilmi Pasha of Egypt Shaykh 'Abd Allah Qwilliam, Sayyid Ahmad Khan, Syed Ameer Ali, the Egyptian nationalist Mustafa Kamil Pasha, and the sultans of Turkey. His public lectures were largely attended by Muslims, particularly the one on the conflict between the Cross and the Crescent delivered on 29th October 1912.

The years 1902-1914 saw some new educational policies brought about by the government in the shape of Town Schools Ordinance and Rural Schools Ordinance. These ordinances did not have much effect, largely because the middle class was not really involved, and in the case of the the Muslims as a whole, education was only peripheral and not a nuclear activity. The position of English, however, was assured, for the middle class was involved and it was strengthened by administrative needs and missionary activity. English has two effects on Muslim middle class. It helped sub-elites to achieve elite status and the elites had to come to terms with English for their commercial and day-to-day work. In turn, this forced upon the Muslim elites and sub-elites a wider awareness of themselves as Muslims.

13

Education

The Schools Character of Medieval Islamic Lerning, Curriculum and Instruction.

The art of reading and writing, which existed to a limited extent in Arabia before Islam, increased after the advent of Islam and especially with the expansion of the empire. In the early stages after the spread of Islam, teachers in the elementary places of instruction (*kuttab*) were mainly non-Muslims, especially Christians and Jews. But the advent of Islam brought for the first time a definite educational instrument of religious culture, the Qur'an and the teaching of the Prophet. This phenomenon gave rise to the controversy that persisted during the first two centuries or so of Islam as to whether one may teach or learn the Holy Book to or from a non-Muslim. The functions of teaching penmanship and of teaching the Word of God were, therefore, entrusted to different persons, a practice which continued for centuries so that Ibn Khaldun writes in the 8th/14th century: 'Penmanship is not to be taught with the Qur'an and religion....Reading and writing are not taught in elementary schools and any one who wants to learn them must have recourse to professional teachers'. Indeed, the emphasis even at the elementary level was on religious instruction, although reading and writing and simple arithmetic were not excluded.

Elementary education, however, was a self-sufficient unit and there was no organic link between it and the higher education. Indeed, to regard elementary education as a systematic feeding-ground for higher learning is a modern phenomenon and in the medieval system the aim was to develop as highly as possible the intellectual capacities of a select few whose educational career was different from those who were intended for an elementary education only. There were, from the early times of Islam, two other types of education only. There were, from the early times of Islam, two other types of education besides the elementary and the higher. The one was the palace-school education instituted for princes with a view to fashioning them into future rulers. This included religious education but laid stress on oratory, literature, etc., and, above all, on 'manly virtues'. The second type of education may be called adult education as it was imparted to the masses, not so much in order to teach them the art of reading and writing as with the purpose of giving instruction in the Qur'an and in the Faith. It was from this latter that schools of higher learning grew through the *halaqas* or 'circles' of pupils gathered around a certain teacher.

The instrument of religious culture for the higher educational circles was the new legal and theological-moral body of thought which was being produced during the early centuries of Islam. Among these schools legal science was the first to mature, and the followers of Abu Hanifa in Iraq, of Malik in Medina and later on those of al-Shafi'i and Ahmad ibn Hanbal developed a legal body of doctrine. But discussions of moral issues and controversies concerning theological problems to which the former led during the 2nd/8th and the 3rd/9th centuries also continued in a climate of ferment. These discussions and disputes were sometimes carried on in the mosques, but mostly in the private houses either of learned men or their patrons in the great cities of Iraq — Basra, Kufa and Baghdad. During the 'Abbasid period, certain Caliphs, notably al-Ma'mun and his father Harun al-Rashid, encouraged holding of learned disputes at their courts on all sorts of questions, logical, legal, grammatical, etc. Before the professional class of the 'Ulama' generally came into being, there was a great fluidity in thought and a remarkable tolerance of different views. Al-Ash'ari, the formulator of the orthodox creed, had himself heard the lectures of his Mu'tazili master al-Jubba'i in a mosque.

The steady and rapid growth of official mosque-libraries and semi-public libraries is a significant feature of medieval Islamic education. Several notable and powerful officials of the state acquired book-collections in large numbers and put them at the disposal of people of learning and sometimes even donated them for the public use. So too did the the semi-independent rulers and chiefs of principalities in the later 'Abbasid period. Towards the end of the 4th/10th century, the philosopher Ibn Sina obtained access to the library of the Persian ruler Nuh ibn Nasr, which he describes as fabulous but which was subsequently to perish in flames. The palace-library of the Fatimid al-Hakim of Egypt is said to have had forty rooms full of books. These libraries contained books on all subjects—literature, specifically Islamic sciences, natural sciences, logic, philosophy, etc. It is striking that the first state-sponsored academy set up by the 'Abbasid al-Ma'mun in the first quarter of the 3rd/9th century was not a venture in Islamic learning but concerned itself with systematic translations of Greek philosophy and science. The interaction of this body of knowledge with the Islamic sciences, which has had such a far-reaching effect on the character of Islamic education throughout the medieval period of Islam, will be dealt with later.

Private and public schools were also founded by individual effort and by donations for special Islamic subjects. General institutions were founded for the teaching of Hadith, law and so on. Abu Hatim al-Busti (d. 277/890) founded in his native town a school with a library and with allowances for non-native students. These institutions multiplied especially in the East in several places like Naysabur, Marv, etc. We must remember,however, that the subjects taught in these schools, notably Hadith, had developed a content which differed from the corresponding disciplines in the Shi'a sect. The teaching of these subjects, therefore, was *ipso facto*, and attack on Shi'ism. The Shi'a movement, which had led a subterranean life until the middle of the 4th/10th century, having attained external political success at the hands of the Buwayhid dynasty in Iraq and the Fatimids of Egypt, began to propagate its cause openly. It developed its own Hadith and partly its own law and placed them both at the service of its central doctrine of Imamate. It seized existing institutions of learning and established new ones, and on the basis of its political power turned these into propaganda machines for the spread of its ideology (*da'wa*). It had already acquired a skill in propaganda work by its long underground activities. In the year 361/972 the famous mosque-school of al-Azhar was founded by the Fatimids in Cairo, an institution which later turned into a Sunni institution and is today the greatest single traditional Islamic university in the world. During the last two years certain new faculties of practical science have been introduced (Agriculture, Medicine, etc.) through a law enacted by the U.A.R. Parliament in 1961. In 395/1005 the Fatimid al-Hakim founded a Sunni 'House of Wisdom' in Cairo, but closed it down in 398/1008 and executed its two learned professors.

While, therefore, the fairly commonly held view that the orthodox *madrasa* originated as a counter-propaganda measure against Shi'ism does not seem basically correct, since Sunni schools had already existed, it is true that the employment by the Shi'a, during their political power, of their academic institutions as propaganda tools, subsequently led the Sunni rulers — the Seljuqs and the Ayyubids— to lend state support, after the overthrow of the Shi'a rule, to Sunni educational institutions. By this time, the earlier Sunni institutions had produced a considerable body of learned scholars who were now appointed in the new *madrasas.* These, in their turn, created both a new core of text-books on various religious disciplines which resulted in a definite curriculum and, above all, the new 'Ulama' who became a distinct class in Muslim society with their own character, ethos and social status. The first of these new *madrasas* was instituted under the Seljuqs in Baghdad and Persia by Nizam al-Mulk (the great and wise wazir of the Seljuq Alp Arslan and Malikshah) who was assassinated in 485/1092 by Isma'ili agents. In course of time, a network of such colleges spread throughout the length and breadth of the Muslim world.

It would, however, be a mistake to suppose that Sunni Islam

emerged victorious primarily because of state-support. On the contrary, the new state-policies espoused the trends that had already taken root among the majority of the population and this is the real reason for the success of these policies. It is quite obvious that the Fatimids, despite their efforts to propagate, through education and otherwise, the Isma'ili doctrine, had failed to make any large scale impact on the populace. Nor did the majority of the people in Iraq and Persia accept Shi'ism under the Buwayhids. The Ash'arite dogmatic, however, did receive state favour but even its large-scale acceptance was due to the influence of men like al-Ghazali who taught at Nizam al-Mulk's college at Baghdad.

From the organisational point of view, the *madrasa* system reached its highest point in the Ottoman Empire where *madrasas* were systematically instituted, endowed and maintained under the Shaykh al-Islam's office with remarkable administrative skill and efficiency. The 'Ulama' were organised in a hierarchy and became almost a caste in the Ottoman society. These traditional seats of learning are still functioning all over the Muslim world outside Turkey: we have already pointed to the most eminent of them, the University of al-Azhar in Cairo. But these are at present in their various stages of adjustment to the challenges and demands that modern education has brought with it. Some, indeed, are still quite outside the sphere of these influences, like Deoband in India, and have refused so far to yield an inch to modern pressures. We shall, however, for the present turn to consider the content and inner character of medieval Islamic education.

The Character of Medieval Islamic Learning

The beginning and spread of Islamic learning in the early days of Islam is centred around individuals rather than schools. The content of Islamic thought is also characterized by individual effort. Certain outstanding personalities, who had learned the tradition and had built round it their own legal and theological systems, attracted students from far and near who sought knowledge from them. The first chief characteristic of this learning, therefore, and the one which has persisted throughout the Middle Ages of Islam, is the individual importance of the teacher. The teacher, after giving his full course, personally gave a certificate (*ijaza*) to the student who was then allowed to teach. The certificate was sometimes given in an individual subject — say *fiqh* or Hadith. Sometimes it concerned several subjects and sometimes it was valid only for specified books which the pupil had read. Later, when the *madrasas* came into existence, a system of examination was often instituted. But so great was the role and the prestige of the teacher as an individual that, even after the organisation of the *madrasas,* the biographies of illustrious men and scholars usually give the names of their teachers and it is relatively rare to find the names of the colleges at which they studied. Even the certificates were issued often in the name of the teacher rather than that of the school. Indeed, it would not be far from the truth to say that even in the later Middle Ages, the majority of celebrated savants were not the product of the *madrasas* but men who had been informal students of individual teachers. If one were to write a history of great and original thinkers in Islam, one would not find many recruits from the *madrasas.*

Connected with this central importance of the teacher is the phenomenon known as 'seeking of knowledge' (*talab al-'ilm*). Itinerant students travelled over long distances, sometimes over the length and breadth of the Muslim world, to follow the lectures of famous teachers. The study of the Hadith, the *putative* reports of deeds and sayings of the Prophet and his Companions, gave the earliest and the most powerful impetus to these scholastic journeys. There are reports in medieval Islam of people who had heard more than a hundred teachers. 'Making ready for the road' (*shadd al-rihal*) is a key-phrase aptly summing up this movement of acquisition of knowledge. The 'knowledge' or *'ilm,* was understood to mean, in the early stages of this movement, traditional knowledge. This was distinguished from *fiqh* or understanding, i.e. the intellectual operation on this traditional body of knowledge. Gradually, however, when the sciences of law and theology were developed, *fiqh* came to mean the legal thought, and 'knowledge' came to mean theology. The perennial rivalry between law and theology for the title of the 'crown of sciences'. But the 'closing of the door of *ijtihad* (i.e., original, free thought)' during the 4th/10th and the 5th/11th centuries led to the general stagnation of both legal and intellectual sciences, especially of the former. The intellectual sciences, theology and religious thought, suffered and became impoverished because of their deliberate isolation from, and the gradual decay of, secular intellectualism, especially philosophy and from other forms of religious thought such as Sufism offered.

The *madrasa* system, based to a considerable extent on state-sponsorship and state-control, has been generally regarded as the cause of the decline and stagnation of Muslim learning and scholarship. But the *madrasa,* with its restricted curriculum, was the symptom, not the real cause of this decline, although, of course, it perpetuated and accelerated intellectual stagnation. We have already said above that out standing and even great original thinkers did continue to arise even outside of the *madrasa* system. But the real reason for the decline of the quality of Islamic learning was the gradual starvation of the religious sciences through their isolation from the life of lay intellectualism which itself then decayed. From their successful opposition to the Mu'tazila and the Shi'a, the 'Ulama' had gained the experience of developing their own sciences and teaching them in such a way that a defence would be erected for this body of teaching. This did not have to do merely with the relatively external factor of a school-system which would be physically isolated against opposition. Even more important was the way in which the *content* of the orthodox sciences was developed so that they would be isolated from any possible challenge and opposition.

The inner constitution of these religious sciences was so created as to make them apparently absolutely self-sufficient; they filled not only their own place but the place of the entire field of knowledge. All other knowledge was superfluous, if not utterly condemnable. The statement quoted from the jurist al-Shatibi, to the effect that pursuit of all knowledge that was not related to action directly was forbidden, is characteristic of the temper of the medieval 'Ulama'.

The judgment, when directed against unrealistic, futile thinking, is valid enough, and modern pragmatism has taken a similar corrective stand against certain types of pure thought in the West. But, as enunciated by its medieval Muslim authors, this principle excludes not only philosophy but even mathematics, except the rudiments of arithmetic. It is designed to give an absolute position to *fiqh*-law. As for dogmatic theology, while vying with law for a position of paramountcy in the scheme of Islamic learning, it erected itself as a *substitute* for rational philosophy. Since the 6th/10th century - and through the genius of Fakhr al-Din al-Razi — it expanded its scope by adopting logic from the philosophical systems, by adding its own theories of physics and natural philosophy, and by substituting its dogmatic theological theses for philosophical metaphysics. The student could, henceforth dispense with all philosophical works since theology had produced a comprehensive rival to it. Such a theological-philosophical scheme by itself is not to be derogated: it is rather a sign of the inner fertility of Islamic thinking, and indeed Thomas Aquinas had done precisely this for Christianity in medieval Europe. But when its content is regarded as absolutely and exclusively self-sufficient, taking the place of all other rational thought, it removes the possibility of all creative challenge that might arise. By organically relating all forms of knowledge and gearing these to dogmatic theology the very sources of intellectual fecundity were blighted and the possibility of original thinking stifled.

Through this process, the curriculum of the *madrasas* was necessarily and harmfully reduced with a resultant narrow outlook as well as causing higher religious education to languish. The Turkish author, Katib Ghelebi (d. 1067/1657) bemoaned the decay of rational sciences and even of higher theology: 'But many unintelligent people ... remained as inert as rocks, frozen in blind imitation of the ancients. Without deliberation, they rejected and repudiated the new sciences. They passed for learned men, while all the time they were ignoramuses, fond of disparaging what they called "the philosophical sciences," and knowing nothing of earth or sky. The admonition "Have they not contemplated the Kingdom of Heaven and Earth ?" (Qur'an, VII,184) made no impression on them; they thought "contemplating the world and the firmament" meant staring at them like a cow.'

In Mughal India an interest in philosophical studies was created during the 11th/17th century, but philosophy itself had become so starved that instead of dealing with the problems of real importance it had degenerated into a pedantic exercise of technical terms. There is hardly a more eloquent and pungent criticism of the narrowness of the curriculum in the later Middle Ages of Islam than the following reported speech of Aurangzeb, the last great Muslim ruler of India (d. 1118/1707), addressed to his erstwhile teacher:

What did you teach me? You told me that the land of the Franks is a small island where the greatest king had previously been the ruler of Portugal, then the king of Holland and now the king of England. You told me about the kings of France and Spain that they are like our petty local rulers.... Glory be to God! What a knowledge of geography and history you displayed! Was it not your duty to instruct me in the characteristics of the nations of the world — the products of these countries, their military power, their methods of warfare, their customs, religions, ways of government and political policies?.....

You never considered what academic training is requisite for a prince. All you thought necessary for me was that I become an expert in grammar and learn subjects suitable for a judge or a jurist....

You told my father that you had taught me philosophy. It is true that for several years you worried my head about unnecessary and nonsensical questions quite unrelated to the issues of life.... When I finished my education, I had no real knowledge of any science or art except that I could utter certain abstruse technical terms which confuse even the brightest mind and by which claimants to a knowledge of philosophy cover up their ignorance....

The same attitude of aloofness was adopted towards Sufism—an attitude that had been so successful from the orthodox point of view against philosophy. But the impoverishment of the soul and the mind through orthodox disciplines in the *madrasa* drove the more serious and bright spirits to the fold of Sufism. In the *madrasas,* attached to the Sufi *khanqahs* and *zawiyas,* Sufi works were included in the normal curriculum, especially in India where, since the 8th/14th century, the works of al-Suhrawardi (founder of the Suhrawardi order), Ibn al-'Arabi and later those of Jami were taught. But in most Sufi centres, especially in Turkey, the academic curriculum consisted almost exclusively of Sufi works. In Turkey there were special places, called *Methnevi-khana,* where the famous Mathnawi of Rumi was the sole work of instruction. Further, the content of these works, largely pervaded by pantheism, was in sharp opposition to the teaching of orthodox seats of learning. There arose, therefore, an acute spiritual dualism in Muslim society, that between the *madrasa* and the *khanqah.* Characteristic of this phenomenon are the innumerable statements of Sufi converts who, 'after finding the true path', burnt their *madrasa* books or threw them into wells. Gradually, however, through the work of certain outstanding personalities, a new *rapprochement* was developed between orthodox theology and Sufi metaphysics, and a new kind of orthodox speculative theology came into existence during the 11th/17th and 12th/18th centuries. In the course of the 13th/19th century the Muslim world felt the sudden and powerful impact of European education and a new and more far-reaching dualism arose.

Curriculum and Instruction

With the narrowing down of the general field of learning through an absence of general thought and natural sciences, the curriculum was naturally confined to the purely religious sciences with grammar and literature as their necessary instruments. The purely religious subjects were four: Hadith or Tradition, *fiqh* or Law (including the 'Principles of Law'), *kalam* or theology, and *tafsir* or the exegesis of the Qur'an. In many *madrasas* of the right-wing Ahl al-Hadith even theology was suspect, and the subjects were accordingly reduced to three. In certain special schools, works on Sufism were added. The total number of works studied was usually very small. Indeed, certain great scholars and original thinkers that emerged from time to time were something of prodigies by themselves and did not owe much to the 'official' curriculum.

Part of the explanation of this gradual deterioration of academic standards over the centuries must lie in the fact that, the number of books in the curriculum being small, the years devoted to studies were also too few for the student to be able to grapple with tough and often abstruse materials of the higher aspects of religious sciences at a relatively young and immature age. This in turn meant not so much the grasping of the subject as such but a more or less textual study of the books. This encouraged memorizing rather than real understanding. The fact that later medieval centuries produced only large commentaries rather than basically original works is well-known. This phenomenon developed fundamentally from the habit of concentrating on books rather than on subjects. There is no doubt that much ingenuity and often considerable originality lies buried in these commentaries, but fundamental originality *in a subject* is relatively rare. It is remarkable that the writings of Sadr al-Din al-Shirazi, written in the 11th/17th century and still displaying a relatively high quality of philosophic thought, remained the highest texts of philosophy in the subsequent centuries, but were (where philosophy was pursued) always the ideal never surpassed. And yet al-Shrazis himself largely a commentator on previous thinkers, especially the philosopher Ibn Sina. This is the case with all the other subjects.

The custom of writing systematic commentaries was, in the beginning, combined with original works. In the 6th/12th century, for example, Fakhar al-Din al-Razi wrote a commentary on Ibn Sina but was also the author of several independent works. But later the habit developed of writing commentaries upon commentaries until the original works, the subjects of commentaries, were almost completely forgotten. Certain works on dogmatic theology found more than half a dozen layers of commentaries. Still later commentary degenerated into mere marginal notes, usually devoted to superficial quibbles and verbal disputes. These, together with short compendia, formed the stuff of the *madrasa* curriculum. In the 12th/18 century, e.g., a curriculum of studies was worked out in India by Mulla Nizam al-Din. This course, known after him as the Nizami Course (*Dars-i Nizami*), had widespread acclaim and, with modifications, was accepted almost all over India. Similar courses in Persia and Central Asia also existed with somewhat different emphasis on different subjects. However, this course, which represented, and was also accused by the right-wing of the orthodox of representing, the highest emphasis on the rational sciences, had three works on pure philosophy. All of these were later resumes, compilations or commentaries, including Sadr al-Din al-Shirazi's commentary on Ibn Sina. In Hadith it had only one book, a late compilation known as *Mishkat al-Masabih.* In Qur'anic exegesis it had only two medieval commentaries, one of which, called *al-Jalayn,* is so brief that its words are the same in number as those of the Qur'an itself. The ingenuity of writing commentaries reached such a pitch that some people used only certain letters of the Arabic alphabet (i.e. only 14 out of 28 letters) to exhibit their linguistic skill ! A concise work of Arabic syntax, known as *al-Kafiya,* found purely mystic interpretations at the hands of some commentators.

Usually, the curriculum was executed on the method of succession of subjects. Thus, to take one example of the serial arrangement, Arabic grammar and language; literature; arithmetic; philosophy; law; jurisprudence; theology; Qur'anic exegesis; and Hadith. The student passed from one grade to another by finishing one subject and starting the 'higher.' This system did not naturally allow enough time to be spent on each subject. But this was by no means the only method; often a student started with a compendium on a subject and in the next grade studied the same subject in greater detail and with commentaries. The job of the teacher was to teach others' commentaries as well as the text usually without any comment by himself on the subject itself. Moreover, there was no agreement as to which subjects were 'higher' than others. We have already referred to the competion of law and theology. Many regarded the

Hadith as the greatest of all subjects since it supplied the materials, so to speak, for other religious academic disciplines. Indeed, there were several schools where almost the only subject taught was the Hadith. There was, however, a great deal of flexibility in the acquisition of learning. A person, after acquiring an elementary religious education, could enter any place of higher learning. But after having completed his course, he might go to another school and enrol in those subjects which were there receiving greater emphasis and thus he could pass from school to school. If he regarded Sufism as the highest spiritual goal, he entered a *zawiya* after graduating from institutions of conventional learning.

Whereas, therefore, one may justifiably speak of the rigidity of the religious disciplines and of the general orientation of the *madrasa* education towards these religious interests, the educational field, as a whole, was far from rigid. An eminent thinker of the eighteenth century, Shah Wali Allah (d. 1174/1761), has left us his own curriculum in his autobiographical sketch. This included mathematics, astronomy and medicine. The *madrasa*-system does not, therefore, represent the whole of Muslim education. Shah Wali Allah did not attend *madrasas* but learnt privately at home from his own father. In the middle of the same century, another Indian author, Muhammad 'Ali al-Thanawi, wrote (1158/1745) a famous book, *Kashshaf Istilahat al-Funun,* on all branches of learning and their technical terms. In his preface to this book he writes: 'When I completed my study of Arabic and the religious disciplines from my father, I prepared myself to acquire the treasures of philosophy, natural sciences, rational theology and mathematics, etc., but I could not obtain these from any teacher. I then devoted part of my time to the study of compendia of these sciences such as I possessed.' The same author has recommended to us his own carefully thought out scheme of the rational sciences for study with their branches — physics, mathematics (including mechanics, etc.), and rational theology.

Other prominent cases of such extra-*madrasa* learning are by no means rare. But the fundamental weakness of medieval Muslim learning, as of all pre-modern learning, was its concept of knowledge. In opposition to the modern attitude which regards knowledge as something essentially to be searched and discovered by the mind to which it assigns an active role in knowledge, the medieval attitude was that knowledge was something to be *acquired.* This attitude of mind was rather passive and receptive than creative and positive. In the Muslim world this contrast became still more acute because of the opposition between the 'transmitted' or traditional (*naql* or *sam'*), on the one hand, and the rational on the other. In this controversy orthodoxy, anxious to safeguard tradition, came out on the whole heavily against reason, which it wanted to keep in strict subordination to dogma. We have already pointed to the phenomenon of memory-work and learning by rote in schools. The emphasis on 'transmission' and tradition had an incalculably damaging influence in this direction, even though enlightened and intelligent men were not altogether lacking who insisted on a real understanding of the tradition. In the logical part of works on dogmatic theology, there were lengthy and sometimes incisive discussions on the nature of knowledge and even special treatises were written on the subject. But since the expansion of the *kalam* theology had been done rather mechanically and its parts had been externally juxtaposed instead of there being any inner and organic relationship of growth among them, these endless discussions on the nature of knowledge failed, in practice, to have any effect whatever on the theological part proper where dogmatic tenets were formally supported by arguments. This is what we mean by saying that the *kalam*-system, instead of stimulating thought, came to be a *substitute* for philosophy and retarded thought in general. Ibn Khaldun very perceptively remarks, in his discussion of the sciences in his Prolegomenon, that this later development in the *kalam* has resulted in a terrible confusion between the topics and methods of philosophy and those of dogmatic theology.

Al-Azhar, now called 'the University of al-Azhar', began as a mosque-school under the Fatimids of Egypt. It was taken over by the Sunnis after the collapse of the Isma'ili kingdom and was devoted to the study of law according to the Shafi'i system. The teaching of other Sunni schools of law was later added, but still in the 9th/15th century it was only one of several places of higher learning in Egypt, although perhaps the most eminent among them. Its fame slowly ousted other rivals, however, and with the decline, in modern times of Sufi centres of religious instruction, it has emerged as the largest and most important place of religious instruction not only in Egypt but of the entire Muslim World.

The 'supervisor' of al-Azhar, charged with the administration of the institution, was replaced by a scholar-head entitled 'the Shaykh of al-Azhar' and now its entire internal administration is vested in a body of scholars, the 'Committee of the Grand Scholars'. During the late 13th/ 19th and the present centuries, through a series of steps initiated by Shaykh Muhammad 'Abduh, its curriculum has been reorganised both in form and in content and certain modern intellectual disciplines of the humanities and social sciences have been introduced together with certain natural science subjects at the high school level. Elementary and secondary teaching have been geared to higher instruction in contrast to the practice prevailing in the Middle Ages (see above) and a vast number of lower institutions, the *kuttabs,* have been created to prepare for the higher learning. This network of lower schools even extends beyond Egypt to certain other Arab countries of the neighbourhood. Various 'wings' (*riwaq*) represent different nationalities, a practice in several *madrasas* which influenced the growth of the 'Nations' in the medieval Western universities.

Although al-Azhar,with more than ten thousand students, is the greatest traditional institution of learning today, it is by no means the only one. The mosque-college of Zaytuna in Tunisia, and that of Deoband, near Saharanpur in India (set up in the second half of the 13th/19th century) are important seminaries for the training of the 'Ulama', although the former institution has, during the last few years, been turned into a kind of higher institute of Islamic studies and has been placed under the direction and control of the Tunisian government. The problem of the relationship of this traditional learning with modern education will be discussed in Chapter XIII which deals with Islamic modernism.

14

The Azhar in the Service of Islam and Arab Contributions to the World

SHAIKH AHMAD HASSAN EL-FAQOURY

Introduction

In the middle of July, 1964, a decree was issued by President Gamal Abdul-Nasser, in which I was appointed rector of the Azhar University… The current usage followed by the Azharites, whenever anyone amongst them is called to hold a high post was to pray two rak'as in the Azhar Mosque, just before starting the discharge of his new duties.

I took upon myself the adoption of such an established usage. Thus, I went to the old qiblah to ask God's blessings, and to begin with what is deemed as good to the highest degree; that is the worship and prayer which had been the sole delight and consolation to the Apostle of God (P.B.U.H). But the Azhar Mosque came to be unoccupied by mujawirs, students, since teaching and studying had been transferred to adjacent buildings.

Hence, circles of learning which had been a prominent feature in the Azhar for almost a thousand years ceased to exist within its precincts.

I had no sooner made a few steps in the court-yard of the Mosque than a feeling of depression overcame me as I beheld the desolate place. It was as if I had been walking around decaying monuments. I imagined I almost could hear the elegies composed by poets in olden times when they used to mourn the ruined remains in lines such as those of Imru'l-Qays.

" O Ruined remains! May God give you a happy morning!." Or in the first verse of his mu'allaqah:

"O my two companions! Let us halt hither to recall in tears the memory of the beloved."

Since that day, I decided to invoke God's help to restore the old-established tradition of studying and teaching in the Mosque, side by side with the Faculties that were developed or newly founded. The resumption of this old practice was done in acknowledgment of the Azhar's credit to Muslim learning, in respect to the feelings of those who are closely attached to it, and to establish a continuous link between its glorious past and promising future in its remarkable career of cultivating noble ideals and the upholding of the principle of Truth.

Muslims, though gratified with the new developments and confident of their adequacy, have not experienced any feelings of approval towards the discontinuance of teaching and studying in the Mosque of al-Azhar; a cessation which was considered by both the Azharites and non-Azharites, from amongst the people of this country as an intolerable trial causing them great affliction; since this blessed Mosque, during an educational career of almost one thousand years had been teeming with the pious performing their prayers, the preachers giving their sermons, and students occupied in seeking knowledge.

Through the Help of God—be He Blessed and Exalted—studying and teaching in the Azhar Mosque have been restored. Thus, the various branches of Muslim learning have regained their former unity, after they had been severed by the Law issued in 1930, which had assigned higher Islamic studies to three Faculties: one for Usul al-Din, (theology), another for the Shari'at (Muslim Jurisprudence), and a third for the Arabic language.

Anyone, however most efficient and imaginative he might be, cannot justify such an amazing partitioning of the Islamic disciplines, since the Shari'at can never dispense with the Quran and the Sunna, its two basic sources. Philological and literary studies in Arabic are thereby most requisite for the Quranic and Sunna disciplines, the thorough understanding of which depends entirely on a well-grounded knowledge of the Arabic language and a full grasp of its characteristics and mysteries.

For this reason, when higher studies were resumed in the Azhar Mosque, they comprise the Quran, the Sunna, the Arabic language and Muslim Jurisprudence, together with the auxiliary disciplines related to them. Hence, the various branches of Muslim learning came to be combined—as before—into a whole body, providing the Azharite student with a thorough grasp and training, rendering him fully competent to propagate the Muslim mission.

As God—Glory be to Him—had granted His Help in restoring studies in the Azhar Mosque, He also aided the Azharite teaching staff to be accorded what they had not hitherto attained; that is to occupy the posts of professors, assistant professors, and lecturers, so as to be on an equal standing with the teaching staffs in the other universities of the United Arab Republic. Praise be to God, by Whose Grace can good deeds be accomplished.

I have said that the cessation of teaching and studying in the Azhar Mosque after the law of tatwir, development, had been issued, was unquestionably a mistake, viewed even by some people as a sin, considering that such cessation had nothing to justify it. Nay, it aroused unavailing doubts and ungrounded rumours, owing to the fact that the Azhar University without the Azhar Mosque is like an infant who has just lost his father. It is the Azhar Mosque that helped the University to emerge and to acquire a status. Without it, the University would be unknown to anybody; but the Azhar Mosque in the absence of a university has a claim to distinction and eminence, well-known in both the Arab and Muslim world, nay even in the world at large.

Yet two briefs notes should be added here to give a clear picture to the inquirer. They might be helpful to him, or perhaps he can make them helpful to others. The one deals with the Azhar of the Caliph al-Mu'issli-Dini Allah (the Exalter of the Religion of the Lord), and the other with the Azhar University as established by President Gamal Abdul-Nasser.

The Azhar

When the Commander Jawhar al-Siqilli (the Sicilian) advanced with his army towards Egypt to repel the menace of the Qarmatians, the Fatimid Caliph Al-Mu'izz li-Dini Illah, sent him a letter in which he said: "Verily, you would enter Egypt with robes, alight at the ruins of Ibn Tulun's buildings, and lay the foundations of a new city called al-Qahirah, the Victorious which would conquer the world."

Certain historians stated this to be the reason why the new city was called al-Qahirah. I should like to support this view, because in my visit to Qairawan, I saw an old Mosque quite similar to Azhar. Close by was a hall which my guides said that it used to be a repository for munitions and weapons, and that the hall was called al-Qahirah. My guides added that the new city founded by Jawhar in Egypt was given the name.

If we consider that optimism is part of man's nature, we can perceive why the Fatimids chose that name for their new city.

It had been the wont of the conquering Islamic states to lay the foundations of mosques within the new cities which they had erected, following a certain trend that goes back to the Caliph 'Umar God be pleased with him. It is to be noted that 'Umar, in this respect, had only been adopting the noble Prophetic Sunna. The Prophet (P.B.U.H), when he established the new Muslim State in Medina, started by the building of his Mosque in that city.

This had been the usage adopted in laying the foundations of the early metropolitan cities in Islam, such as Kufa and Basra. Whenever a new Muslim capital was established, there arose in its midst a cathedral mosque. Such mosques were intended to represent the Muslim State; their pulpits were used to propagate its policy and to secure the loyalty of congregations.

Such was the case of Fustat, the first Muslim capital in Egypt, the foundation of which symbolized the Arab conquest of one of the Byzantine province in the eastern Mediterranean. Its mosque, the mosque of 'Amr, representing the mastery of Islam, was also a centre of study and learning.

Egypt witnessed before the foundation of the Azhar Mosque three other cathedral mosques. These were Amr's, 'Askar Mosque, and that of Ibn Tulun. The fourth was the Azhar Mosque, the building of which took two years and three months. It was inaugurated for worship on Friday the 7th of Ramadan, 361 A.H. (23rd June, 972 A.D.).

Thus, by 1972, the long career of the Azhar had attained one thousand years, throughout which its call has always been for humanity's welfare and the linking of man's sentiments with the Creator of heaven and earth, in a way that secures full right of freedom, prosperity and peace.

The Azhar, since its foundation, has striven to banish uncertainty and bewilderment in human society, since no distress is severer than the one experienced by souls tormented with shaken beliefs. The Azhar has always been expounding the Muslim Faith in all its mildness and tenderness; thus ensuring for mankind confidence and tranquillity.

Muslim dogma, in its bare simplicity, can be summed up in the fact that this universe has but one God, with no partner, and that His will for the good and happiness of mankind has been revealed through His Holy Messenger whose teachings epitomize all those of the previous Prophets. He is Muhammad ibn Abdullah (P.B.U.H.).

The Muslim Faith calls people to annihilate their egoistic and capricious tendencies so as to emancipate themselves from their tyrants. In this way the Azhar has mustered up around it, through its Call, considerable forces drawn from various parts of the world, tending to uphold the banner of true freedom which asserts that submission to any authority other than that of God is ignominious humiliation. The salaf, pious predecessors used to say in their prayers: "O God! Grant me power through my submission to Thee, and render me rich through my utter need to Thee."

If the Azhar, by upholding the noble mission has rendered great services to mankind, it is in this country that its impact has been more beneficial and enduring.

But prejudiced views might lead to an agreement on error, and accordingly the credit given to the Azhar comes to be disowned and refuted. Perhaps those most attached to it and well-aware of its high standing might be led to denounce it as Malik had denounced intoxicating drinks and as advocates of freedom have condemned imperialism.

Yet prejudice is quite unable to suppress two major facts that reveal certain endurable advantages our country has drawn from the Azhar.

The first is shown in the "intellectual harmony," characterizing the outlook of our citizens; a prominent feature we owe to the Azhar. Hence, hardly had it been possible for doctrinaire ideologies to find in this country a suitable environment where hatred and sedition could break out from time to time to disrupt its unity and subvert its institutions.

The second is the high eminence to which our country has risen and become unique amongst others. In this respect, the Azhar had done a great deal and is still doing. It is what had been rendered by the Azhar that added to the awe felt by our enemies and the sympathy entertained by our well-wishers.

Thus it is quite legitimate for the Azhar since it had done such services to our country to be accorded full acknowledgment by all sorts of citizens whether they be in agreement or disagreement with its mission; because the good accruing from its accomplishments had been beneficial to the whole body of our compatriots: Christians and Muslims.

Yet if prejudice and hatred lead to a denial of what is true and what is right, God's rewards to those who do good out of devotion to Him, is that best compensation. How much did men renounce what is due to their Creator and how often did they let loose their tongues against Him!

It is transmitted in our religious literature that Zachariah (P.B.U.H.) prayed his Lord to save him from the evil talk people disseminated against him. But God—Glory be to Him—said, "You ask for something

I have not chosen for Myself; how can I choose it for thee?"

However, it might not be out of place to remind the oblivious and the neglectful to the mistaken view, approaching to sin, of ignoring the care the Azhar accorded from old to the teaching of women, and thereby attributing what is really due to the Azhar, in this respect, to other institutions.

Those who happen to read what had been written by the late Sheikh Mahmoud Abul-Uyun about women students in the Azhar could realize that their participation in the circles of learning in the Mosque continued until very recent times. This remarkable fact led us to establish a faculty for girls in the Azhar University which we hope to acquire further extensions in the near future, if God will.

The Azhar had been, and still is rendering memorable services of Islam which will inevitably go on so long as human life persists on this planet. Yet a true picture of what had been accomplished by the Azhar to mankind at large, through Islam, may be summed up in two basic principles: FREEDOM and SOCIAL JUSTICE.

As to *freedom*, we find it to be issuing from the tenets of Islam which had been strenuously propagated by the students who came to acquire their Muslim education in the Azhar and had since become proud of being affiliated to it.

Freedom, emanating from faith and confidence in God is the most elevated and ardently sought in every age. It is this kind of freedom, most conformable to the Islamic viewpoint, that had been established by Muslim jurists and raised to a supreme ideal hitherto unthought of nor identically appreciated.

Such an ideal is referred to in an established legal rule that can be summed up as follows:

"If two men: a Christian and a Muslim sued each other about a child of unknown parentage whom the Muslim claimed to be his slave, and the Christian to be his son, the Qadi's decision should be in favour of the Christian and not the Muslim, asserting the child to be the son of the Christian and not the slave of the Muslim."

The moral significance of such a legal rule, lies in the fact that the Muslim jurist has to place his zeal for freedom on a standing higher that his zeal for religion, thought the latter is unquestionably much more persuasive and compelling.

As regards *social justice*, we find that it is closely related, in the Muslim's soul, to the creed in which he believes and the faith he has in God, Glory be to Him.

Justice has different aspects that are dealt with in the Quran as recited by Muslims in their worship. Passing from the Quran to the Sunna Muslims find in the Prophet's exhortations to establish justice, a vivid picture, representing Paradise as the rightful reward for the just, and hell-fire as the due retribution to wrong-doers. Nay torment would, even, be the lot of those who accede to be wronged, though it be within their power to avoid oppression.

We cite from amongst the aspects of justice as mentioned in the Quran, fairness in giving testimony, as stated by God—Glory be to Him—in His saying: "O ye who believe! Stand out firmly for justice, as witnesses to God, even as against yourselves, or your parents, or your kin, and whether it be (against) rich or poor: for God can best protect both. So follow not passion lest ye lapse (from truth), and if ye distort (justice) or decline to do justice, verily God is ever well-acquainted with all that ye do." (IV, 135).

Most significant in these aspects of justice is the one of which mankind is in dire need; it is justice in the distribution of wealth. It is the call which is clearly expressed in the Holy Quran where it is closely associated with prayer. The underlying reason is the fact that man is made up of body and soul, each of which has certain characteristics and requirements.

If man's soul is in need of close relation to God, his body cannot retain its living functions without sustenance. This will lead the Muslim to realize the meaning of destitution, and why the call to prayer in the

Quran is invariably combined with the call to Zakat, so as to provide for man's need for both his body and soul.

This is fully explained in one of the Quranic Surahs which goes to say: "For the taming of Quraysh for the taming. (We cause) the caravan to set forth in winter and summer. So let them worship the Lord of the House, Who that fed them against hunger and hath made them safe from fear". (CVI, 1:5).

A third item in the theme of justice, in the appeal to which the Azhar has taken in major part, is the one that led mankind to the relinquishment racial and colour prejudice. Scarcely had there been any torment more trying and painful to humanity than the differential discrimination based on the pretentious assertion of belonging to a higher breed or race.

The Quranic call for men to vie each other in merit and excellence—if they have to strive for such emulation—had been in the field of good deeds that promote righteous living in human society. Such is the purport of God's saying:

"O mankind! We have created you male and female and made you into nations and tribes that you may know each other (not that ye may despise each other). Verily, the most honoured of you in the sight of God is most righteous of you. Verily, God is Knower Aware". (XLIV, 13).

This is in brief the mission of the Azhar, offered to humanity under the banner of Islam. It is a mission that enhances Azhar's dignity and honour amongst the people to whom it belongs. Hence, in prestige and veneration it has gained much than any other mosque or university.

After having dealt with the Azhar of al-Mu'izz, it remains to say a word about Nasser's University.

The Azhar University

At the end of October, 1965, the new faculties of the Azhar

University were inaugurated in the suburb of Madinat Nasr, in premises that had been built for the occasion.

God has bestowed upon us His Favours so as to realize our aspiration in forming a new generation of Azharites whose outlook would adjust religion to secular affairs and the latter to be dealt with from a religious stand-point.

No doubt the suburb would enthusiastically welcome the staff and students of the new faculties of the Azhar University. It is to be noted that the area of Madinat Nasr had long been assigned to the British occupation forces for whom it was so exclusive that no Egyptian would dare trespass upon its precincts.

Since the Azhar University adds, at present, to the embellishment of Madinat Nasr with learning and culture, and takes part in purifying it from the stains of colonialism, we have to praise God for the favours He lavished upon us...We have also to thank President Nasser, and pray God to destine for him an ample reward in the Hereafter, after having accorded him great honour in this worldly life.

The word 'tatwir', development which is always mentioned in any reference to the Azhar University, can signify two meanings. It is either to make a thing pass through a totally new stage of evolution, or to recover a former one that had been left off and discontinued; but efforts are made to get it back by reviving it.

Which of these two renderings is intended as regards developing the Azhar into a university? Is the teaching of medicine and engineering together with the other disciplines of modern culture a new state of development to be applied to the Azhar, or were these studies a feature in a past phase of its evolution that has been abandoned and now sought to be recovered?

The answer to these questions requires admitting the validity of two postulates the well-informed has to take for granted.

(a) *The First Postulate* is that Islam is an integrated culture and not only a religion in the narrow sense of the term. This rendering might be fitting with God's saying: It is He Who hath sent amongst the unlettered an apostle from among themselves, to recite unto them His Revelations, and to purify them, and to teach them the Book and Wisdom, though heretofore they were indeed in error manifest, along with others of them who have not yet joined them. He is the Mighty, the Wise." (LXII, 2,3).

In these the Quranic verses are mentioned three aims Divine Providence has decreed to be realized through the mission of His Apostle to mankind: his contemporaries and the succeeding generations until the day when God inherit the earth and all who would be thereon.

1. The first aim is the recital of God's Plain Revelations enjoining faith in God, His Scriptures, Apostles and the Hereafter. The Revelations in the divine Scriptures and the sayings of His Apostles (P.B.U. Them) comprise exhortation, admonition, warning and good news.

2. The second aim is calling people to moral conduct, so as to purify them (tuzakkihim) and to prepare them in a way as to reveal their goodness and righteousness. Zaka' and Zakat indicate in Arabic progress towards higher grades of merit and excellence.

3. The third aim is teaching men the Book and Wisdom. The word 'Book', mentioned in the above verse, is taken by Quran Commentators to mean the Holy Quran.

But the word kitab, Book, may possibly signify kitabah, writing, as the latter had been practised as a means to guard what is written against disappearance through failure of memory. Hence, there are two remarks which might prove the validity of this interpretation.

1. In linguistic usage the Arabs say: kataba al-shay'a. (= he wrote something), yaktubuhu (= he writes it,) katban, kitaban, and kitabatan (= the last three words are nouns, meaning: writing), Katabahu (= he wrote it), means: khattahu (= he used signs in writing).

2. The Apostle (P.B.U.H.) told his Companions to write down the Quran. Thus it was written on 'usub (sing. 'asib), date-leaves, and likhaf (sing. lakhfah), tablets of white stones, until it was finally

recorded in al-Mushaf al-Imam the Canonical Codex, known as the Mushaf of the Calip `Uthman, God have mercy on him.

Thus, kitabah, writing as rendered, according to this viewpoint is something that should be well-cared for, learnt, and practised by the Arab nation who had been on the point of conveying the Islamic Call to mankind at large; since it is the Call that combines the *summaun bonum* of both the worldly life and the Hereafter.

The ransom of the captives of war after the battle of Badr reveals how Islam and the Prophet (P.B.U.H.) attached considerable importance to (the acquisition of the most indispensable elements of knowledge through) writing. The Prophet stipulated that the release of any prisoner of war depended on three conditions:

(a) the payment of a sum of money to the Muslim community.
(b) amnesty granted by the Prophet with due regard to the interest of Muslims.
(c) that the captive should teach ten Muslim boys how to read and write; and as soon as the pupils had attained the stipulated degree of progress, his teacher was set at liberty.

Therefore, the word al-kitab (= the Book)—alongside of its rendering as referring to the Holy Quran — can be taken to mean writing in an allegorical sense.

As regards hikmah, wisdom, it signifies, according to the usage of the Arabs, the truest kind of knowledge (and the ability of good judgment). We have to remark here the mention of writing together with wisdom in instruction as if the two elements were indissolubly associated.

The Second Postulate, to be taken for granted, equally with the former one, stating that Islam is an integrated culture, is that the Azhar is more to be identified with a religious and scientific mission than signifying merely the buildings, the foundations of which had been laid by the Fatimids, in Cairo.

Such mission was inherited from Jami' 'Amr, the earliest mosque to be built in Africa. The prototype, however, goes back to al-Masjid al-Haram, the Holy Sanctuary, the first House in Mecca, appointed by God, to mankind, as a blessed place, affording protection, mercy, and guidance, from which Muhammad, the Messenger of God conveyed to humanity at large the tenets of Islam which are the sum and substance of all heavenly revelations.

The Arab nation had carried out the dissemination of the Islamic Mission through mosques and the schools derived therefrom, which had been the means for awakening the heedless and teaching the ignorant. Thus, Islamic science and art had paved the way for the flourishing of a higher form of civilization that could realize universal brotherhood, unblemished with any sort of prejudice or fanaticism.

No wonder that Islam in its broad cultural significance had gained worldwide appeal and appraisal. Arabs came to be, in their golden age, the unchallenged masters in engineering, medicine, philosophy, music and industry. These are no idle claims, attributing undue credit to our nation, through a chauvinistic attitude of mind. But they are solid historical facts stated in full detail by non-Arab and non-Muslims scholars in both East and West; though these facts might be overlooked by the later generations of Arab and Muslim peoples.

It gives me great pleasure, in this connexion, while preparing this lecture to be delivered to the Azhar students, to quote at length the views of various authorities, notably the French scholar Dr. Gustava Le Bon in his monumental work: La Civilization des Arabes, and Sigrid Hoenke in her book about the Impact of Arab Civilization on Europe. I avail myself of the opportunity of following these authorities; since they could know what he had been unable to know concerning the achievements of our Arabo-Muslim nation.

Discerning in such light our glorious contributions, we come to perceive that the new developments in the organization of the Azhar signify the revival of a remarkable phase in the history of Arab culture. The various disciplines covering all the aspects of civilization had been an integral part of medieval Muslim learning of which the Azhar ranks as its foremost representative. Today the Azhar is simply recovering the full import of its true missions, the adequate performance of which had been hindered (during the ages of decline).

1. The Arab Contribution to Geography

Siyahah or travel is considered as the first step in getting acquainted with the basic data of geography. Siyahah, taken to mean wandering in various places for the sake of pondering the reflexion, is considered a meritorious act for which the faithful had been praised in Quran.

God, Glory be to Him, said: "Those that turn (to God) in repentance; that serve Him and praise Him; that wander in devotion to the Cause of God; that bow down and prostrate themselves in prayer; that enjoin good and forbid evil; observe the limits set by God; (these do rejoice). So proclaim the glad tidings to the Believers". (IX, 113).

Describing faithful women, God, the Almighty, also said, "It may be, if he divorced you (all) that god will give him in exchange consorts better than you,—who submit (their wills), who believe, who are devout, who turn to God in repentance, who worship (in humility), who travel (for Faith) and fast,—previously married or virgins." (LXVI, 5).

Adopting this noble Quranic meanings, we find that Muslim travellers had made long journeys in many countries, and wrote down books that were the first treatises in geographical sciences.

The earliest among those travellers was an Arab Muslim named Sulaiman. He went so far in his journeys as to visit China. He wrote down a book about his travels in which he added further information he drew from other Arabs who had equally journeyed to China. Sulaiman's book, (silsilat tawarikh) was translated into French (by Reinaud, Paris, 1845) and considered as one of the early works about China.

I recall, in this connexion, when I had been to that country in 1955, that I paid a visit to a mosque in the city of Canton which is called "Masjid al-Shawq ila al-Nabi", the Mosque of Yearning to the Prophet. My Chinese guide told me that it had been built in first century of the Hijra by Muslims who had come to China and could not go back to Medina. So they dwelt in Canton and built that Mosque which they called "Masjid al-Shawq ila al-Nabi."

Al-Sharif al-Idrisi is well-noted among Arab geographers and is accorded full credit for his geographical learning. From his works, Europe learnt a great deal about geography in the Middle Ages. The numerous maps he had drawn were considered by Europeans as authoritative references for three centuries. His standard work (entitled: Nuzhat al-Mushtaq fi Ikhtiraq al-Afaq = the Recreation of him Who yearns to Traverse the Lands, written before 1166 A.D.) embodies certain data about the sources of the river Nile, and the equatorial lakes.

In dealing with this subject, he said, "This Nile comes out from the Mountains of the Moon, bordering the equator. There are five rivulets which flow into a spacious batiha or lake. Other rivulets flow into two other big lakes. On the shores of the biggest batiha lies a town called Tarmi."

In reading today the above quotation, it is easy to perceive that those batihas are no other than the lakes known, at present, by the lakes: Victoria, Albert, and Albert Edward. These facts about the sources of the Nile (known to Arab in the Middle Ages) had been ignored by Europeans.

Perhaps the most striking case of disowning Arab achievements in geography is clearly shown in ascribing the first discovery of America to non-Arabs. Five years ago a Chinese scholar published a book in which he proved beyond doubt that the Arab sailors had been the pioneers in making such a great discovery. Yet the credit had been mistakenly given to Cristopher Colombus.

It would not be out of place to cite in this connexion the concluding remarks of Dr. Gustave Le Bon, concerning the contributions of the Arabs the geography in which he said: "The Arabs, through their astronomical observations, acquired precise data, deemed as most requisite for the art of making maps and charts... They published their books of travel, dealing with countries of which Europeans had never heard nor reached... as regards geographical literature, the Arabs wrote down monumental works, the Western nations used to copy and adopt for long centuries."

2. The Arab Contribution to Astronomical Studies

Islam came while the life of the Arab in his homeland depended entirely on weather phenomena. Day and night, he looked intently at the sky, either waiting for the clouds that would bring rain, or seeking guidance for his night journeys, in the light of the stars.

He used to say that the stars forboded rain, ignoring or forgetting the true tenets of Islam. To be reminded of these, the Messenger of God (P.B.U.H) is reported to have said: "He who said the star had brought him rain, would be believing in the star and disbelieving in God; but he, who said the God had brought him rain, would be believing in God, and renouncing belief in the star."

Nevertheless, 'Umar, God be pleased with him, followed the Arab usage, giving a new interpretation to the Prophet's prohibition of any belief in stars and their alleged effect upon sustenance. Umar prayed for rain in the mosque; then he called at al-'Abbas, the Prophet's uncle, asking him what was still remaining as regards the Pleiades foreboding rain. Al-'Abbas said that forecasters claimed that it had appeared over the horizon seven times. Later, rain poured down abundantly.

The Arabs felt great interest in observing the heavens, as shown in the multiplicity of Arabic terms, respecting stars, planets, and weather phenomena, (some of which still survive in European languages).

With the advent of Islam, the Arabs perceived the earnest call in the Quran, enjoining them to consider the sovereignty of the heavens and the earth; since reflexion upon the universe is the surest way leading to full realization of God's existence, and providing evidence for His Glory, Wisdom, Omnipotence and Omniscience.

One is struck with awe and wonder in reciting such a Quranic verse, in which God, the Almighty, said, "Furthermore I call to witness the setting of the stars—and that is indeed a mighty adjuration, if ye but knew—that this is indeed a Quran most honourable, in a book well-guarded, which none shall touch but those who are clean: a Revelation from the Lord of the Worlds". (LVI, 75:80).

The point in the above verse, is that the Arab people, despite their extensive knowledge of the stars, had been as if they know nothing about them. Moreover, prayer, zakat, fasting, and pilgrimage, the main ordinances which are known as the pillars of Islam, require for their performance precise details about their appointed times, so as to conform to the rules for which they had been prescribed.

For these reasons mostly related to be physical environment, the requirements of the Islamic call, together with the love of knowledge, the Arabs became deeply interested in astronomical studies. After the establishment of the Muslim State, they availed themselves of the scientific heritage of India. Babylonia, Ancient Egypt and Greece. Yet, they maintained their impact on everything they had offered to humanity.

Historians recorded that Caliphs, princes, and leading scholars had incessantly been preoccupied with the establishment of observatories in different parts of the Muslim World. Ma'mun built one in Baghdad and another in Damascus. Others were built by the Fatimid Caliph: al-Aziz and al-Hakim, in Cairo; by the Seljuqs in Naisabur, by 'Adud al-Dawlah in Baghdad, and by Hulagu in Maraghah. The vizir of the last named, was the illustrious Nasir-al-Din al-Tusi who spent thirty years engaged in astronomical observations.

Al-Biruni (973-1048 A.D.) was an adviser to Sultan Mas'ud ibn Mahmoud of Ghazna, to whom he produced (an account of the science of astronomy, entitled: al-Qanun al-Mas'udi fi al-Hay'ah wal-Nujum.) He composed another work entitled: Tashih al-Toul wal ='Ard li-Masakin al-Ma'mur min al-'Ard, (in which he explained the earth's rotation, and made accurate determination of latitudes and longitudes). Al-Biruni sojourned in India where he imparted to the Indians the learning of Baghdad.

Equally did historians record that the Suljuq Sultan (Jalal al-Din Malikshah) patronized astronomical studies. He established in 1074-5 A.D. at Naisapur an observatory, where there was introduced into the civil calendar an important reform based on an accurate determination of the length of the solar year. It proved to be more accurate than the Gregorian calendar, adopted six hundred years later; since the latter leads to an error of one day in 3,330 years, whereas al-Tarikh al-Jalali (the calendar of Jalal al-Din) leads to an error of one day in about five thousand years.

Le Bon said, "Today we know that the Chinese astronomers, especially Kush-Keng, borrowed their basic knowledge about astronomy from the works, written by the scholars of Baghdad and Cairo. So it is safe to say that the Arabs had been the disseminators of the science of astronomy in thc world at large."

3. The Arab Contribution to Mathematics

It might be unknown to some people that the numerals used nowadays by Europeans were derived from those invented by the Arabs, and that they had been borrowed by the peoples of Europe from the Moors in Spain.

A scholar, once, paid me a visit; and coming across certain books in my study that had been presented to me by some Moroccan friends, he saw, to his great surprise, that their pagination followed the European signs of numerals. He exclaimed that the Maghrebis have been so impressed with colonialism that they adopted signs (in the publication of their Arabic books). Yet he was much more astonished when I told him that these are the Arabic numerals that had been formerly borrowed by Europeans from the Arabs.

But they were not the only things offered by the Arabs. The names of certain numerals still survive in the corrupt form, so different in pronunciation as to seem quite unrelated to Arabic.

Most notable, among these, is the word sifr, which is a genuine arabic world signifying void or emptiness. It is mentioned in a Prophetic tradition, which goes to say: "Safratun emptiness (meaning hunger) in the Way of God is better than possessing the choice part of a flock of camels."

Arabs say: "Yadun sifr, an empty hand, and in a sifr, a vessel devoid of anything. Europeans adopted the word together with the meaning it indicates or implies, though variously pronounced as zero, contracted from zefiro, (and cipher in English, cifra in Italian, and chiffre in French). Its arithmetical meaning was later extended as to cover secret writing or writing in cipher.

Algorizmus is another loan word borrowed from the Arabs and used to signify calculation and thought also to be the word from which logarithm was derived. The latter word has been arabicized in the mathematical literature of modern Arabic. The word is a corrupt form derived from al-Khwarizmi, as stated by the French scholar Reinaud, in 1845.

(Al-Khwarizmi, Muhammad ibn Musa (d. 850 A.D.) was the principal figure in the early history of Arabic mathematics, and is one of the greatest scientific minds in Islam. He was librarian and astronomer to the 'Abbasid Caliph al-Ma'mun. He influenced mathematical thought to a greater extent than any other writer.).

Arabic numerals found its way to Europe through his work on arithmetic. He composed, as well, several works that were translated into Latin, three centuries later, of which the most well-noted is his book entitled: Hisab al-Jabr wal-Muqabalah (= the Calculation of Integration and Equation).

There is also brief manual on Indian arithmetic in which he explained the principal rules of addition, subtraction, multiplication, and division, together with fractions. Manuscripts of this manual are found in certain libraries in Europe, and given in the catalogues the Latin name: Liber Algorismus meaning the Book of al-Khwarizmi.

It is a pleasure to me to quote what the German scholar Hoenke, had written in this connexion. She said, "Arabic numerals had invaded Europe, and started to exercise its prominent influence on physical sciences, industries, economics, and the various means of communications amongst progressive nations throughout the ages."

4. The Arab Contribution to Physics

How much are modern Arabs grieved when they know of the loss of the physical works written by their predecessors. One can hardly imagine what mankind had missed through the destruction of this valuable scientific heritage, caused by the ravages of the Tartar invasions in the East, and Catholic fanaticism in Spain.

No doubt had been lost important works on physics of which nothing remained but the mention of their bare names in bibliographical and biographical dictionaries, or brief passages quoted from them by writers whose works have fortunately survived.

I should like to mention in this connexion, an Arabic work on optics (entitled: Kitab al-Manazir, of which the original was lost but before the disappearance of its manuscripts was translated into Latin, and the Latin version was later published in Europe in 1572).

This monumental work as written by the great Muslim physicist al-Hassan Ibn-Haytham, (known to medieval Europe by the name Alhazen). This work was most influential in the development of optics in the Middle Ages, as stated by Europeans themselves. Almost all medieval writers on this subject base their works on Alhazen's Opticae Thesaurus.

(In his work, Ibn al-Haytham opposes the theory of Euclid and Ptolemy that the eye sends out visual rays to the object of vision, and discusses the propagation of light and colours, optic illusions and reflection, with experiments for testing the angles of incidence and reflection.).

We find also in his work the first record of the camera obscura. In detailing his experiments, Alhazen comes very near to the theoretical discovery of magnifying lenses. He is also credited with the attempt of calculating the thickness of the atmosphere surrounding the earth.

Historians, however partial, can never minimize the achievements of Ibn al-Haytham, nor can they overlook the great debt Europe owes to him. The same holds true, respecting 'Ali ibn Sulaiman, of Cairo, another physicist who formulated a theory about the atom. In a treatise dealing with this subject, he asserted the possibility of dividing the substance into particles; and these divisions can go on indefinitely, until one is met with a particle which is indivisible.

5. The Arab Contribution to Mechanics

Le Bon said, "The Arabs had a comprehensive knowledge of practical mechanics of which we have ample evidence in the surviving remains of their machines and the description they had written about them." Then, he added, "No doubt, the Arabs knew the making of clocks moved by weights which differ in many respects from the water clocks". This is confirmed by the writings of many authors about the famous clock of the Umayyad Mosque in Damascus.

In describing the clock, Ibn Jubair (1145-1217 A.D.) the Andalusian traveller, said in the Rihlah: "Anyone coming out from the Umayyad Mosque, through the door of Jiroun, would find at his right hand, near the pavement, in front of him, a room in the shape of a big round vault, embodying brass arches that are equal in number to the day hours. These are mechanically arranged as to the let fall two weights from the mouths of two brass falcons standing on two bowls. As the bowls, have holes pierced in them, they go back inside the wall of the arch with the fall of these two weights.

"Then you see the two brass falcons extend their necks with the weights to the two bowls, hastily throwing them in a way so wonderful as to make the beholder imagine that they were made to move by magic.

"There is another contrivance for the night hours. The curve of the arches comprises twelve pierced circles made of brass, coming across each of them a bottle inside the wall. Behind each bottle lies a lamp that turns with the lapse of an hour with the passing of which the bottle is illuminated with the light of the lamp.

"Thus a ray will cover the circle facing the bottle, causing it to be visible as to look like a red circle; a procedure that will go on, until all the circles turn red. A man in charge looks after the room, reopens the doors, and puts back the weights in their proper places."

6. The Arab Contribution to Chemistry

I do not recall that I had been so much surprised as when I, once, read, what had been written by Muslim scholars, respecting chemistry. Dealing with the subject, Sheikh Ibn Nubatah, one of the notable figures of the eighth century of the Hijrah, said: "Chemistry is known by name; but it is devoid of any meaning."

The amazement aroused by such a statement, is due to the plain contradiction it shows to the tribute paid by Western authorities on science to the achievements and discoveries made by the Arabs in chemical research. (It is well-known that the Arabs, in the field of chemistry introduced the objective experiment, a decided improvement over the hazy speculation of the Greeks. The Arabs were accurate in the observation of phenomena and diligent in the accumulation of facts).

Such great progress that paved the way for the rise of modern chemistry, was done by the Arabs; yet it was overlooked by their later generations. Thus, forgetful posterity went on reiterating the statement that chemistry is known only by name, while it is, in fact unfounded and useless.

But Western historians of sciences, well-known for their authority, assert that Arab chemistry was mixed with alchemy, as did their astronomy with astrology; but a mingling of science with illusion could not hinder the Arabs from making important discoveries.

Le Bon said, "Meagre had been the chemical knowledge that was transmitted from the Greek to the Arabs. The Greeks had had no idea about the important compounds that were discovered by the Arabs, such as: alcohol sulpheric and nitric acids, aqua regia, etc. Arabs found out, as well, the main principles of distillation". He also added,

"Some authors asserted that Lavoisier is the founder of the science of chemistry; but they forgot that we do not know of any science, the factual body of which had come right away into existence. The experiments made, and the facts accumulated by the Arabs were so essential and substantial that Lavoisier, without them, would have been unable to make his discoveries."

Ibn Nubatah, in his refutation of alchemy, said, "As regards Jabir ibn Hayyan, credited with being aware of the secret of alchemy, I know of no biography of his in any reliable historical work. This confirms a widespread view that alchemy is a fanciful subject dealt with by certain compilers who assume that such a discipline existed in the time of Ga'far al-Sadiq; and that if Jabir says in his works that his master told him, he means Ga`far'.

Western scholars, however, consider Jabir ibn Hayyan—who flourished in the second half of the eighth century A.D.—as one of the early and well-noted Arab alchemists. (His name after that of al-Razi is the greatest in the field of chemical science). He composed a considerable number of works, some of which were translated into Latin.

His work entitled: Kitab al-Istitmam (or Kitab al-Tajmi' = the Book of Concentration) was translated into French in 1672; an indication that his scientific impact on Europe continued for a long time.

Jabir's works constitute a comprehensive encyclopeadia, summarizing the stage of progress chemical science had attained in his age. They comprise descriptions of many chemical compounds that were hitherto unknown such as silver nitrate, aqua regia, potash, sel ammoniac, etc. Jabir is credited with making improvements on the methods of evaporation, sublimation, melting and crystallisation.

Arabs made also accurate researches in pharmacology. They distinguished themselves in chemical industries, as they excelled in the art of dyeing, manufacture of steel, and the tanning of leather. They used gunpowder in a way hitherto unadopted. Though gunpowder was evidently invented in China, where it was used mainly as an incendiary,

Arabs contrived to apply its explosive force for the propulsion of missiles. They threw those projectiles behind fortified walls, causing terrible havoc.

These weapons unknown to Europeans, were used by the Egyptian Commander Fakhrel-Din against the Crusaders of the fifth Crusade who were eventually stricken with panic.

Referring to this, Le Bon said, "The terror Arab weapons aroused amongst Crusaders was mentioned in the latter' narratives. Joinville stated that they were the most formidable he had ever seen in his life. He added that these weapons were like flying giants. One morning Joinville knelt beside Saint Louis, the King, raised his hands to heaven and said, "O Lord Jesus! Preserve our people".

Before 1300 A.D. Hasan al-Rammah Najm al-Din al-Ahdab composed a treatise on war, in which he mentioned saltpetre, a component of powder, containing pyrotechnic recipes. He described these firearms as explosive shells which fly, emit flames, make a thundering noise, and cause fire and destruction. (Another early reference to the use of gunpowder is in the book of al-'Umari (d. 1348 A.D), entitled: Al-Ta'rif bil-Mustalah al-Sharif).

The German scholar Hoenke, after dealing at length with this topic, said, "Arabs are credited with being the precursors in making mines and throwing projectiles."

Arabs used firearms in defending Algeeiras in Spain, when it was attacked by Alphonso XI, in 1342 A.D. Historians related that the Moors in the besieged city threw against the attackers many shells. They added that two English nobles: Count Derby and Count Salisbury attended the siege and witnessed the consequences to which led the use of gunpowder. They managed to introduce that remarkable invention into their country, where it was adopted four years later.

7. The Arab Contribution to Medicine

Most remarkable are the achievements made by our nation in medical studies, as recorded in historical works. (Muslim physicians, through their practice and learned treatises had been held in high repute and could exercise world-wide influence in the Middle Ages. Prominent among them in the East was Abu-Bakr Muhammad ibn Zakariyya al-Razi (865-925 A.D.), known to Latin Europe as Rhazes, and considered by historians of medicine as: "the greatest and most original of Muslim physicians and one of the most prolific as an author").

In the West (in Spain) flourished Abul-Qasim Khalaf ibn 'Abbas al-Zahrawi (known to Latin Europe as Abulcasis). He is also deemed as the greatest surgeon of the Arabs. Most important among his many works is the one entitled: Al-Tasrif li-man 'Ajaza 'an al-Ta'lif (=An Aid to Him Who is no Equal to the Large Treatises); a comprehensive medical encyclopeadia on which rests his claim to distinction. In its last section al-Zahrawi sums up the surgical knowledge of his age. The work introduces or emphasizes such new ideas as cauterization of wounds, the crushing of a stone inside the bladder, and the necessity of vivsection and dissection.

This surgical part was translated into Latin, and various editions were published at Venice in 1497, at Basel in 1541, and at Oxford in 1778. Thus it continued to be the authoritative manual on surgery in European universities up to the second half of the eighteenth century.

Dr. Hoenke stated that hospitals were unknown to Europeans till the end of the twelveth century. Only after the contacts with the Arab Orient did they borrow that system for the treatment of the sick. Europe, however, had been, for a long time, prejudiced against physicians, refraining from appointing them in hospitals, urged by the mistaken belief that the mission of the church, respecting the sick is solely to relieve pain and not to gain recovery. In these words did the German scholar depict the attitude of medieval European towards medicine and medical services.

Quoting from an eye-witness is a medieval chronicle, describing one of the most notable of these hospitals, she said, "Its floor was laid with bricks and covered with straw, on which were herded the sick: young and old, women and children, among whom were those who suffered from contagious diseases: fevers, tuberclosis and skin disorders. No less repulsive were the vermins infesting the hospital and the horrid smell coming out of corpses that were left for a long time without burial.

In great contrast to the above description, is the great care shown by Muslims to their hospitals, their intense eagerness to keep them neat and tidy, and to secure for their inmates adequate treatment and nutrition, besides providing them with clothes.

Most noteworthy in this connexion is the way Muslims adopted in choosing the sites of their hospitals. In selecting a new site for the great hospital at Baghdad, of which Abu Bakr al-Razi was the chief physician, he is said to have hung up shreds of meat in different places, choosing the spot, where they showed the least signs of putrefaction.

Again when Saladin wanted to turn one of the Fatimid places in Cairo into a hospital, he chose the one that was least infested with ants.

In Damascus, extreme care was given to the hospital established by Sultan Nuriddin ibn Zangi. As regards its well chosen site, neatness, treatment and diet, it stood comparison with none but modern hospitals.

There is a story confirming this fact, (related by the Egyptian official and author Khalil ibn Shahin al-Zahiri who visited the Damascus Hospital around 1428). He was accompanied by an amiable pilgrim, who, attracted by the comforts accorded the patients, feigned illness and was admitted.

On feeling his pulse and examining him thoroughly, the head physician realized there was nothing wrong with the gentleman; but nevertheless prescribed fattened chickens, fragrant sherbets, fruits, savoury cakes and other delicacies. When the time came, however, he wrote a new prescription: Three days are the limit of the hospitality period.

It is to be noted that Qalawun's hospital, standing today near al-Husein's quarter, owes its existence to the one that had been built by

Sultan Nuriddin at Damascus. Sultan Qalawun is said to have received the inspiration while lying ill in the Nuri Hospital, where he made a vow to establish a similar institution in Cairo in the event of his recovery. When he became well, he fulfilled his vow, and the building is situated in what is known today in Cairo as the street of Nahhsin (= Coppersmiths).

The structure, including not only the hospital proper with annexes, but also a school and a mosque, was completed in 1284 A.D. It comprised special wards for segregating various diseases, such as fevers, ophthalmia, and dysentry, and was provided with laboratories, a dispensary, baths, kitchens and store-rooms. There were wards for young and old, men and women.

The patients who recovered were given clothes; and those who died were provided by the hospital with everything needed for their burial.

Qalawun's hospital was staffed with physicians specialized in the various branches of medicine. Thus, there were pathologists, surgeons, oculists (sing, kahhal), and setters of broken bones (mujabbirs). The services, rendered by the hospital, were, however, not confined to the inmates; but were also extended to those patients who preferred to have their treatment at home. They were provided with the specific medicine and diet prescribed for them.

The rich vied with rulers and princes in the establishment of hospitals and assigning to them rich endowments. These hospitals used to provide their patients with money after their recovery and return to their homes. The money given to them was intended to cover their expenses within a month, so that they would not have to work for their living during their convalescence.

Muslims adopted certain therapeutic methods that are still overlooked even by highly civilized countries. As stated by Shakib Arslan (and notably by the Egyptian medical doctor and linguist Ahmad 'Isa, in the standard work: "History of Hospitals in Islam", Damascus, 1939), there were in Muslim hospitals, men especially appointed to inspire the patient—through concealed suggestion—with hope for speedy recovery. Two of these men would stage a dialogue between them, in a way as to let it be overheard by particular patient. One of them would ask the other about patient's illness; and the other would answer that there was nothing to worry about if the prescribed medicine was punctually taken. Thus the patient would be relieved from the anxiety, and reassured about his recovery.

We have only dealt in brief with Arabian hospitals: yet the technical and practical side is more striking. As stated by Ibn Ali Usaibi'a (Muwaffaqal-Din Abul' Abbas Ahmad (1203-1270), the most distinguished historian of medicine the Arab world produced—in his monumental biographical dictionary of physicians, entitled: 'Uyun al-Anba' fi Tabaqat al-Attiba' (= Sources of Information on the Classes of Physicians), medical students used to accompany their lecturer in his visit to the patients, and to study clinically with him the various cases of disease, and to listen attentively to the conversations that later took place between him and the chief physician.

Examinations were held for medical students, and those who passed were awarded certificates (sing. ijazah) in which was stated after the 'basmalah' the permission to practise the medical profession: to cut open veins, remove piles, extract decayed teeth, dress wounds, and circumcise infants. At the same time, the would be physician had to consult his more experienced professors and lecturers.

The Egyptian vizir 'Ali ibn Yusuf al-Qifti, stated in his book Ikhbar al-'Ulama' bi-Akhbar al-Hukama' (= Acquainting the Learned with the Story of Philosophers and Physicians) that following a case of malpractice, Sinan ibn Thabit ibn Qurrah was ordered by the Abbasid Caliph al-Muqtadir in 931 A.D. to examine all practising physicians, and grant certificates only to those who satisfied him. Over eight hundred and sixty such men in Baghdad passed the text, and the capital rid itself of its quacks.

(On the orders of al-Muqtadir's virtuous vizir 'Ali ibn 'Isa, Sinan organized a staff of physicians who would go from place to place, carrying drugs and administering relief to ailing people. Other physicians made daily visits to jails. Such facts show an intelligent interest in public hygiene unknown to the rest of the world at that time.).

Men of letters cannot ignore the verses composed by a certain poet in the court of Saiful-Dawlah, the Hamdanid, in praise of Thabit ibn Qurrah. The poet said:

"There is none to cure the patient, after having excepted the Deity, save ibn Qurrah; but is there anyone to stand the patient in good stead?

"My bottle had been shown to him where he saw what lay hidden in my ribs and pericardium.

"The mysterious disease is quite visible to him, as when the eye beholds the ripples of a limpid rivulet".

But men of letters, in reciting these verses, or hearing their recital, find nothing to draw their attention but their exquisite diction and elegant rhyming as is the Arabs wont in dealing with literary themes in our cultural heritage. Yet, the word 'qarurah', bottle has further indications in other fields rendering it more significant and worthy of consideration in these verses. It shows that Arab physician had, for a long time, made use of the bottle (containing the urine of a sick person) in diagnosing diseases, which is something similar to the analytical methods adopted nowadays by medical science.

There is no doubt that the reader, after having followed this survey, could come back to the starting-point of our paper; and this will reveal to him the fact that the new developments intended to change the Azhar Mosque into a university are not a deviation from its basic mission. Rather they are an integral part of the teachings of Islam, and had been the field in which Muslims made their great achievements.

For this reason, Muslims, today, should have received the new developments changing the Azhar Mosque into a university with cheerfulness and welcome, instead of disapproval or apprehension of pernicious consequences. But I surely believe that the promoters of these reforms, meant entirely to realize fully the mission of the Azhar in the building up of souls and bodies, would be accorded ample reward of God, the Almighty, for the great services they have rendered to the Arabo-Muslim nation, in the world at large.

Before concluding this paper, I must not miss reporting once more, on behalf of the Azhar, our heartiest thanks and sincerest loyalty to President Gamal Abdul-Nasser, in compliance with the moral rule laid down by the Prophet (P.B.U.H.) who is reported to have said, "He, who failed to thank people (for the good they had done to him, would not be in a position to thank God". It is reported in another genuine tradition. "O My servant! How can you thank Me, if you fail to thank the one whom I enabled to do good to thee?"

If the new developments in the Azhar led unfortunately to the cessation of teaching and studying in the Mosque, considering that the Azharite faculties would be adequate in supplying these needs, such discontinuance persisted only for a short while. Teaching was soon restored once more in the traditional and familiar rings. Thus were completed the regulations, embodying both the Mosque and the University of the Azhar.

Peace and blessing be on the Holy Prophet Muhammad, his Family, his companions, and those who devoutly had adopted and still adopt their guidance, up to the Day of Judgment.

Peace and blessings be on other fellow Prophets and Messengers.

15

The Theological Colleges of Najaf

MOHAMMED FAHDIL JAMALI

Among the well-known higher institutions of Islamic learning are al-Azhar University in Cairo, az-Zeitunah College in Tunis, and Qurawyin Mosque in Fez. In recent years all of these institutions have undergone modernization and drastic changes in their programmes and methods.

The theological colleges of Najaf in Iraq, on the other hand, still retain the traditional contents and methods of Islamic education, and thus represent the basic principles in accordance with Islamic traditions.

My acquaintance with Najaf and its system of education began in my childhood when my father was a scholar there. He spent some nineteen years studying theology in Najaf. I myself, started the same education at the age of fifteen, not in Najaf, but in Kadhimain, the Shi'i holy city near Baghdad. Najaf is the site of the tomb of 'Ali, the fourth Caliph and the first Imam of the Shi'ah. It ranks fourth after Mecca, Medina and Jerusalem as a holy place in Islam.

Because of its theological colleges, Najaf is a great centre of Shi'ah religious learning. It acquired special significance because of the development in it of the principle of *Ijtihad*, whereby the scholar is able to interpret and deduce religious precepts from three sources, the *Qur'an*, the *Hadith* (sayings of the Prophet Muhammad), and the Sunnah (his practices).

Such a scholar (*Mujtahid*) expounds the application of Islam to the changing conditions of the times. Every member of the Shi'ah is required to follow the teachings of a living *Mujtahid*, whose teachings, however, loses authority on his death. Thus the Shi'ahs must always have living *Mujtahids*, who are characterized, in theory at least, by deep scholarship, original thinking, and training in the thorough examination and analysis of religious precepts.

Apart from Najaf, the main centre of Shi'ah religious education in Iraq are Sammarrah, Kadhimain in Karbala. They all have their own theological colleges, but in general they do not rank as high as Najaf in importance. Today (1976) the leading *Mujtahid* is Sayyid Abul-Qasim al-Khu'i who attained prominence after the death of the great *Mujtahid,* Sayyid Muhsin al-Hakim.

Najaf has some twenty-four colleges of which those of Burujurdi, Kadhim al-Yazdi, Hindi, Qawam, al-Jaza'iri, Sadr, Ahmadiya, Kashif al-Ghita, and Mahdiyah are among the best known. At the time of my last visit in 1957 the colleges were attended by around two thousand students representing several nationalities. The greatest number of students came from Iran (896), but there were also others from Iraq (326), Pakistan (324), Afghanistan (270), India, Kashmir and Tibet (71), Syria and Lebanon (47) and from Hasa, Qatif and Bahrain (20), a total of 1954.

I have had my education in American universities. I have studied the systems of education in Western universities and visited French, German an British universities, Oxford and Cambridge included. But none of these, not even the German universities which pride themselves on *Freiheit* (freedom), is comparable to the colleges of Najaf in the freedom and independence enjoyed by students in planning their own programmes of study and in self-management.

The whole of the theological system, including the twenty-four colleges at Najaf, is free of government control. It is not financed or supported by the government, nor is there a board of external authority which controls or directs the colleges. There are no presidents, deans, or masters of colleges. Any person of any academic standard who has the desire to study, and who can find a free room in any of the colleges can occupy it and thereby become a student. Religious piety and self-discipline are the only unwritten rules that guide the operation of these colleges.

Each college is built around an open court, usually square or rectangular, with a pond in the middle, and sometimes with trees around the pond. The open square is surrounded by rooms each for the lodging of one or two students. The rooms are about one meter higher than the level of the court. In most colleges the building consists of only one storey. A modern college, that of Burujurdi, consists of two. Each college has a guardian and a janitor. But that is all.

I have visited some of the students' rooms. They contain no bedsteads; at night the student places his mattress on a mat or rug. Some rooms are ventilated either by a window or a chimney; other have no ventilation except through the door. Most of the colleges have *sirdabs*, or underground cellars, which the students use during summer when the days are very hot. Some of these *sirdabs* are noted for their depth. One can go down into one, two, or three, each below the other. The lower one goes the cooler it becomes.

Scholars usually wear a massive black or white half-spherical turban on their heads. The blacks denotes that the wearer is a Sayyid or Hashimite, which means that he is a descendant of the family of the Prophet Muhammad. The wearer of a white turban claims no such descent. Students who live in a college do their own cooking and washing, unless they can afford the expense of restaurants and laundries. They receive bread free, the price being paid from donations given by benefactors through the great *Mujtahids*. Ayatullah Burujurdi, the great Iranian *Mujtahid* who lived in Qum, used to send 6,000 Iraqi dinars per month to Najaf, Karbala and Samarrah to pay for bread, and the monthly allowances to some 5000 needy scholars. In 1957 most of them received about two dinars a month (about £ 2). Today the great *Mujtahid* Sayyid Abul-Qasim al-Khu'i carries this burden.

Non-resident scholars are about half the total number of students in Najaf. Some of them depend on their families for support while others are supported from benevolent sources. The colleges themselves have no fixed budged and no fixed income.

A student receives instruction free of charge, and a teacher teaches without pay. Most scholars in Najaf are student and teachers at the same time. An advanced scholars who studies with a *Mujtahid* teachers those who are less advanced; those less qualified teach those who are still less advanced, and so on. Thus anybody studying in Najaf soon becomes both a student and a teacher at the same time. There is no fixed number of years for education. A student may stay for as many years as he chooses; five, then, fifteen, twenty years, or a lifetime. And some do indeed spend their whole life studying and teaching.

There are no examinations to be passed. Najaf resembles a great fountain of learning to which anybody can go and drink. But the courses of study make up a well-defined curriculum in Arabic language studies, logic and theology. Other subjects like philosophy, astronomy and mathematics, according to traditional curricula, are offered as optional studies. The student is, however, at liberty to use his free time to study any subject, such as a foreign language or literature. He is free to choose his teacher from among the scholars, to agree with him on the time and place of study. This place may be in a college, in a mosque, or in the teacher's own home.

Al-Hindi Mosque is one of the largest centres of teaching, whether for small circles, or for larger gatherings when lectures are given. A class may be formed of two or three or up to twenty-four in number. Advanced courses are usually taught through lectures in mosques when the lecturer discourses from the pulpit.

The rate of progress varies considerably from one student to another, depending on natural capacity and diligence. There is no rush since there is not time limit, and no examinations to be followed by certificates. But once a scholar distinguishes himself he attracts attention and becomes a centre for those who desire to associate with him and study under him.

Teaching starts early before sunrise after the morning prayer and continues until an hour after the evening prayer. Apart from teaching students in groups there are arrangements for discussion and recitation when students of the same teacher meet to discuss the last lesson he gave. It is usual for one of the students to recite or repeat that day's lecture, acting as the teacher, and then for his colleagues to ask him questions.

Education in Najaf is divided into three stages. The first stage is called the *sutuh* or surface education. This includes the study of Arabic grammar, rhetoric and logic. Among the texts used is one on advanced grammar called *al-Qatar*, which may be replaced by another book called *jami'al-Muqaddimat*, or 'The Sum Total of Introductions'. After this the student moves on to a still more advanced book of grammar which is a commentary on a thousand verses (*al-Aliyyah*) composed by Ibn-Malik, which summarize the whole of Arabic grammar. These thousand verses are usually memorized. The most advanced book on Arabic grammar is *Mughni al-Labib* which contains all the delicacies and intricacies of Arabic grammar. After finishing with Arabic grammar the student moves on to *al-Mutawwal* by at-Taftazani which is on Arabic rhetoric. After that he moves on to Aristotelian logic in a book called *al-Hashiyah* by Mullah 'Abdullah. The time taken for this *sutuh* stage is normally seven years.

The second stage of learning is that of *al-Fudala* which is comparable to the term 'sophomore' used in American universities. In this stage the student studies methodology and jurisprudence. The former consist of the methods of examining evidence and original sources of religious teachings. The latter consists of the ruler and dictates of Islam, whether pertaining to ritual practice like purification, prayer, fasting and paying alms (*zakah*), or individual and social dealings, like commercial transactions, marriage, heritage, etc. The books taught in methodology are *al-Ma'alim, al-quwanin, ar-Rasa'il* and *al-Kifayah*. A student takes these successively and usually moves from the simpler one to the more complex. The books on jurisprudence are *at-Tabsirah, ash-Sharai', al-Luma, al-Makasib* and *al-'Urwat ul-Wuthqa*. Here again the books rise gradually in complexity and technicality.

The third stage of study is called *al-Khariji*. During this final phase the students attend lessons given in public lectures by the *Mujtahids*. These lectures consist of very highly specialized analysis and examination of religious problems. Among the famous *Mujtahids* who gave such lectures in 1957 were Sayyid Muhsin al-Hakim, Sayyid Husain al-Hammami and Sayyid Abul-Qasim al-Khu'i.

I attended a few of these lectures in December 1957. One of them was al-Khu'i's lecture in al-Khadra Mosque. There were some 150 students attending, all sitting on the floor with legs crossed. The lecture did not last more than thirty minutes. It was on juridical methodology. I also attended a lecture by Sayyid Husain al-Hammami in al-Hindi Mosque. Some 150 students were present. The lecture analysed the meaning of intention and its relation to the act of prayer. The discussion included a great deal of psychology as well. Another lecture I attended was given in at-Tusi Mosque by Ayatullah Sayyid Muhsin al-Hakim.

There is no limit in time for this stage of study. The aim is to attain the high state of *Ijtihad*, which may be compared to a doctorate in theology. The stage of *Ijtihad* is reached not by learning alone, but by gaining, in addition, an insight 'which is God-given'. 'for *Mujtahids*,' I was told, 'ability is not to be measured by the amount of learning amassed, but by the light which God instils in a scholar's mind.'

Unless he is a *Mujtahid* himself, a Shi'i has to follow in his daily life the teachings of living one. He is called simply a *Muqallid*, which means a follower or imitator. A scholar who reaches the stage of *Ijtihad*, but is not standing for leadership remains in abeyance and is called a *Muhtat* or 'reserved'. There are many *Muhtats* in Najaf whose *Ijtihad* may one day be recognized in public. Najaf possesses a number of great *Mujtahids*, very learned and impressive leaders in the Shi'ah world, while most of them are devoted to scholarship, others assume public duties and deal with human welfare.

When I visited the colleges, I asked one student Shaikh Muhammad Rida Shams-ud-Din, to tell me his schedule for one day. He said that he rose from bed half an hour before sunrise to perform the morning prayer. After sunrise he attended an external lecture in jurisprudence with Sayyid Abul Qasim al-Khu'i. After that he himself taught rhetoric. Then he studied Islamic philosophy in a book called *The Explanation of the Eleventh Chapter* by Miqdad al-Suisi. Then he attended another external lecture in jurisprudence based on *ash-Sharai'*. Then a third external lecture dealing with the subject of *zakah* (alms) based on the same book. Then he attended still another external lecture by Sayyid 'Ali al-Isfahani. Besides, he studied by himself, performed the prayers and attended to the needs of daily life. That was certainly a very full schedule.

To sum up—the religious education at Najaf is entirely free from external control; this education is sought for its own sake and the service of God; it is conducted with complete freedom regarding the subjects of study and the manner of discussion and enquiry; its tempo and absence of rules provides an excellent atmosphere for individual differences; the scholars lead an ascetic life devoted to study and performance of acts of piety; their serenity is not disturbed by the ordeal of examinations; above all their education is conducive to the building of the character of the upright Muslim.

However, some criticism must be made and one or two problems involved may be pointed out in conclusion:

First, the content of education is archaic, and the scholars have very little contact with modern science, philosophy, psychology or hygiene.

Some of the colleges still had a central pond in which all wash—a very unhygienic practice. I remember talking to a professor of Islamic philosophy who was unacquainted with the name or the ideas of Henri Bergson. The response to my suggestions made to scholars and great *Mujtahids* about the need for introducing subjects like modern philosophy, psychology, sociology, natural science and some hygiene was generally negative.

Second, there is an obvious need for a system of licensing the graduates and the scholars. One does occasionally meet former students of Najaf who are not well qualified, although they may claim to have religious knowledge. It is left to the public to discover whether any such former student is worthy of his claim or not. There is risk that he may achieve prominence in society by outward piety and personal charm and this compensates for what he lacks in scholarship. Some kind of licensing is therefore essential.

Third, the colleges must be assured of a more regular source of income that does not fluctuate according to circumstances. Without it the life of the student may suffer anxiety and actual hardship when his income from donations may not be adequate to satisfy his needs in food, clothing and pocket money.

16

The Arab College, Jerusalem

MAHMUD ABIDI

Arab College made a distinct contribution in Palestine.

The truism that great institutions begin very small applies exactly to the Arab College in Jerusalem, the highest educational establishment in Palestine during the period of the British mandate. Four months after General Allenby entered Jerusalem in December 1917 the British military authorities began a modest scheme of educational reconstruction in the occupied parts of Palestine, roughly the Ottoman *sanjaq* (district) of Jerusalem, south of a line from the Mediterranean, three miles north of Jaffa to the River Jordan.

Under Ottoman rule this district, like the rest of Palestine, was served by state elementary and secondary schools, apart from private schools both native and foreign. But there were no schools higher than the secondary level. For teacher training and higher education students went to Beirut or Istanbul or to Europe and America. After the Turkish revolution in 1908 there was an increasing stress on the Turkish language in state schools, so that it became the medium of instruction in higher elementary and secondary schools in towns. Arabic, the language of the indigenous population, was taught as if it were a foreign language. This was one of the major grievances of the Arab nationalists on the eve of the 1914 war.

The British military authorities recognized the justice of the Arab demand for making Arabic the sole medium of instruction. But shortage of teachers competent to teach through the medium of Arabic was a major difficulty. To overcome it, in the beginning of March 1918 a modest boarding school for training teachers was opened in Jerusalem.

It was staffed mainly with seconded teachers from Egyptian schools who brought with them the required textbooks in Arabic. To start with, the school had some thirty students coming from diverse backgrounds. They received free board and tuition and in addition some pocket money. The period of training was six months only, and the whole course was quite elementary.

Because the British administration was military, educational reconstruction was entrusted successively to two army officers, the one with experience of teaching Muslim children in India and the other in Egypt. A board of education was formed with Isma'il Bey Husaini, member of one of the leading Arab Muslim families in Jerusalem, as chairman. But the British army officer assumed the post of Director of Education, with a Palestine Arab Muslim as an assistant. This was unacceptable to the Arabs in general, and accordingly Husaini resigned, soon to be followed by the assistant director.

It was the British Director who renamed the school as the Men's Elementary Training College. It remained true to describe the first eighteen months of its life as the Egyptian period, if only because of the staff, methods and textbooks. Almost all the Egyptians returned to their country with the exception of Husain Ruhi. He was of Persian origin and a follower of the Baha'i sect. He had served the Oriental Secretary at the British Residency in Cairo as in intelligence agent, and when the chief became military governor of Jerusalem, he brought his protege to serve, rather incongruously, as a teacher at the college and later, even more incongruously, as an inspector of schools.

In the following academic year 1919-1920 the British Director of Education appointed Khalil Sakakini, a well known Christian Arab teacher in Jerusalem, as the first native Principal of the College. He was a man of letters who taught Arabic to private students and for some time before the war conducted a private school in Jerusalem. Very little is known about his short term as principal of College except the reason for its termination. He wrote in his diaries that he resigned in protest against the appointment of Sir Herbert Samuel, a Jew and a Zionist, as the first high commissioner for Palestine, charged with the task of establishing a civil government in place of the military administration, and of putting into force the policy of establishing a national home for the Jews in Palestine.

In that year 1919-1920 the college gained some prestige from the appointment of Ma'ruf ar-Rusafi as Lecturer in Arabic. The well-known poet had been a member of the Turkish Parliament before the war representing a district in his native Iraq. He allowed his loyalty to the Sultan-Caliph to override his loyalty to his Arab nation, and composed a poem hostile to the Sharif of Mecca who in June 1916, proclaimed the Arab revolt in the Hijaz with the aim of achieving Arab independence from the Turks. Arab nationalists never forgave Rusafi for his aberration. So after the war that ended in Turkish defeat he appeared in Damasucus which was then under an Arab government with Amir Faisal, son of the Sharif of Mecca, at its head. Needles to say, Rusafi was snubbed and no notice was taken of him. But through a discreet British move he was invited to Jerusalem. The British authorities in Iraq were then in trouble with the Arab nationalists and were not keen on seeing Rusafi in Baghdad. Thus the was side-tracked to Palestine.

The college was also fortunate in the appointment of the first really qualified principal. Khalil Totah was a Christian Arab from Ramallah who obtained the Master's Degree from Teachers College at Columbia University. It was he who improved the academic standards and professional training. The period of training was raised first to two years and then to three. However, the curriculum remained quite elementary because the students came from incomplete elementary schools, and had to be taught the subject matter of what they were expected to teach, in addition to a smattering of the theory of education and some perfunctory teaching practice in a primary school attached to the college.

Meanwhile, the opening of new schools in towns and villages increased the demand for teachers. Hitherto, students were admitted to the College for training from the most developed town schools. But through Totah's foresight, a preparatory class was opened to receive students from less developed schools in villages, inevitably nicknamed

'The Villagers Class'. From 1924-25 the period of training was raised to four years.

From the beginning the college was conducted in the hired building, and for seventeen years it continued to be housed in three adjacent buildings outside and near Herod's Gate of the city wall. These hired buildings were designed as dwelling houses, and had to be adapted without structural change for use as a boarding school: classrooms, dormitories, dining hall, kitchen, and other essentials. Except for the principal's apartment, which was part of one of the buildings with a separate entrance and conveniences, staff and students had to use cold water taps and showers and toilets in a separate block constructed at the edge of the playground and reached by a badly paved path that became muddy in winter. There was no running water in the rooms and no internal sanitation for some 60 students, and ten lecturers. Once a week hot water was provided in a small room next to the kitchen for student to use in shifts of four at a time. Occasionally the personnel of the whole establishment went to a Turkish bath in the city.

The playground used for football, basket-ball, athletics, and recreation was also improvised. It was an open space behind one of the three buildings. It remained an open space for such uses for some ten years. Then the landlord began to construct on it new buildings for rent. That made the situation virtually intolerable, and the government was persuaded to acquire a spacious plot on the outskirts of the city to the south on a commanding height not far from government House. But it took several years more to build on this site the really satisfactory accommodation.

Under Totah the college began to build a reference library in Arabic and English. A small laboratory was started for the chemistry and physics lessons. With discreet supervision the students ran a Debating Society and published a magazine. The latter was printed every month of the academic year and published the best of the talks at the Debating Society and contributions by Totah and other members of the staff, mostly on educational subjects useful for teachers.

Three unsettling events took place in quick succession during Totah's five years in office. The first was concerned with Rusafi. Although all his life he was a weathercock, in Jerusalem he seems to have been manoeuvred into an awkward situation. In December 1920, an Arabic-speaking Jew, whose family originally came from Baghdad, gave a lecture in Arabic under the auspices of Raghib Nashashibi, the Mayor of Jerusalem, on Arab civilization in Spain. The attendance of Samuel who knew no Arabic was extraordinary and so were his thanks to the speaker followed by the promise to establish a college for Arab higher education in Jerusalem. Rusafi was among the guests, and as if by pre-arrangement produced a polished poem in some thirty verses. It was not exactly a panegyric for Samuel, but he regarded it as such and ordered a high official to have it published in the press. This official did so in a letter addressed to each editor. *Al-Karmil*, well-known for its opposition to Zionism since before the war, delayed publication until it published a reply in the same number: another poem composed in the same metre and rhyme by Wadi Bustani. In justice to Rusafi his poem contained much praise of the Arabs and called upon Samuel to fulfil his promise, but exception was taken to the whole idea, even though the poem ascribed Arab hostility to fear of expulsion. Bustani's poem chided and castigated in remarkably gentle tones, but Rusafi's conduct aroused a wave of protest and condemnation that rendered his position at the college untenable and led to his exit scarcely a year and a half after joining it.

The second episode received little publicity at the time, largely owing to Totah's discretion. He was the co-author with 'Umar Salih al-Burghuthi, a nationalist with scholarly tastes, of a History of Palestine for schools from ancient times to the British era. It was promptly banned on Samuel's orders. Totah told the story in 1937 before the Royal Commission when he appeared as the Arab expert on education. The book was banned because Samuel took exception to a statement of fact concerning his policy. The author stated that Samuel endeavoured to reconcile the Arabs of Palestine to the Zionist policy of the British government but failed.

As an introduction to the more serious and third episode it is necessary to refer to the augmentation of the staff in 1922-23 by a contingent of three graduates of the American University of Beirut. The most controversial of the three was the lecturer in history, Darwish al-Miqdadi, an ardent Arab nationalist. He was an inspiring teacher, and his extra-curricular activities were as extensive and stimulating as his teaching. His talks at the Debating Society were very popular, and his organised tours of his historic sites in and around the city were most exciting and illuminated by well prepared expositions. His first clash with authority was concerning his attempt to organize an Arab Scout Group independent of the Baden-Powell Association of which the British Director of Education was county Commissioner and Samuel the chief scout. Miqdadi was as popular with the Arab leadership outside the college as with the students inside. Among the staff he had two very close allies, both graduates of the American University of Beirut.

The Arab nationalists in Palestine always maintained that they, and not the British, should control Arab education, especially since the Jewish minority was allowed to control its own schools. Although the Arab leadership was in constant political conflict with the British authorities, and often declared political strikes particularly on the 2nd of November, the anniversary of the Balfour declaration, schools were never specifically asked to join. But they often did spontaneously. Such was the case in the spring of 1925—the third unsettling episode during Totah's term of office. Balfour himself was then coming to Jerusalem to inaugurate the Hebrew University and the Palestine Arab Executive Committee was busy organising protests.

Agitation among students was spontaneous and limited at first to demonstration in the playground and singing national songs. But soon students from private Arab schools joined, and the noisy demonstrations could but attract the attention of the Chief Secretary of the Government of Palestine whose residence was almost next door to the college. Totah's position as principal became very delicate: he could neither discourage nor encourage the students. As a Quaker he was against violence. He was unjustly suspected of sympathy with the government (which his evidence before the Royal Commission twelve years later proved unfounded). Accordingly he resigned, and the government decided to close down the college and send students home under police escort to the railway station. The college remained closed for several weeks, and was re-opened only after making every student sign an undertaking to conform to discipline. Miqdadi and his two allies were dismissed.

Ahmad Samih Khalidi, one of the inspectors at the headquarters of the Department of Education, was the new principal. Scion of one of the oldest Muslim families in Jerusalem, he studied pharmacy at the American University of Beirut, but through personal study he obtained the M.A. in education, and in due course translated into Arabic or adapted a number of English books on education and psychology. He combined personal charm with administrative ability. He soon won the confidence of the students and the cooperation of the staff.

The aftermath of the shocks and upheavals was short lived, and the college began a period of consolidation and progress. All teaching continued to be through the sole medium of Arabic, and English was taught as the only foreign language, mostly by non-English teachers. Admission of students was by selection from the best in the top classes in the town and large village schools, and thus represented the most intelligent boys in the country. That fact was reflected in the results of the first matriculation examination held in 1926 under the auspices of the newly formed Board of Higher Studies. Out of the thirteen students who passed it eleven were from the college.

From 1927 its name was changed to the Arab College, ostensibly because it was for Arab students and taught through the medium of Arabic, but in reality it was a conciliatory gesture on the part of an unpopular government which was repeatedly accused of having usurped the Arab right to control their own schools. After 1927 substantial reorganization was gradually introduced. By that year the college had become the only complete secondary school in the state system, but it remained also the only institution in the state system for the training of men teachers. This training was now given for one year after matriculation. These developments raised the academic and professional standards of teachers. The raising of standards was further facilitated by the recruitment of more graduate lecturers, mainly at this stage from the American University of Beirut.

At the same time a handful of outstanding students were sent as government scholars to this university with a view to their future employment in the secondary classes newly opened at town schools. These classes, the first and the second, were formed by selecting the best pupils in the top elementary classes. The development of those two secondary classes in town schools led to a further re-organization on the college. It no longer had first or secondary classes. Admission to its third secondary class was by selection from pupils in the second secondary classes in all the schools in the country with such classes. Parallel with these improvements in standards three graduates of the American University of Beirut, then serving teachers, were selected for further training at Oxford, Cambridge and London. They returned eventually to be lecturers at the college. For the first time an Englishman, with an Oxford degree, was appointed as lecturer in English.

An innovation that accompanied these developments was the introduction of payment for tuition and board, albeit at the low rate £24 p.a. There was, however, provision for exemption, partial or total, on grounds of exceptional academic merit or the inability of parents to pay. The recommendations for exemption by headmasters, were as a rule accepted by the authorities. The number of students remained around 75, largely controlled by the available accommodation. Students came from towns and villages. On average two-thirds of the students were of village extraction.

Thus by the 1930's the college had a double role: training teachers for the state schools and providing liberal education for those wishing to go to universities in Beirut, Cairo or further afield in Europe and America. With the return of the scholars from England and elsewhere to be lecturers at the college, a further advance was made first by adding a fifth and finally a sixth form and the introduction of the teaching of Latin, higher mathematics and philosophy. The courses were so arranged as to allow for either literary or scientific trends, leading to the Higher School Certificate and the Teachers Diploma. That was the highest limit of academic development.

A word is now necessary on the new building. Financial stringency was often advanced as the reason for delay. But in 1935, the building was completed and the college moved to its new home. However, in the following year the Arab general strike began and soon assumed the dimension of a national revolt against British rule and its Zionist policy. Troops were called in to help the police in a very dangerous situation which continued with varying degrees of intensity for three years. And as was the unfortunate custom, school buildings were used as billets including the new buildings of the college. As a result teaching was interrupted for a considerable time, and inevitably the building and its equipment suffered some damage which had to be made good.

The site of the new building was a beautiful one with commanding views of the city from the south. Apart from the main building with all the amenities and offices there was a separate residence for the principal, and spacious playing fields with well-laid out gardens. But the college was destined to enjoy its new home and indeed life itself only till the first months of 1948. For at the end of November of the previous year, following the U.N. resolution to partition Palestine, widespread disturbances broke out which quickly assumed the character of civil war. That settled the fate of the college: students had to be sent away and the staff soon dispersed. That last to leave was Principal Khalidi.

It is sad that this paragraph on the role of the college is necessarily in the nature of an obituary. After the early and short lax period, admission to the college was possible only after successive selections that began at the fifth elementary class. Thus in 1944-45, the aggregate for the first elementary class in the state system was 17,590 pupils, but only 1,995 completed the seventh elementary class. The lower secondary cycles (the first two classes) had 892 pupils, and the higher (the third and fourth classes) 232 pupils. The fifth and sixth forms at the Arab College, the apex of the pyramid, had only 58. These 58 represented the cream of the cream of the intelligence of the country. The College truly provided education for the very select elite.

Small wonder that former students, both those that continued their education at universities and those that went out straight to teaching have distinguished themselves in all walks of life in practically every Arab country and in many parts of Europe and America; teachers, writers, university professors, doctors, engineers, bankers, businessmen, administrators, politician, ambassadors and ministers.

17

Libraries and Academies During the Buwayhid Period

The Buwayhid period witnessed unprecedented literary development under the patronage of the Amirs and Wazirs, some of whom were themselves great men of learning. The purpose of this short paper is to enumerate the famous libraries and academies of the period as an evidence of the great cultural interest shown by individuals—Amirs, Wazirs and nobles alike-throughout the period.

The second Buwayhid Amir of Baghdad Bakhtiyar, son of Mu'izz al-Dawla, though an unworthy ruler, was himself a poet of no mean order, and one of the causes of his quarrel with his cousin, 'Adud al-Dawla, was his refusal to part with some valuable documents which he wanted to monopolise. Another son of Mu'izz al-Dawla, Habashi by name, who rebelled against Bakhtiyar, was a great lover of books. After the defeat of Habashi, among his confiscated treasures in Basra was found a library containing 15,000 books, exclusive of loose volumes and unbound sheets.

The greatest of the Buwayhid rulers, 'Abdul al-Dawla, was a bibliophile, His love of books can best be realised from a remark of Yaqut that he never parted company with the *Kitab al-Aghani*, whether at home or on journeys. This great monarch, who was a man of multifarious interests, adorned his palace in Shiraz with a library commensurate with his honour and dignity. Its organisation shows the care with which this great Buwayhid devoted himself to its efficient running. The geographer al-Maqdisi, who visited it during the life-time of Adud, reports that it was housed in a building by itself and was looked after by a trustee a treasurer and an inspector chosen from among the trustworthy people of the town.

The library consisted of a long vaulted hall with rooms on all sides. In the walls of the hall and the rooms 'Adud al-Dawla had contrived cupboards of veneered wood, full-size of a man in length and three cubits in breadth and the doors of these cupboards were let down from above. The Books were all arranged upon shelves. Every branch of learning had its own cupboards and catalogues in which the names of the books were registered. 'Adud al-Dawla had collected therein, so says al-Maqdisi, every book published upto his time in all branches of learning. The library was well-guarded by porters and only persons capable of appreciating its value found an entry into it.

Al-Maqdisi also visited two other libraries in the Buwayhid dominion, one at Ramhurmuz and another at Basra, in both of which the readers were awarded regular stipends by the founder. Of the two, the one at Basra was bigger and more frequented by people, while the peculiarity of the one at Ramhurmuz was that a Mu'tazili Shaykh used to lecture there on Mu'tazili principles.

Sharaf al-Dawla, son of 'Adud al-Dawla, who took keen interest in astronomy, also established at Shiraz a new library which he committed to the care of one Qadi.

Majd al-Dawla, the last Buwayhid ruler of the branch of Rayy, also had a big personal library. When Sultan Mahmud ibn Sabuktagin invaded Rayy in July 1029, he plundered all the treasures of Majd al-Dawla, including 50 loads of books, exclusive of those which dealt with Mutazilism and Philosophy and which were therefore burnt under the corpses of the crucified heretics.

The great Wazirs of the period also had their own libraries. Ustad Abu'l-Fadl ibn al-'Amid, the celebrated Wazir of Rukn al-Dawla, had a big library, including volumes on every form of learning, estimated to be one hundred camels load, and the eminent Buwayhid historian Abu'Ali Miskawayh was put in charge of this.

The Sahib Isma'il ibn 'Abbad, the Wazir of Mua'yyid al-Dawla and Fakhr al-Dawla, had a vast treasure of books in his library. When invited to accept the Wizarah of Khurasan by the Samanid Nuh ibn Mansur (976-997 A.D.), the Sahib refused the offer and among the reasons stated was the difficulty of transport of his books which would have required the services of 400 camels. These books were catalogued in ten big volumes, but unfortunately for the world of learning these were all committed to the flames by Mahmud of Ghazna, along with the library of Majid al-Dawla mentioned above, when the Sultan conquered Rayy.

Al-'Adil Bahram ibn Mafannah, the Wazir of Abu Kalijar, the pen-ultimate Buwayhid Amir in Baghdad, established at Firuzabad in Fars a library consisting of 7,000 volumes, including 4000 leaves, in the hand-writing of the calligraphers of Banu Muqla.

Apart from these libraries which are generally referred to as *Khizanat al-Kutub*, there developed during the period another type of institution known as *Dar Al-'Ilm,* "Academy of Learning", which combined library and reading room with a seminar attached to it. There the elite met together and had discussions and debates. `Adud al-Dawla fixed a room next to his own suite in his palace for discussion among the savants. Since these discussions were held at a high level, utmost care was taken lest the scholars should be disturbed by the general folk.

An ideal academy which combined a library with a seminar was established in Baghdad by Sabur ibn Ardashir, the Wazir of Baha al-Dawla, in 383 A.H./993-94 A.D. in the Karkh quarter-the Shi'i stronghold in the place known as "between the two walls." Sabur dedicated this building to use by men of learning. Among the books collected, numbering 10,400, there were a hundred copies of the Qur'an written by Banu Muqla and many autographs of other famous writers. Sabur also prepared a catalogue of the books in the library entrusting it to the care of two responsible `Alids and appointing one Abu Bakr al-Khwarizmi as supervisor of the establishment. Though as a Wazir Sabur had to suffer severe reverses owing to the whims of the Amir, yet his institution survived unmolested till 451/1059-60, when a fire broke out in the area and the books became objects of plunder among officials and the mob.

The academy of Sabur became a rendezvous for men engaged in literary pursuits. When the Syrian poet-philosopher Abu'l-'Ala al-Ma'arri visited Baghdad in 399-400'1008-9, he visited this academy and there came in contact with outstanding literary figures of the period whom he mentions by name. Not only did he join there in the discussions of eminent men of learning but also on one occasion he was also entertained by the music of a sprightly songstress, a fact which he has immortalised in the famous couplet;

Another noble of the court of Baha al-Dawla, a descendant of the Prophet, the Sharif al-Radi founded an academy, also called *Dar al-ilm*, where scholars were provided with everything necessary in connection with reading. A treasurer was entrusted with the task of supplying the needs, but when on one occasion slight inconvenience was caused to one of the readers in the absence of the treasurer, al-Radi provided each scholar with a key to enable him to take himself whatever he needed from the store without waiting for the treasurer.

18

The Libraries of the Arabs

OLGA PINTO

The history of books among the Arabs, so important for the knowledge of the development of Arabic Culture, is almost completely ignored in the larger works dealing with the History of Libraries. Neither in the work of Petit-Radel, nor that of Edwards, nor that of Axon, of Olschki, nor even in the most recent by Hessel, is any mention made of them. Only in Lalanne, a collector of the most curious notes on bibliography, and in the steps of Cim, are short notes found about the libraries of Cairo and Tripolis of Syria.

Among few peoples, however, has the cult of books and literary tradition had such importance in the spiritual and cultural life as with the Arabs.

At first sight it appears strange that a people, uneducated, coming from the desert, to become rulers in youthful energy of a vast territory at one time ruled over by two large empires, the Roman-Byzantine and Sassanide-Persian, should in a short time exhaust the originality of its impulsive creativeness and impress upon its own civilisation the characteristics of a reflective, traditional and typically "book"—culture. The reason for this apparent incongruity must be sought (as is demonstrated by the recent enquiries into the formation of Islamic civilisation by Goldziher, and Becker), in the facts that the Arabs, especially on account of their own imperfect cultural development at the time of the conquests, absorbed more rapidly the essential elements and the inquisitive spirit of the three civilisations which they had subjugated politically and ethically: the Greek, Persian and Jewish. All three, on account of their secular, evolution, had arrived at a state of saturation and petrification, so that the Arabic-Muslim civilisation presents at its formation almost all the characteristics of what is called "Mediaevalism."

For the Arabs, every book, commencing with the great book, "the Kur'an", represented a whole world in itself; more than for any other people of antiquity it was the only and inexhaustible fountain for the inner life. This people is accused at the time when it appeared on the stage of the history of the world, of having committed an act of vandalism in the first century of the Hijrah, of having destroyed, at the command of 'Umar Ibn al-Khattab, the greatest library of antiquity, the library of Alexandria. This accusation, which has long been relegated to legendary fiction, is also in complete contrast to the spirit which animated the Arabs at the time of the conquests, which was not that of violent proselytism or fanatic destructiveness, but rather that of respect for the superior civilisations with which they came into contact, and of which they appropriated the greater part of the spiritual heritage.

It must be well understood that at the time of 'Umar one could not speak of Arabic books, much less of libraries, but a little over a hundred years later we see in Baghdad, the capital of the empire, the rise of the first, what may be called "public", library.

The Arabs always speak with affection and respect of books as if they were things dear to the heart and faithful friends :

"What a good companion a book is when you happen to be alone with it! You can find consolation with it, even if those whom you loved have betrayed you!"

"It does not betray the secret which is confided to it, and out of itself bears fruit of wisdom and truth!"

Yet another says:

"The book is a companion who does not betray, does not annoy nor make reproaches when harshly treated."

The most celebrated poet of the 'Abbaside times, Al-Mutanabbi, says:

"The most honourable seat in this world is in the saddle of a horse, and the best companion will always be a book."

Sometimes it is considered of equal value with arms, as al-Muhallabi advised his sons :

"My sons! Whenever you stand in the market before a shop, stand only before those where weapons and books are sold."

Everything that had relation to books had a great and, stupendous development; they were copied, embellished and sumptuously bound. At the same time they were most carefully preserved and also they were communicated to others; all that was the aim and preoccupation of Muslim culture. There arose veritable schools of calligraphy, from which the Banu Muqlah and Ibn al-Bawwab issued as real artists. Among the calligraphists were authors and scholars like Al-Jauhari, the author of the dictionary *As-Sahah,* the celebrated traditionist Ibn al-Jauzi and the musician 'Abd al-Mu'min of Isfahan. Not only were books produced by celebrated calligraphists, but also the art of painting in miniature originated in this manner. At first this art confined itself to painting plants and flowers, but soon also animated beings were introduced and the artists displayed remarkable skill in the technique of their pictures.

Binding of the books was not neglected and often mention is made of books bound in valuable leather, of various colours and tooled with silver and gold.

A great impulse was given to the development of the book by the importation of the art of paper-making, because it made them less expensive and consequently within easier reach of the masses. As late as the fourth century of the Hijrah (Xth century A.D.) books were still written upon parchment and papyrus, but this made the books very expensive. The art of paper-making having come from China by the way of Samarqand to the Muslim world, made very rapid progress and in many centres of the extensive Muslim empire paper-factories were established on a large scale. It was principally in Egypt where flax was cultivated extensively that most factories arose; here the Arabs substituted linen rags for the silk-waste which had been the material of the Chinese in the manufacture of paper. From the fifth century of the Hijrah (XIth century A.D.) the whole of Europe was supplied with paper from the Arab world, from the factories of Baghdad and Cairo in the East, or from those in Spain in the West, where the principal centre of the industry was in the town of Shatiba (to-day Xativa).

With the introduction of paper and the increased traffic in books caused by the fall in prices, in every Arab city book-shops were opened, which assumed a great importance because they became the meeting-places of scholars and students, who, seeking and examining the books, conversed and discussed their value.

Baghdad for example had already in the third century (XIth century A.D.) one hundred book-shops. These were in small shops in close proximity to each other and generally in the vicinity of a mosque. The books exposed for sale on trestles had a label on the back to facilitate the search for them, whether by the book-seller or the purchaser, or to be copied. These labels were affixed either by the seller himself or by his assistants, whether for sale privately or by auction, a custom which was much in vogue in all parts of the Arab world. The proprietors of such shops or their agents were at times well-known scholars. The poet al-Haziri (died 568/1172) was, on account of his profession, called *Dallal al-Kutub, i.e.,* book-agent; book sellers were Abu Hatim Sahl ibn Muhammad as-Sijistani, one of the chief pupils of al-Asma'i, and the geographer and historian Yaqut (died 626/1229).

The price of books, though made cheaper by the introduction and use of paper, was always high, and one can understand the necessity of public libraries for persons who could not afford the luxury of acquiring a library of their own.

In the fifth century (XIth) a copy of the dictionary *Al-Jamharah* of the Ibn Duraid cost sixty Dinars (1 dinar = 10 sh.); a copy of the vast historical work of at-Tabari one hundred Dinars, a copy of the poems of the Omayyad poet Jarir ten Dinars. In the year 248/862 a copy of the dictionary *Kitab al-'Ain* of Al-Khalil was sold for fifty Dinars. The translation of the commentary of Alexander of Afrodisia upon the "Acrosis" of Aristotle was sold for one hundred Dinars; and Al-Hakam, caliph of Cordoba, paid to the author one thousand Dinars for the immense poetical and literary collection, the *Kitab al-Aghani*. In the seventh century (XIIIth A.D.) books cost already less. The above named Yaqut, mentioning the loan of books which he had at the Damiriyah library at Marw, says, "My house was never clear of 200 volumes, taken on loan, or more, and I had never to give a deposit though their value was 200 Dinars." This would mean an average price of one Dinar per volume.

In spite of the high price of books we find in the Arab world many bibliophiles who collected fine libraries; among these are mentioned in the 3rd/9th century the prolific writer on all matters Al-Jahiz, Al-Fath ibn Khaqan, the courtier of the caliph Al-Mutawakkil, and the judge Isma'il ibn Ishaq.

Al-Jahiz (died 255/868) was a real devourer of books for in addition to his eagerness in reading and absorbing the books which he could buy, he took on deposit, as agent, books from booksellers, and no book ever fell into his hands but he read it from cover to cover. But the books which he loved were the cause of his death like a true bibliophile. As it was his habit to heap up round him all the books which he needed for his studies, and being on account of his great age partially paralysed, one day a heap of books fell on him and killed him. Also Isma'il ibn Ishaq (died 282/895 or 286/899) passed all his time among his books; and one of his contemporaries relates that he never entered his presence except that he found him handling some book.

A -Fath ibn Khaqan had a magnificient library probably at Baghdad, collected and arranged by 'Ali ibn Yahya al-Munajjim (died 275/888) another patron of learning who will be mentioned shortly. No one could see a more marvellous library than his for the quantity and beauty of the books, and his house was open to the Bedouies and scientists of al-Basrah and al-Kufah. Always did he carry a book with him, which he carried either in his sleeve or in the legging of his boot and whenever be found a spare moment he began to read it. If ever he had cause to leave the table of the caliph, he fetched out his book, even when he went to the lavatory.

The habit of carrying a book in the sleeve was also adopted by another book-lover, Abu Da'ud as -Sijistani, the celebrated author of the *Sunan* or collection of traditions. For the purpose of being able to carry books of greater volume he had his sleeves made larger so as to be able to accommodate such books. Also the above-named 'Ali ibn Yahya al-Munajjim collected a large library in his magnificent castle in the village of Karkar, near Qufs in the neighbourhood of Baghdad, and called it *Khizanat al-Hikmah* "Treasury of Wisdom." Yaqut relates: Many people from all countries travelled to it in order to study various sciences. In it the books were completely at the disposal of students and all were entertained at the sole expenses of 'Ali. This library was known in the whole Arabic world and attracted students in such manner that the astronomer Abu Ma'shar (died 272/885) coming from Khorasan with the intention of going to Mecca to perform the pilgrimage, decided to go and see it. He was so enthusiastic about it that he remained there and did not continue his journey.

The historian of the 5/11th century, Ghars an-Ni'mah of the celebrated family of scientists as-Sabi, collected at Baghdad a small library of 400 volumes to which admission was granted to a limited number of students. He sold it later when the instalment of the library of the Nizamiyyah college drew the students away from his more modest establishment.

We have much less information about the private libraries in Egypt. In that province were but few large town-centres, and as in Cairo existed one of the most marvellous public libraries in the world, private persons did not feel the necessity to possess their own collections of books.

A private character had the library of the Fatimide caliph al-'Aziz Billah (reigned 365/975—386/996) probably collected and arranged by his Wazir Ya'qub bn Killis, who was himself a book-lover; for among its heritage was found among other treasures a rich library. The collection of manuscripts of the caliph, the librarian of which was the author Abu'l Hasan 'Ali ibn Muhammad Ash-Shabushti, has been described as being rich in books, distributed in forty rooms. 18,000 books dealt with theology alone. Of the Kur'an there were 2,400 copies, written by celebrated calligraphers, like Ibn al-Bawwab and the Banu Muqlah already mentioned; they were embellished with gold and silver. But there were also many other manuscripts of celebrated authors, among them several autographs. This library was incorporated in one of the greatest public libraries of the world, the "Dar al-'Ilm" or "House of Knowledge" by his successors, the caliph Al-Hakim bi Amr Allah. This remarkable ruler, who was responsible for many wise ordinances but also for extravagance, towards the end of his life conceived the mad idea of having himself proclaimed a Godhead, and as such he is worshipped to this day by the sect of the Druzes in the Lebanon.

At the time of the conquest of Egypt by Salah ad-Din (Saladin) in 567/1171 his Wazir Al-Fadhil formed out of the books presented to him by his sovereign an immense library consisting of 68,000 volumes. Being, however, sequestered after a few months, they came back to their owner diminished by about 12,000 volumes.

The Wazir of the Ayyubi dynasty founded by Saladin, Abu'l Hasan 'Ali al-Qifti, known also by the title Al-Qadhi al-Akram, had a fine library at Halab, valued at 50,000 Dinars, which by his will he left to An-Nasir, the ruler of that city.

Also, in the Western provinces of the Arab empire, arose everywhere private libraries to some of which foreign students were admitted.

The Sultans of the Persian dynasties who in the 4/10th century wrested the power from the Caliphs, made their courts the protectors of sciences. Besides the large library founded by 'Adhud ad-Daulah (reigned 338/949-372/982), which has been mentioned before, there existed smaller libraries of the princes like that of Majd ad-Daulah, of Mu'izz ad-Daulah, (and of some of the wazirs of this dynasty like Abu'l Fadhl ibn al-Amid and as-Sahib ibn 'Abbad. The latter (died 385/995) declined the office of wazir of the Samanid princes, making the pretence that it would be impossible to carry with him his library, the theological works in which alone amounted to 400 camel-loads.

Of Ibn al-'Amid the historian Ibn Miskawaih, who was his librarian, treats at length in his history. The house of this wazir having been plundered by the soldiers of Khorasan so that not even a cup remained to drink from nor a thing to sit on, he did not worry; his mind was solely occupied with his library because he did not know what had become of it and nothing in the world was so dear to him. "He had many books", says Ibn Miskawaih, "on every science and every branch of philosophy and literature, more than a hundred camel-loads. He hardly had seen me when he asked me about them and when I informed him that they had been saved and none had been lost he became happy and said to me: Thou art a man of good omen, everything can be replaced, but this, meaning his library, could never have been made good. I saw his face become serene.

The Samanid Sultans, also, in the third (9th) century, who reigned over the Eastern part of the Arab realm, cultivated an intense cultural life at their courts. The Sultan Nuh ibn Mansur (reigned 366/976-387/997) had his private library, praised by Avicenna, who was permitted to visit it and became some time after its librarian. To him is wrongly attributed the mad act of having set the library on fire.

Spain, which had but few public libraries, was instead rich in libraries collected by private persons, not only such formed by princes and rich nobles at great expense, but also by poor students who spent for books their meagre means. They were collected gradually, as was done by Muhammad ibn Hazm, a schoolmaster, who by degrees was able to bring together in Cordoba a fine library, envied by many scholars who frequently made use of his manuscripts which he himself had carefully copied, and guarded with the utmost care. One of the greatest book-lovers in Spain was the judge Futais ibn Sulaiman, known as Abu Mutrif, of Cordoba, he had a rich library in which six scribes were continually working and the great value of his collection was not revealed till through misfortune which befell his family the books were sold by auction. The sum realised was 40,000 Dinars.

The love for books was inherited by the many small kings, Muluk-at-Tawa 'if, who divided Spain among themselves at the death of the caliph Hisham in 423/1031. Known are the libraries of the Aftasid Al-Muzaffar, prince of Badajoz (Batalyaus), of the Banu Hud of Saragossa, the Banu'l Ahmar of Granada, the Banu Dhu Nuh of Toledo, who to enrich their own collection did not hesitate to rob those of Al-Araushi, and many others.

Also the Hasside princes of Tunis followed the cultural movement of the whole Arab empire. The founder of the dynasty, Abu Zakariya (reigned 625/1228-647/1249) collected a library which was sold much later by one of his successors Abu Yahya Zakariya' al-Lihyani (reigned 711/1313-717/1317) when the retired to private life to Cairo.

There were also not lacking in the Arabic empire people of high rank who considered it their duty to collect a library equipped with the utmost luxury, with shelves filled with books, bound artistically, but which were never taken from the shelves except now and then to be dusted and cleaned. A clear example of this occurred at Cordoba to a great book-lover and passionate scholar, al-Hadhrami. He used to visit every auction of books in search of a manuscript of a work in which he had the greatest interest. Having at last found one at one of the auctions, there ensued between him and another bidder a struggle by which the price rose by leaps and bounds till it reached a sum out of all proportion with the value of the book. Al-Hadhrami at last decided to give up, but he wanted to know the person who bid against him as he believed him to be a student as ardent as himself, but possessing larger means. His disillusion and anger were immense when he learned that the fortunate purchaser did not know any thing at all about the work he had bought but was attracted solely by the beautiful binding and the size of the book, as it would just fill a gap on his book shelf in his library.

An indication of the civilization of a people however are not private libraries, but public ones; and it is these which in the Arabic world found their greatest development. It must be noted as a curious fact that, while those regions and provinces of the extensive empire which were nearest to Europe (then buried in the obscurity of the

Middle Ages) could boast of many and rich private libraries, they were practically destitute of public ones; as, for example, Spain, where no library existed which was open to every-body. The contrary was the rule in the great centres of the Orient, like Baghdad, Cairo, Shiraz, etc.

The Arab sovereigns and government-officials in general, following a conception which we may call "democratic," which always ruled in Islamic countries, by which studies and science were not considered the monopoly of a few privileged persons, but ought to be assessible to all people of good intentions, be they rich or poor, free or slaves, understood early the necessity for consulting books. At first they commenced by admitting to their private libraries persons desirous to study, later they undertook professedly to found real public collection.

The centre in which undoubtedly the first public library saw its initiation was the capital of the empire, Baghdad, where in fact in the third (9th) century, by order of the great caliph al-Ma'mun (reigned 198/813-218/833) the first library was instituted as an annexe to the *Dar al-'Ilm* or *Bait al-Hikmah* "The House of knowledge" or "Abode of Wisdom." After this there arose in the capital as well as in other centres many similar institutions, which gained world-wide fame, and perhaps gave to Louis XI of France, when he was in Eastern lands, the idea of imitating them and initiating at Paris a collection which was to become in later time a public library.

Commencing at Baghdad, the principal centres of Mesopotamia and Syria, followed, then Egypt which was a very important cultural centre, then the Eastern provinces which, though divided into many small principalities, still maintained a vivid sentiment of Arabic culture, and at last that distant branch of the Arabic world, Spain where, as in all countries conquered by the Arabs, their culture penetrated gradually, and attained a wonderful development, perhaps greater than in any other part.

I have thought it advisable to arrest my enquiry with he collapse of the Arab Empire and the end of the Abbasid dynasty, partly because the sources of information concerning the later period are scarce and scattered, but also on account of the great decay of Arabic Culture and the rise of new nations, the Persians. Turks and Mongols; except that at the end of this article I shall try to trace a brief review of the condition and growth of modern Arabic libraries, to show the relationship between them and the ancient ones, and point out the new aspects which belong to them and the importance they have for Oriental studies.

As I have already pointed out concerning the private libraries, many of these were open to students. Like that of 'Ali ibn Yahya, of Ghars an-Ni'mah and others, but the public character arose and developed gradually from three types of large libraries. Those of the sovereigns who with their ample means were able to found vast collections worthy of being placed at the disposal of the public, those of the mosques and those of the Madrasahs.

In ancient times education, elementary as well as advanced, came from the mosques, each of which had its own small library in which the necessary books were brought together, but only such as were strictly connected with theological studies, a custom still in vogue. Later and gradually, under lay influence which flourished most in the 3/9th century, the advanced studies remained no longer confined to the mosques. The Madrasahs arose, resembling our colleges. In these the instruction had a wider scope, for in Baghdad as well as in Damascus and elsewhere history, grammar and philosophy were also included. In the Madrasah founded in Cairo by the caliph Al-Hakim, which was in reality the first Lay University also Mathematics, Astronomy, Medicine and Methaphysics were taught.

These great institutions had their libraries which, at the time of their foundation or soon after, were made public and did not remain the preserve of the professors and students alone.

The same process can be noticed in the West, for we see the great public libraries arose out of those of princes given to the State or of libraries belonging to monasteries, which in Europe were the first places where a love for books and their preservation can be traced and finally the libraries of the colleges or universities. But while in the

East the institution of the Waqf conferred upon private libraries an inalienable public character, this characteristic is not to be found in Europe till much later, in the 15th century.

The development of the Arabic libraries was much quicker and more extensive. These institutions, a sign of high culture, received not only admirable support from the Abbasid Caliphs, masters of a realm worthy to stand at the head of the greatest empires of East and West, but also from the ambition of many small princes from the early centuries of the Hijrah onwards to gain favour with the Caliphs of Baghdad. First, these princes acted as governors, later as independent rulers of the various provinces of the Arab empire. The same process can be noticed in Arabic civilization which we find in the Italian renaissance. While the splitting up and dismembering of the State into small semi-independent principalities certainly meant a weakening of the power of the State, it nevertheless gave greater impulse for cultural life on account of the continual rivalry of the small princes. So it happened in Halab (Aleppo) in the case of the Hamdanid dynasty, especially under Saif ad-Daulah (reigned 333/944—356/967) when the city became an important cultural centre, or in Tripolis under the Banu 'Ammar. The same occurred in distant Persian provinces under the dynasties of the Samanids. Buwaihis and Ghaznawis; also in Spain under the Banu Dhu-Nun in Taledo, the Aftasis in Badajoz, the Banu Hud in Saragossa, the Banu-'l Ahmar in Granada and others. Al-Qalqashandi (died 812/1418), author of a voluminous encyclopaedia for the instruction of State officials under the Mamluk Sultans (the *Subh al-A'sha)* speaks with pride of the great libraries which had once existed and laments that they had been left abandoned in his times:

"The Caliphs and kings had in ancient times great libraries and bestowed much care upon them, which enabled them to get the most beautiful and numerous collections. It is said that the greatest libraries in Islam were the following three : First, the Library of the Caliphs in Baghdad. It contained an enormous quantity of books of inestimable value. It existed till the Tatars came to Baghdad and their king Hulagu murdered the Caliph al-Musta'sim, the last of the Caliphs. The library disappeared like so many other things and was lost and its traces disappeared. Second, the library of the Fatimide Caliphs at Cairo. This was one of the largest libraries and one of the richest collection of books in all sciences. It remained in existence till the death of the last of their caliphs, when Salah ad-Din (Saladin) ibn Ayyub made himself master of the kingdom... The third was the library of the Omayyad Caliphs of Spain. This library also remained intact till the end of the dynasty when the smaller kings divided Spain among themselves. It was then that the books were dispersed for ever. As regards to-day, kings have but little interest in libraries, they content themselves with the libraries of the Madrasahs because these are a greater necessity."

I have compiled in the pages which follow a list of all the public libraries which existed in the Arab empire during the time of the Abbasid Caliphate of which I have been able to find any mention. Some of the sources simply enumerate them while others tell us about their foundation, their utility and management.

Baghdad

(1) The library attached to the Dar al'Ilm or Bait al-Hikmah founded by the Caliph Harun ar-Rashid (170/786—194/809) or by Al-Ma'mun (198/813—218/833) which was still in existence at the time of Al-Mu'tasim (218/833—227/842).

(2) A library attached to another Dar al-'Ilm, founded in 381/991 or in 383/903 in the street *Bain as-Surain* in the town-quarter Al-Karkh by the Buwaihi wazir Abu Nasr Sabur ibn Ardashir (died 416/1025), praised by many writers for its beauty and size and also that it contained more than 100,000 volumes, among them some copied by the most celebrated calligraphists. This library survived the death of its founder for a short time only, because it was completely plundered and burned to the ground by the soldiers of the Saljuq Sultan Toghrul Beg when he conquered Baghdad in 401/1059. A certain quantity of books were saved from destruction and incorporated in the library of 'Amid al-Mulk al-Kunduri, the wazir of Toghrul Beg.

(3) The library attached to the Nizamiyah Madrasah, founded in 457/1064 by Nizam al-Mulk, the wazir of the Saljuq Sultan Alp Arslan.

(4) The library of the Mustansiriyah Madrasah founded in 631/1233 by the last but one Abbasid caliph al-Mustansir (624/1226—641/1243).

All these libraries, and in the seventh century of the Hijrah (XIII century) there were thirty-six in all, were probably destroyed at the entering of Baghdad by the Mongols under Hulagu Khan in 656/1258.

Mosul (Al-Mausil)

(5) The library of the Dar al-'Ilm founded by the scholar and poet Ibn Hamdun in 323/935.

Al-Basrah

(6) and (7) Two libraries, one founded and opened to the public by a certain Ibn Sawwar, the other mentioned by al-Hariri, the author of the *Maqamat,* were both probably burned down when the Bedouins invaded the town in 483/1090.

Ramahormuz

(9) A library founded by the same Ibn Sawwar who founded the library at Al-Basrah.

Halab (Aleppo)

(10) A library founded by the Hamdanide princes who reigned there in the fourth (10th) century.

Tripolis in Syria

(11) The library founded by the rulers, the Banu 'Ammar towards the end of the fifth (11th) century and destroyed by the Franks at the time of the First Crusade (503/1109).

Cairo

(12) The library attached to the Azhar mosque founded by the Fatimid Caliph Al-'Aziz (reigned 365/975-386/996).

(13) The library attached to the Dar al-'Ilm founded in 395/1004 by the Caliph Al-Hakim, successor of Al-'Aziz. This library was still flourishing under his successor Az-Zahir, but was later neglected and partly plundered, though it still existed at the time when Salah ad-Din

took the city in 567/1171. He made a present of part of the library to his secretary, Al-Fadil 'Abd ar-Rahim, while the remainder was sold by auction.

(14) The library attached to the Fadiliyah Madrasah founded by the above named Al-Fadil, in which were incorporated the books which he had received from Salah-ad-Din. Very soon after, the books were sold by the students (!) and scattered in all directions.

Ghaznah

(15) Libraries enriched by the books plundered from ar-Ray in 420/1029 and from Isfahan in 425/1033 by the Ghaznawi troops, but they were a century later destroyed and scattered when the city was taken in 550/1155 by the Ghuri Sultan Husain.

Marw. possessed ten libraries, among them :

(16) The Nizamiyah founded by the above-named Nazim al-Mulk.

(17) The 'Aziziyyah founded in the sixth (XIIth) century by 'Aziz ad-Din, a court chamberlain.

Nishapur

(18) Libraries are mentioned only on account of their being burned by the Ghuzz Turks in 548/1153.

Ray

(19) The library which in 420/1029 was removed to Ghaznah by the conqueror Mahmud of Ghaznah.

Shiraz

(20) The library founded by the Buwaihi ruler 'Adid ad-Daulah (reigned 367/977—372/982), but it was already neglected at the time of his son Baha' ad-Daulah.

SPAIN

Cordoba

(21) The library founded by the Caliph Al-Hakam al-Mustansir

(349/961—365/976). The wazir of his successor Hisham (365/976—396/1006) named al-Wadish, a freedman of Al-Mansur Muhammad ibn Abu 'Amir, had all materialistic and philosophical works in it burned; part of it was sold at the time of the Berber invasion (5/11 century) and what remained was plundered by the conquerors.

MAGHRIB

Fas (Fez)

(22) The library of the Madrasah as-Saffarin founded by the Merini Sultan Ya'qub ibn 'Abd al-Haqq (591/1195—614/1217) formed to a great extent from the books found in Spain, which the Sultan demanded from the defeated Sancho, king of Spain.

The princes took great care concerning the buildings which were to serve as public libraries. Some of them like those of Shiraz, Cordoba and Cairo were placed in separate structures, with many rooms for different uses : galleries with shelves in which the books were kept, rooms where the visitors could read and study, rooms set apart for those in charge of making copies of manuscripts, rooms which served for literary assemblies, and even in some cases rooms for musical entertainment, etc. All rooms were richly and comfortably fitted; on the floors were carpets and mats, where the readers in Oriental fashion squatted with crossed legs, reading and even writing, holding the sheet of paper or parchment adroitly in the palm of the left hand. The windows and doors were closed with curtains, the chief entrance-door having a specially heavy curtain to prevent the cold air from entering.

The Arab historians have described some of these libraries at some length as if they were finding a great delight in their beauty and riches. So, for example, al-Maqrizi describes a library in Cairo :

"On the 8th day of Jamada II. 395 A.H. (1004) was opened the building called *"The House of Wisdom."* The students took up their residence. The books were brought from the libraries of the Inhabited Castles (residences of the Fatimid Caliphs) and the public was admitted: Whoever wanted was at liberty to copy any book he wished to copy, or whoever required to read a certain book found in the library could do so. Scholars studied the Kor'an, astronomy, grammar, lexicography and medicine. The building was, moreover, adorned by carpets, and all doors and corridors had curtains, and managers, servants, porters and other menials were appointed to maintain the establishment. Out of the library of the Caliph al-Hakim those books were brought, which he had granted—books in all sciences and literatures and of exquisite calligraphy such as no other king had ever been able to bring together. Al-Hakim permitted admittance to everyone, without distinction of rank, who wished to read or consult any of the books."

Al-Maqdisi has left an interesting description of the rich library at Shiraz :

"Adad ad-Daulah founded in Shiraz a residence which had not its equal East to West : no ignorant person entered it but was enchanted, nor any learned person but his imagination was filled with the delights and perfumes of Paradise. He made it intersected with water-courses, the buildings were crowned with domes and surrounded by gardens and parks, lakes were excavated and every kind of comfort that could be thought of. I have heard the servants say that there were 360 rooms and pavilions, in each of which he resided one day of the year, some were on the ground-floor and some above. The library constituted a gallery by itself; there was a superintendent, a librarian and an inspector chosen from the most trustworthy people of the country. There is no book written up to this time in whatever branch of science but the prince has acquired a copy of it. The library consists of one long vaulted room, annexed to which are store-rooms. The prince had made along the large room and the store-chambers, scaffoldings about the height of a man, three yards wide, of decorated wood, which have shelves from top to bottom; the books are arranged on the shelves and for every branch of learning there are separate scaffolds. There are also catalogues in which all the titles of the books are entered. Only persons of standing are admitted to this library. I myself inspected this library, downstairs and upstairs, when all was still in order. I observed in each room carpets and curtains, I also saw the ventilation chamber, to which the water is carried by pipes which surround it on every side in circulation."

The rooms set apart for the books had along the walls shelves which did not surpass the height of a man, so that it was not necessary to use dangerous ladders to reach the books on the top-shelves. The scaffolds were all furnished with shutters some on hinges while other were let down from the top, and with locks. These locked shelves though not very commodious for the distribution of the books had the advantage that they preserved the rich and beautiful bindings from dust and sunlight. They certainly added to the books being infested by vermin on account of the want of ventilation.

The books were placed on the book-shelves divided in sections so as to form little heaps as can be clearly seen in the miniature taken from a manuscript of Hariri, published by Blochet, which reproduces the wall of a public library, most probably at Mosul.

The name of the author and the title were written on the back of the book. The arrangement was according to subjects, and to facilitate the search for a work required the contents of each section of a bookshelf was registered upon a strip of paper attached to the shelf outside; these strips had also indications of works which were incomplete or lacking in some part.

The number of books in libraries naturally varied considerably. The library founded by Sabur ibn Ardashir contained 100,000 to 140,000 volumes, among them a hundred copies of the Kor'an written by the celebrated Banu Muqlah. The library at Tripolis, according to Ibn al-Furat, possessed three millions, certainly an exaggerated figure, among them 50,000 copies of the Kor'an and 80,000 commentaries upon the same. That of Cordoba consisted of 400,000 volumes, and six whole months were required to remove it from its old building to a new one. The number of the volumes in the library of the Fatimid Caliphs is very uncertain because the various Arabic sources used by al-Maqrizi, author of a very extensive topographical description of Egypt, do not state explicitly the number of books in total, but here and there one or the other portion of this library. One of these, for example, speaking of the library of Al-'Aziz, later incorporated in that of al-Hakim, says that it consisted of forty chambers each containing 18,000 books upon the *"ancient"* sciences and that of the *Kitab al-'Ain* the great dictionary of Al-Khalil, thirty copies were found, and of the colossal historical work of Tabari twenty copies, while the Jamharah of Ibn Duraid was represented by one hundred copies, besides 2,400 copies of the Kor'an. Another source states that the library was accommodated in one single room which housed about 200,000 volumes, a notice which is incredible as one room could not possibly hold such an enormous quantity of books. Another source states that the library contained 1,600,000 volumes, among them 1,200 copies of the history of At-Tabari; and finally another author limits the number to only 120,000 a figure which agrees with that of another historian, Al-Qalqashandi, who has drawn from other sources independent of al-Maqrizi. Though we are unable to arrive at a correct figure, the library must have been composed of a much greater quantity that 120,00 because, though frequently plundered in the time of the Fatimids, Salah-ad-Din, at the conquest of the city of Cairo, after having given to his secretary Al-Fadil 100,000 to 120,000 books, had the remainder sold at auctions which were held twice a week and lasted for a whole year.

In order that the public might use with ease all the material collected in these great libraries there existed proper catalogues collected in booklets or larger volumes, as was the case with the libraries at Cordoba, Ar-Ray, Bukhara and Shiraz.

Additions to the library were made either by the purchase of manuscripts or by copying for which special copyists were employed.

Immense sums were spent by the founders of libraries for the acquisition of new books; the pride and ambition of many was to be the first to possess the work of a well-known author. For this purpose princes like Al-Hakam of Spain, and the Banu 'Ammar of Tripolis employed specialists and merchants who undertook this class of trade to acquire books in all foreign lands.

Probably some founders or directors of libraries acquired books at the auction sales, much in vogue in oriental countries, which was also one of the means adopted by private persons.

Besides the direct purchase of books it was also the custom to make copies of a work of which a copy was wanted. For this work the great libraries employed in a room set apart for the purpose a number of special copyists. Their manner of working varied. Sometimes a copyist would work by himself, in other cases several scribes would copy to dictation, so that at the same time several copies were made of the same original. The library at Tripolis is stated to have employed 180 such scribes, 30 of whom never ceased working day and night; such scribes were also employed in the libraries of Cairo and Shiraz. The same method was used by private persons like the Caliph al-'Aziz in Cairo, Al-Hakam in Spain, the historian Al-Waqidi (died 208/823), the Spanish scholar Abu Mutrif and others, when for some reason they were unable to purchase the book they required.

The large private libraries as well as the public ones had their librarians and attendants and among these we find at times distinguished authors and scientists. The historian Ibn Miskawaihi (died 421/1030) was librarian of the wazir Abu'l Fadl ibn al 'Amid of Ar-Ray, the historian Ibn as -Sa'i (died 674/1275) was director of the Mustansiriyah library at Baghdad, Avicenna (Ibn Sina) as mentioned before, was librarian of the Samanid prince Nah ibn Mansur at Bukhara, the author 'Ali ibn-Muhammad ash-Shabushti (died 389/998) was librarian of the Fatimid Caliph Al-'Aziz.

In the large public libraries the work of one librarian was absolutely impossible and he had under him as a rule one or more sub-librarians. In fact the librarians, though primarily in charge of the administration and cataloguing of the books, was supposed to keep the public informed and to overlook the loan of books and the handing of books to the students; as it was difficult work the ordinary servants attached to the establishment could not take charge of it. For this post it was imperative to be able to read, while the ordinary attendants may have been analphabets. One interesting notice has come down to us : In the large library of the *Dar al'Ilm* at Baghdad the charge of handing the books to the copyists was a negro woman's named Taufiq.

The administration of such an establishment incurred large expenses, especially as nearly all libraries supplied the students with paper, ink and pens. A survey of the fixed sums for the needs of the library at Cairo at the time of Al-Hakim shows that the expenses incurred by this institution were not inconsiderable.

		Dinars
Price of 'Abbadani matting	..	10
Paper for the copyists	..	90
For the librarian (perhaps his salary)	..	48
For water	..	12
For servants	..	15
Paper, ink and pens	..	12
Repairs to the curtains	..	1
Repairs to books and missing leaves supplied.	..	12
Felt curtains for winter use	..	5
Carpets for winter use	..	4

The large public libraries were open to all without distinction; upon this the sources insist continually, saying that anyone who could read, write or study a subject was admitted. Such was the free admission in the libraries at Tripolis, Cairo Shiraz and Mosul. It is not clear from the original sources whether the library of the Caliph Al-Hakam at Cordoba was open to the public. The explicit statement that the public were admitted cannot be found but the words of the informant: "Al-Hakam was very generous towards the people, collecting many books, seem to indicate that the library was open to the public, for if the Caliph had only collected a fine private library, he could hardly have done any service to the people even if, as Mr. Ribera believes, some scholars were allowed to use it. In such case the modest schoolmaster Muhammad ibn Hazm would have been infinitely more generous towards the public who freely permitted many scholars of Cordoba to work in his library. The same can be said of 'Ali ibn Yahya al-Munajjim and many other private persons.

To facilitate in every way the use of books by students and scientists the public libraries also permitted their loan to places far away, sometimes against a deposit of money, at others, even without such deposit. An example is the Damiriyah library at Marw from which Yaqut had borrowed 200 books, and others visited by the Spanish historian Abu Hayyan (died 745/1343) who would not buy any books, because, he says : Whatever book I want to have I can get on loan from any library, while if I wanted to borrow money to buy these books I should find no-one who would lend it to me.

But not all were so generous. Some donors, leaving their books in *Waqf,* made the condition that such books should not under any circumstances be lent out, as was done by the Qadi Ibn Hibban of Nishapur. Many books lent were not returned to the library they belonged to, and the verses of a certain Ar-Rabbat of Halab composed in 1216/1801) were a cry from the depth of his heart :

"Never lend a book, but rather make an excuse ! Take some lien for it, for such is a just way of acting. If you do not pay attention to my words you will certainly lose the book!"

Also the verses of a certain Ibn as-Sarim (964/1556) "Whoever borrows my book and then keeps it is certainly not noble, but of low breed and a traitor."

After all the life of these wonderful libraries was not long, through carelessness of the librarians, change of government, acts of vandalism by conquerors who tried to eradicate everything they found made by the hands of the defeated, these immense intellectual riches gradually vanished. In Arabic history not infrequent are notices of the loss of this or that library. One of the most frequent causes was destruction by fire. So ended the library founded in Baghdad by Sabur ibn Ardashir, which did not long survive its founder who died in 416/1025, being burned down with the whole quarter of the city where it was situated by the soldiers of the victorious Saljuk Sultan, Toghrul Beg.

A similar fate had several other libraries in Baghdad, burned and destroyed by the Tatars under the leadership of Hulagu so that all traces of them were wiped out; that of Ghaznah, burned by the troops of the Ghuri prince Husain, when he sacked the city in 550/1155; that of Marw, destroyed by the Tatars in 606/1209; that of Nishapur laid to ashes by the Ghuzz turks in 548/1153. Less disastrous was the fate of the library of Ar-Ray. Of its books only those were burned by the conqueror, Mahmud of Ghaznah, which were against the Sunni doctrines of which the Sultan was a fervent supporter.

The rich library at Shiraz, on the contrary, decayed gradually; at the time of the successor of its founder it was already neglected. In fact one of the copyists, Ibn al-Bawwab, complained one day to the sultan Baha' ad-Daulah about the disorder which reigned in it, so that a manuscript of the Kor'an copied by the celebrated calligraphist Ibn Muqlah in thirty sections had lost one section and it took a long time to bring the fragments together to make the copy complete.

Neither was the library of the Banu 'Ammar in Tripolis spared from being destroyed by fire, the incendiaries were in this case not Tatars or Turks, but Christian bands. In fact this library was burned down by the Frank soldiers in the First Crusade 503/1109.

This fact has been recorded by the historian Ibn al-Furat (died 807/1404) as follows :

"The Shaikh Yahya ibn Abi Tayy Humaid an-Najjar Al-Halabi says : In Tripolis was an academy the like of which there was nowhere else in the world on account of the abundance, beauty and excellence of its books. Yahya said that his father informed him on the authority of a Shaikh of Tripolis who said: I was with Fakhr al-Mulkibn 'Ammar, lord of Tripolis, at Shaizar. He received the news of the conquest of Tripolis (by the Franks) and he fell down in a faint; then he regained consciousness and tears fell from his eyes. He said : By God! Nothing has caused me greater sorrow than (the destruction of) the Academy. In it were three million books in all sciences of theology, Kor'ans, traditions and literature. There were fifty thousand copies of the Kor'an alone and eighty thousand commentaries on it. My father said that this library was one of the wonders of the world and the Banu 'Ammar had bestowed the greatest care upon it. There were 180 copyists employed in it, and thirty worked day and night, and all were well paid for their services. The Banu `Ammar had in all lands agents who bought for them choice books and Tripolis during the reign of the Banu `Ammar became one whole Academy; from all countries came students and eminent persons, and under the Banu 'Ammar all sciences flourished, especially the doctrines of the Imami sect; as a matter of fact the Banu `Ammar had recalled to life this doctrine and its followers. When the Franks entered Tripolis and conquered it they burned the Academy down to the ground. The cause of the burning was that a priest (may God curse him) when he saw all those books became beside himself. It happened that he entered the rooms where the Kor'ans were stored and he picked up a volume and behold! it was a Kor'an. Then he took a second book and it was again a Kor'an like the first; so he went on till he had picked up about twenty Kor'ans. Then he exclaimed "All that is to be found in this library are Kor'ans of the Muslims!" After this they burned it, only a few volumes were carried away by the Franks—May God curse those who are gone down to perdition already, and may He send to perdition all those who remain! And these are those who afterwards wander through Muslim lands."

A slower but nevertheless inexorable agony underwent also the libraries of Cairo and Cordoba. At the death of the Caliph al-Hakim the Cairo library was still cared for; the wazir of his successor Abu'lQasim 'Ali ibn Ahmad al-Jarjara'i in 435/1043 caused a new catalogue to be made of the books and had the bindings repaired. But gradually the library fell into decay, especially under the Caliph al-Mustansir (426/1094). During this reign a serious revolt occurred in Cairo by the negro soldiers in the service of this prince against the Turkish soldiers, commanded in this civil war by the Egyptian general Nasir ad-Daulah ibn Hamdan, who, having, after much trouble, defeated the rebels in 461/1068, demanded from the Caliph for himself and his followers large recompenses. One of his partisans, was the wazir Abu'l Faraj Muhammad ibn Ja'far al-Maghribi who as reward received many books which were carried by 25 camels, while the sum of money which was due to him was 5,000 Dinars, but the books which he had selected were valued at well over 100,000.

The same Nasir ad-Daulah and his partisans were the same year compelled to flee from Cairo driven out by the same Turkish soldiers, who were exasperated by their preponderance and assumed excessive power and many houses, among them the library of the castle were plundered. The books which were in the so called "Internal Library" of the castle escaped out of the large library. This library, it appears, had a secret entrance.

Other books ended by falling into the hands of the governor of Alexandria, who is not known, but on being sent back to Cairo they were again plundered by slaves, and the negro slaves tore off the bindings to make sandals of them, burning the leaves, making the pretence that the book had come from the castle of the Sultan, who was a Shai'ah in opposition to their own creed. Other books were thrown away and scattered in all directions. The remnants which were not burned were covered by heaps of dust and formed hillocks and remained in the vicinity of the ancient deposits called to-day "Hills of Books."

The experiences of the books included in the libraries of the Fatimids had not finished here. In 567/1171 Salah ad-Din made himself master of Egypt and also took a share in the fate of the libraries. As already mentioned he gave to his secretary the Qadi al-Fadl 'Abd ar-Rahim ibn 'Ali 100,000 books while he ordered the remainder to be sold by auction. The sales were twice a week and lasted for years as they were still going on in the year 572/1176, and among the purchasers was the historian 'Imad ad-Din al-Isbahani, secretary of Salah ad-Din, who, however, was by his master absolved from payment for the books he had purchased.

The library of Cordoba also perished miserably. Under the caliphate of the weak Hisham II., the power passed into the hands of the wazir al-Mansur Muhammad ibn Abi 'Amir who, hating everything that dealt with philosophy, religious controversy or similar themes, invited some theologians to the library of Al-Hakam, made them sort out all books of a materialistic or philosophical nature, and had some burned while others were cast into wells and cisterns of the palace where they soon decayed under the dust and stones thrown upon the top of them.

A few years later when Cordoba (in the 5/11the century) was menaced by Berber troops the wazir al-Wadih, freedman of Al-Mansur, had part of the remaining library sold, while what was left was plundered and destroyed by the conquerors; only a very small remnant of the books which escaped was taken to Toledo, where they probably served to form the beautiful library of the Banu'n-Nun of Toledo, when after the death of the Caliph Hisham III, Spain was split into a number of small kingdoms (the Muluk at-Tawa'if).

The 7/13th century, fatal for the independence of the Caliphate, was also disastrous for Arabic culture and libraries. Almost simultaneously this immense realm, already diminished and enfeebled by the continual struggle of the princes who had divided the power among themselves, was invaded from two sides by two great movements of nations totally different in civilization and religion but both intent upon destroying and eradicating all that was dear and sacred to their common enemy; the Mongol horde and the Christian armies of the West.

But while the Christians of Spain were able to drive out the Muslims and supplant their civilization for that of the Arabs, though being to no mean degree influenced by them, the Mongols, less civilised, allowed themselves to be converted to Islam and the religion transfused gradually into the new converts the love for books. The Mongol dynasty established in India was the first to feel the need for intellectual food and became the initiator and protector of all sciences. It was then that in the great cities libraries saw the light which collected the remnants of the great cultural heritage of the Arabs. They were followed by the Othmanli Turks who, in their capital, Constantinople, especially in the 16th and 17th centuries, collected great libraries, most of which were attached to the mosques while the richest and most important one was comprised in the heritage of the Sultans themselves.

Principally, however, in the 19th and more so in the 20th century there has arisen in so many oppressed nations a sentiment of patriotism, of independence and a pride in the sacred and inalienable heritage of their own civilization, and this feeling has also roused the Islamic Orient from its torpor. After the example of Europe all cultural manifestations have revived and flourished, and with these, libraries have taken a new lease of life. If those which exist in the Islamic world are only in part a poor step towards the revival of a glorious past they nevertheless represent this renewal of Muslim culture and the tendency to collect and put into order the cultural treasures. Egypt, most closely in contact with Europe, first felt the need for establishing libraries of European type, and the Khedivial, now National, Library was arranged by distinguished German Orientalists, Spitta, Vollers and Moritz. In this library are brought together the most precious manuscripts which were scattered in the various mosques of Cairo, arranged with modern acumen in such a manner that they can be utilised and studied by the learned of all nations. Since the time of the first European director, Spitta, this library, has had a special staff of qualified copyists able to produce exact copies of the manuscripts for scholars who made a request for such, and recently has been introduced the more commodious and exact process of photographing.

Besides this Public Library, Egypt boasts also of private collections of valuable manuscripts, among which the most important is that of Ahmad Taimur Pasha, one of the most learned modern Egyptians.

Constantinople has not remained behind in this movement so much more so because, as already mentioned, this city boasted of flourishing libraries in the 16th and 17th centuries, and the contents of the collections scattered in many mosques and madrasahs are set out in a large catalogue (in 40 volumes) which catalogue unfortunately leaves much to be desired. Precious mines for students are the Koprulu, Yeni Jami, Top Kapu Sarai, Hamidiyeh and other libraries in which some of the most precious and unique Arabic manuscripts are found. It is certain that the Government of the Turkish Republic will consider it a duty to preserve these treasures and make their use more easily accessible to European students than has been the case hitherto.

The influence of the West has made itself strongly felt in Syria in recent years; at Bairut, where, besides several small libraries, through the efforts of the Jesuit fathers who direct the University of St. Joseph an important collection of manuscripts has been formed. In Damascus, where the first impulse was given by the far-seeing governor, Midhat Pasha, about 1870, several libraries have come into existence.

The libraries of Baghdad, capital of the 'Iraq and once the seat of the Caliphate, underwent during the last fifty years a deplorable decadence, which commenced in the 16th and 17th centuries. Inundations, plague, and last but not least the sale of manuscripts to Europeans have almost completely dispersed the manuscripts. In 1909 there still existed public libraries attached to mosques, the most important of which was that of Shaikh 'Abd al-Qadir al-Jilani. To-day, principally by the interest taken and under the guidance of the learned Carmelite, Father Anastase, a very learned Arabic scholar and himself the possessor of a valuable collection of manuscripts, an important cultural movement has taken place there also.

The libraries of the principal cities of the interior of the Arabian peninsula, like Mecca and Medina, are too little known, but are sure also to contain precious material, if we can judge by the copies made by the learned Shaikh ash-Shinqiti, and others made for Court Landberg.

Other collections exist in the Yaman especially in the city of San'a, where the Lombard merchant Caprotti acquired at intervals large quantities of Yamanite manuscripts which, forming an important collection, are now preserved in the Ambrosian Library at Milan. Professor Griffini commenced to make a catalogue of this collection but it was left unfinished on account of his premature death. Other collections of smaller size, coming from the Yaman, are among the manuscripts preserved at Berlin and at the British Museum in London. The cordial relations between Italy and the Yaman make us hope that the time is not far distant when this extreme portion of the Arab world can be explored scientifically.

Under the influence of the French, libraries have also been established in the cities of Tunisia, Algeria and Morocco, which are gradually being enlarged and enriched by continual new acquisitions. At the present time the following libraries are well-known on account of the precious manuscripts which they contain : the library of the Zaituniyah mosque at Tunis, the library at Algiers, the fine collection in the madrasah at Tlemsen and that of Rabat (Morocco), a catalogue of the latter having been published recently.

Also India, with the very great number of its collections of manuscripts found in the larger cities, like Madras, Bombay and the cities of Bengal and the Punjab, continues with pride, aided by England, the cultural movement commenced by the Mongol dynasty in the 16th and 17th centuries.

But all that has been done up to the present for the preservation of manuscripts in the East is not sufficient. Many precious manuscripts are still scattered everywhere, sometimes in the hands of private people who perhaps do not know even the value of them, or in small mosques or madrasahs where they remain buried and unknown. These ought not only to be saved from destruction and loss and collected in larger institutions, but should also be catalogued rationally and correctly and, in case of need, photographed so that they can be studied in other parts of the world. For this purpose Western Orientalists and learned Orientals should collaborate, the former bringing their scientific methods, the latter their practical knowledge of the language and the cultural tradition of their country. In this manner the study of Arabic culture and civilization, which has in latter years shown such a great development, may continue more rigorously and more successfully.

19

The Founders of the Buhar Library

HIDAYAT HOSAIN

The famous Buhar Library which is an annexe of the Imperial Library, Calcutta, was founded by Sayyid Sadr-ad-din, the Mir Munshi of Warren Hastings. The Library received its finishing touch from his great-grandson, Maulvi Sadr-ad-din Ahmad al-Musavi who presented it to the Imperial Library, Calcutta. It is worth while to make some research into the lives of these two historic, though scarcely remembered, personages.

Munshi Sayyid Sadr-ad-din comes of a Sayyid family of Buhar, also known as the Munshi family. This Munshi family is one of the very ancient and respectable Muhammadan families of Bengal. The Munshi Sahib of Buhar is the hereditary *Mutawalli* and *Sajjadanashin* of the Dargah of Pandooah, famous in Bengal as the Estate of *Ba'is Hazari* which extends over parts of the three districts of Malda, Dinajpore and Rajshahi. The Buhar family is directly descended from the Prophet of Islam through the 7th Imam, Imam Musa al-Kazim, whence the family is known as al-Musavi.

Most of the members of this family were well-known for their piety and devoutness, and reputed as saints of a very high order. One of them, Sayyid Shihab-ad-din by name, being the ninth in descent from Imam Musa Kazim and the fifteenth from the Prophet, came to India as a soldier of fortune during the reign of Sultan Altamish (A.H. 607-633, A.D. 1210-1235), the third king of the Slave Dynasty in Delhi. One of his descendants, Sayyid Hamid Shah, was a distinguished saint, though at first he had chosen the career of a soldier. His tomb is situated in Manickpore in Allahabad and is held in high esteem. His son, Sayyid Raji Nur, a worthy successor of his saintly father, for his piety and his spiritual sanctity won the veneration of the general public. Sayyid Husam al-Haqq son of Sayyid Raji Nur married a princess of Gour, who was the daughter of Nasrat Shah (A.H. 925-939, A.D. 1518-1532), an independent King of Bengal, who bestowed on his son-in-law the Jagir of Pargana Ranihati in Burdwan. This Pargana yielded an income of no less than three lacs of rupees annually in those days. Sayyid Husam al-Haqq settled with his wife at Utra, a village known as Utrasan, now situated within the Kalna sub-division of Burdwan.

As time rolled on, the descendants of Sayyid Husam al-Haqq went on multiplying, and split up into many branches. Sayyid Muhammad Sadiq, the eleventh descent from Husam al-Haqq, married the daughter of Shaikh Karam Allah of the village of Buhar where he settled down. His two sons (1) Sayyid Sadr-ad-din and (2) Sayyid Siraj-ad-din were born at Buhar.

Sayyid Sadr-ad-din, son of Sayyid Muhammad Sadiq, has a remarkable history of his own. His career was a chequered one, being sprinkled with scenes of joy and sorrow, success and failure throughout. For sometime he worked as a clerk under Holwell in Calcutta. Probably he was the first Bengali Muslim to serve under the British. As he was a man of enlightened views he took off the mask of prejudice against private service and did not feel the least scruple to enter the service of Holwell. This took place before the fateful battle of Plassey. Then he acted as the Mir Munshi of Nawab Mir Ja'far 'Ali Khan, to which capacity he united the Dewanship of Munni Begum who approved of his services so highly that she used to call him her son.

As Sadr-ad-din was a friend of Mir Ja'far 'Ali Khan from childhood, for they had read with the same tutor, and as Sadr-ad-din never served under Siraj ad-Dawla, Mir Ja'far naturally trusted him very much, and later events show that his confidence was not misplaced When Mr. John Shore (afterwards Sir John Shore) wanted to extort the secret movements of Mir Ja'far 'Ali Khan from Sadr-ad-din he refused to inform and was imprisoned for four months and fifteen days. On the last day of his imprisonment two European sergeants came to his cell, held loaded pistols to his breast and demanded an immediate disclosure of all the secrets of Mir Ja'far under threat of instant death. The undaunted Sadr-ad-din replied: "It is better that you should kill me. I shall then be relieved of all this pain and misery which are unendurable. You can not expect to have a word from me. My reply throughout has been the uniform denial of all knowledge." This ended in the honourable release of Sadr-ad-din. The author of the *Akhbar as-Sidq* says that afterwards, when he asked Sadr-ad-din why he did not speak out "the secrets" if there were any as it was a question of life and death with him, Sadr-ad-din replied: "Had I spoken out the truth the result would have been the execution of the noble soul of a Sayyid (descendant of the Prophet), meaning Mir Ja'far 'Ali Khan, and that of the very best wearer of the sacred thread (meaning the Brahmin, Maharaja Nanda Kumar). Mir Ja'far 'Ali Khan, who held Sadr-ad-din his most faithful friend and well-wisher, appointed him *Ataliq* (Tutor) to his son by Munni Begum, Nawab Najm-ad-Dawla. It is gratifying to note that Sadr-ad-din proved in no way unworthy of the trust placed in him by his friend and master, Nawab Mir Ja'far ' Ali Khan, and during Nawab Najm-ad-Dawla's rule, when Mr. Johnston fell out with him, he said, "The servants of the Nazim cannot be disloyal, faithless and false to the salt of their master." The history of Nawab Najm-ad-Dawla is inseparably connected with Sadr-ad-din. His advocacy of the cause of Nawab Najm-ad-Dawla against Nawab Muzaffar Jung before Lord Chitty was admirable. Even the last moments of the Nawab were not dissociated from the aforesaid Sayyid. The Nawab passed whole nights in restlessness on the lap of Sadr-ad-din and towards the morning breathed his last quietly in his arms. During Nawab Saif-ad-Dawla's time also he was a figure of no mean importance. It was not till his enemies rose to power during the time of the next Nawab, Mubarak-ad-Dawla, that they got the better of him and pulled him down. They whispered into the ears of the thoughtless Nawab that Sadr-ad-din was rather too intimately familiar with Munni Begum. This incensed the young Nawab who unhesitatingly gave orders for his execution at once. It is said that the Sayyid was enjoying his *Huqqa* when the old Chaprasi who had served him for years ran to him and informed him of his immediate danger.

He at once got up, saying, "If ever better days dawn for me again

I will return your kindness—Now salam, " and off he went. Immediately after, Nawab's men arrived, but only to find the house deserted to their surprise and disappointment. When his enemies found that all their endeavours were thus frustrated by the vigilance of Sadr-ad-din, they prevailed on the Nawab to set a price upon his head and to confiscate all his properties both at Murshidabad and at Burdwan. This was done. His brother Siraj-ad-din who was left at home to look after the affairs there, finding that the family was being driven to a state of penury and distress, sought for an appointment under Mr. John Graham, Collector of Midnapore, and became his Sirishtadar. In this way he managed to keep up his family.

A homeless wanderer, Sadr-ad-din was passing his days in exile from forest to forest till he reached Midnapore, where he found in the Sirishtadari of Mr. J. Graham of the East India Company his own brother, Siraj-ad-din. The two brothers embraced each other tenderly. Sadr-ad-din sought, through Siraj-ad-din, for protection under the British, and this was most sympathetically extended to him by Mr. Graham,[10] who recommended him to Mr. Barwell, Collector of Burdwan and a friend of Warren Hastings. Mr. Barwell again recommended him most highly to the Governor-General, who afterwards found him a most valuable hand in the affairs of the *Nizamat* particularly during the transfer of the Diwani from Murshadabad. Under Warren Hastings, he was at first appointed his Mir Munshi and then the Darugha of all the '*Adalats* (or the Superintendent of all the Courts). In the latter capacity he first made the acquaintance of Sir Elijah Impey, the first Chief Justice of Bengal, and this acquaintance ultimately blossomed into life-long friendship. During the administration of Lord Cornwallis. Sadr-ad-din's services were also utilised in the Decennial Settlement of Bengal. The *Aimma* lands were settled by Sadr-ad-din. The Governor-General was so highly pleased with him that he bestowed on him a *Ja'igir* (hereditary possession) consisting of the Parganas of Baharband as a reward for his services. Diwan Janga Govinda Singh, the founder of the Raj family of Kandi in Murshidabad, who owed his position and fortune to the influence of Sadr-ad-din, wanted to have the above Parganas, Baharband, for his favourite Kanto Mudi, and therefore, played a trick with his benefactor. While congratulating him on the occasion, he artfully requested him to maintain a hundred Brahmins on his behalf, whereupon Sadr-ad-din asked him what he meant by such a request. Ganga Govinda replied that the *Zamindari* of Baharband is required to maintain many a temple and consequently a large number of Brahmins Shebaits for the worship thereof. When Sadr-ad-din heard this, his religious spirit revolted against the idea of worshipping idols (he being a Muslim) and he at once wrote to the Governor-General expressing his unwillingness to accept the *Ja'igir*. This result was that Ganga Govinda won the prize for his friend and co-religionist, Kanto Babu.

Sadr-ad-din was as deeply learned as he was strictly pious in his private life. He built several mosques and rest-houses where travellers were freely fed. The mosque, a pretty big structure, at Buhar is still extant, and travellers are still fed free there. The nice little annexe to the mosque which contains the tombs of Sadr-ad-din, his two wives and a little child, is beautifully situated towards the south-east corner, and at the base of this tomb-house the ground forms the graveyard of his family. The mosque was built in A.H. 1187, A.D. 1773. He constructed many a village road and excavated numerous tanks in the district of Burdwan. His services were recognised not only by the local authorities at Murshidabad and at Calcutta, but also by the East India Company and by the Emperor of Delhi, Shah'Alam, (A. H. 1173-1221, A.D. 1759-1806), who was pleased to bestow on him and his descendants, in the oldest male line, the endowment Estate of the *Pargana Ba'is Hazari* in the districts of Malda, Dinajpore and Rajshahi under *Sanad* bearing the Imperial Seal and the sign manual of the Emperor in the thirteenth year of his reign and subsequently the *Ja'igir* of Pargana Ranihati in Burdwan which now forms the principal factor of the Burdwan Raj, under a similar Sanad. The *A'imma* of Buhar was also granted to him under a royal warrant. Many other properties at Calcutta, Murshidabad and in the Mofassil were granted to him as *Muqarrari Maurusi.* The well-known building in Upper Chitpore Road, Calcutta, named the "Munshi ka Chakla" belonged to him, and the lane to the south of the house still bears his name. Sadr-ad-din married twice, first at Jhillo near Mangalkot in Burdwan, the daughter of Qazi Hafiz Talib Allah Rais and Zemindar of the village;

secondly at Murshidabad the widowed daughter of Sayyid Wajid 'Ali, a member of the well-known Sayyid family of Barh in Bihar. He had no issue by his first wife, while by his second he had a girl and a son Kafil-ad-din al-Musavi. He died on the 14th, of Ramazan, A.H. 1211, A.D. 1796, in his favourite cottage famous as Rangin Ghar. He left behind him an inheritance worth several lacs of rupees.

Sadr-ad-din's zeal for works of public utility was indeed remarkable. He was a sincere well-wisher of his country. In A.H. 1189 (A.D. 1775) he established the famous Buhar Madrasah, as the following chronogram indicates:-

> When Sadr-ad-din erected this auspicious Madrasah;
> The foundation of Knowledge came into being.
> Aziz! I wanted (to know) the year (of its foundation) from heavenly regions.

The angels replied! "Let this auspicious Madrasah be luminous (with learning)" Date: A.H. 1189 and the nucleus of the Buhar library was then started. This Madrasah diffused the light of Oriental learning in Bengal and became the last seat of Oriental education during the Musalman regime in India. It was in this Madrasa that he utilised the services of Maulana 'Abd al-'Ali, Bahr-al 'Ulum, or the Sea of Learning, at a monthly salary of Rs. 1,000. Students from all parts of Asia used to flock there to get education and, on the completion of their course, an examination used to be held to confer academic degrees on the successful candidates in accordance with their acquirements, together with the usual presentation of turbans. He also attached a free boarding-house for 800 students who were all fed free of charge, and were supplied with light for study. Most of the Qazis of all the Courts of Bengal, from the Supreme Court downwards, were in-debted for their education to the Buhar Madrasah. The Calcutta Government Madrasah was built after its model five years afterwards in 1780 A.D. The aforesaid Maulana Bahr-al-Ulum was not the only person who adorned the professorial staff under Sadr-ad-din. The most erudite scholar of the six schools of Indian Philosophy of that age, Pandit Dulal Chandra Tarkabagis, who defeated quite a host of Sava

Pandits who gathered at the Sradha ceremony of Raja Naba Kissen's mother, held service under Sadr-ad-din, at a monthly salary of Rs. 300. The well-known caligraphist of the time Ghulam Qadir, who had not a second in the land, was also in his service; while writers like Munshi Muhammad Yasin and Munshi Lal Chand, each of whom was a master in the literary sphere, worked under him and used to draw Rs. 300 a month each. The caligraphist used to receive Rs. 250 a month.

Kafil-ad-din was only a boy when his father died. So, the British Government gave him protection and his whole estate was managed by the Court of Wards. Kafil-ad-din, when of age, took over charge of his property; but on account of his extravagance he left a debt of over two lacs of rupees when he died in A.H. 1243, A.D. 1827, at the age of 43. He had married a daughter of Khundkar Sayyid Muhammad Kirmani and had a son, called Karim-ad-din Ahmad al-Musavi, who, unlike his father, was a man of prudence and tact and managed his affairs with wisdom and skill. His frugality became a household word and the immense debt of his father was eventually paid off by him although he had to part with some of the most valuable portions of his property. However, when he died he left an estate yielding an annual net income of not less than a lac of rupees. He married a daughter of Maulavi Muhammad Sajid Siddiq, who was a Munsif. He had three sons—(1) Sadr-ad-din Ahmad, (2) Siraj-ad-din Ahmad, (3) Safi-ad-din Ahmad, and a daughter. All these children were minors, except Sadr-ad-din Ahmad, at the time of his death in A.H. 1274, (A.D.1857).

Sayyid Sadr-ad-din Ahmad al-Musavi was born in 1259 A.H. , (A.D. 1843). When he was about seven he was admitted into the Buhar Madrasah and studied with Maulavi Sayyid Rasul Bakhsh. At the age of fifteen he was reading *Sharh Jami*. At this time he lost his father, and the management of the estate developed upon him, he being the eldest child. He spent some of his time in the estate affairs and some in his studies, history and biography being his favourite subjects. He was an important member of the Muslim Community of Bengal, being an Honorary Magistrate, Municipal Commissioner and a Juror in the District Court for 30 years, and having been exempted from the Arms Act with four of his retainers. He did a good deal for the public benefit. He was a great Oriental scholar. He compiled in Persian, first the *Rawa'ih al-Mustafa min Azhar al-Murtaza,* a biography of the Prophet's descendants. His second book was *Zarb al-Malahi,* a treatise justifying sober music and mirth according to the principles of Islam. He also edited *an-Nasa'iz al-Khasa'is.* Lastly, he wrote *Al-Murtaza* which is the biography of 'Ali bin Abi Talib and is still unpublished.

He was so engrossed in his books that he could not take proper care of the estate which ultimately came to partial ruin. He even sold some of the property to buy books.

He died in 1905 A.D. and left behind him two sons, 'Abd-al-Waris and 'Abdullah, both of whom are now dead, and two daughters.

The Buhar Library contains 485 Persian MSS. and 465 Arabic MSS. Maulavi Sayyid Sadr-ad-din presented the Library to the Government of India under an agreement on the 22nd August, 1904. In accordance with the agreement the Buhar Library, which is always to be so designated, is preserved in a separate room in the Imperial Library, Calcutta.

Among the Persian MSS, the following are of special interest:-

Kitab 'Aja'ib-ul-Makhluqat

This is a very valuable and extremely rare cosmographical work, composed in the beginning of the latter half of the 6th century A.H.

This work, of which I have seen no notice anywhere else, is one of the earliest, Persian works on cosmography and is, therefore of considerable interest.

On an ornamented blue ground in the beautifully illuminated head-piece the title of the work written in gold letters is Kitab 'Aja'ib-ul-Makhluqat, but in the preface, on fol. 3[a] the full title of the work, as given by the author himself, is "Aja'ib-ul-Makhluqat wa Ghara'ib-ul-Mau-judat."

From a passage on fol. 7[b] we learn that the author wrote the work for Tughril bin Arslan bin Tughril. This royal personage is evidently

Sultan Tughril bin Arslan (A.H.571590-A.D.11-75-1193) the last of the Saljuqian monarchs of Persia.

On fol. 132[b] he deals at some length with Hamadan. He speaks of the place with a certain predilection and relates some stories from his father and his teacher Imam Sa'id bin Majd-ad-din Abu-'I-Fata-al-Tali. Again on fol. 9 he says that a man who has spent his whole life in the place where he was born may not necessarily know everything that can be known about the locality, and cites the following incident. He relates that on one occasion when he was Isfahan a certain person wanted from him some particulars of the inscription on the Arwand Mountain (Koh-i-Arwand) (a mountain in Hamadan noticed by our author on fol. 63[b]). In reply the author said that he had no knowledge whatever of the existence of such an inscription. Subsequently, when he came to Hamadan, he went to the mountain, saw the inscription and was surprised with its curiosities.

This points to the author's having been a native of Hamadan.

The above facts point to the conclusion that our anonymous author was born before A.H. 551—A.D. 1156, and that he wrote this work entitled *'Aja'ib-ul-Makhluqart wa Ghara"ib-ul-Maujudat* for Sultan Tughril III bin Arslan between A.H. 571 and 590—A.D. 1175 and 1193.

An anonymous treatise of about 52 folios, called "*Ri-sala-i-`ib-ul-Makhluqat,*" which seems to bear a close relation with the present work, is noticed by Dr. Ethe. in the Bodl. Lib. Cat. No. 405. The beginning of the said treatise is quite different from that of the present work, but the subject headings, so far as enumerated in the said catalogue, closely agree with those of this work. We learn that the division of Dr. Ethe's copy is not quite clear and that the headings are very often omitted. Strangely, the division in this copy is also vague and confusing, but the headings here are seldom omitted.

Like Ethe's copy our work begins with wonderful stories from the lives of Iskandar Luqman, Jamshid, etc.; then follows the index of the work in beginning which the author says that the work is divided into ten Qanuns and ten Rukns.

Each page containing the miniature, with its opposite page, is beautifully illuminated.

Written on thick and glossy gold sprinkled paper in a clear Nasta'liq within gold and coloured borders with a double-page, beautifully illuminated '*Unwan.* The headings are written in red and blue throughout.

Dated Muharram, A.H. 125, evidently meaning 1025.

Al-Mu'jam fi Ma'ayir-i Ash'ar-ul-'Ajam

A work on prosody, rhyme and poetical figures, by Shams-ud-din Muhammad ibn Qays of Ray.

The work has been edited by Mirza Muhammad with introduction and indices in "E.J.W." Gibb Memorial Series (London,1909).

The title of the work given in the preface is *Al-Mu'jam Fi Ash'ar-al-'Ajam* but it has been labelled and entitled by some former owner "Hada'iq-us-Sihr or Hada'iq-us-Sihr-Fi Daqa'iq-ish-Sh'ir which, as we know, is a work on the same subject by the famous poet Rashid-ud-din Watwat (died A.H. 578-A.D. 1182) and which Shams-i-Qays mentions in the preface, Fol.4[a].

The present copy is somewhat abridged. Most of the poetical quotations found in the printed edition are omitted, while the prose part is merely an abstract. The system of divisions and arrangement, found in the printed edition, is maintained. The year in which the author began to write the book is given here as A.H. 615 (A.D. 1218) instead of A.H. 614, as in the printed edition.

Of the two Qisms into which the work is divided the first on Prosody, subdivided into four Babs, begins on fol.5[b]; the second on Rhyme, subdivided into six Babs on fol. 55[a]. The Khatimah on poetical figures begins on fol.111[a].

Written in a careless Nasta'liq. Dated A.H. 1236.

Diwan-i-Nizami

A collection of lyrical poems attributed to Nizami. His full name was Nizami-ud-din Abu Muhammad Ilyas bin Yusuf bin Mu'ayyid al-Ganjawi. He was born in A.H. 535 (A.D. 1140) and died, according to reliable authorities, A.H. 599 (A.D.1202).

The Diwan consists chiefly of Qasidahs (fol.1[b]-12[a]) without any alphabetical order.

The MS., an incomplete one, is written in fair Nasta'liq within gold and coloured-ruled borders. Folios have been misplaced in several cases.

Not dated, apparently 18th century.

Khamsah-i-Sarfi

A unique and valuable, but defective, copy of the Khamsah of Maulana Shaikh Ya'qub, poetically surnamed Sarfi, of Kashmir. He was a friend of the celebrated historian Bada'uni, who devoted a long notice to the poet's life. Sarfi died on the 12th Zulqa'da. A.H. 1003 (A.D. 1594).

The poet composed this Khamsah in imitation of the five poems of Nizami.

The poems in the present copy are arranged in wrong order. The right order seems to be as follows:-

I. Maslak-ul-Akhyar, foll. 87[b]-111[a], written in imitation of Nizami's Makhzan-ul-Asrar, and completed (A.H. 993 A.D. 1585). This seems to be the first poem of the poet's Khamsah.

II. Wamiq wa Azra, fol. 1[b]-24[a]. It is in imitation of Nizami's Khusrau wa Shirin, and treats of the love adventures of Wamiq and Azra. This is the second (Masnawi) poem of the poet's Khamsah.

It was completed in (A.H. 993 A.D. 1585), as expressed by the chronogram "*Ma'shuq wa 'Ashiq*" in the concluding line of the poem.

III. Layla wa Majnun, foll. 25[b]-50[a]. This is in imitation of Nizami's poem of the same name. This is third poem of the Khamsah.

The date of completion is (A.H. 998 A.D. 1589), as is expressed by the chronogram "Sharh-i-`Ishqbazi" in the concluding lines of the poem.

The fourth poem which he has written in imitation of Nizami's Iskandar Namah and to which he refers in the prologue of his fifth poem, is wanting.

V. Maqamat-i-Pir, fol. 50^b- 86^b, is in imitation of Nizami's Haft-i-Paikar.

It was completed in (A.H. 1000 A.D. 1591), for which year the title forms a chronogram.

Written in small Nastaliq within gold and coloured-ruled border, with an illuminated head-piece at the beginning of each poem. The headings are written in red throughout. The original folios are placed in new margins.

Not dated, apparently beginning of the 17th century.

Tuhfat-ul-Faqir wa Hidayat-ul-Haqir

A very rare and valuable copy of an Arabic and Persian anthology, compiled by Sharaf-ud-din 'Ali Yazdi (d.A.H. 858—A.D. 1454), the author of the well-known history of Timur, entitled Zafar Namah. Sharaf enjoys a vast reputation as an elegant prose-writer, but at the same time he was a poet of no mean order. He was well-versed in the art of composing verses and his Hulal-Mutarraz and Muntakhab-i-Hulal-i-Mutarraz, on riddles and enigmas, were held in high estimation by later poets of distinction, so much so that the celebrated Jami based on them his own treatise on the same subject entitled Mu'amma-i-Kabir or Hilayat ul-Hilal.

The present work, which seems to be hitherto unknown, contains a vast collection of the choicest specimens of the different branches of Arabic and Persian poetry by various authors, arranged according to the topics of which they treat.

Unfortunately there is a lacuna after fol. 2, otherwise we might possibly have got some valuable information about the work. This folio suddenly breaks off in the middle of the praise of a certain royal personage to who our author dedicates the work.

After which fol. 3[a] abruptly opens in the middle of the description of the contents.

The subjects, consisting of sixty-four Babs, are enumerated on fol. 3[a]- 4[a].

The first Bab begins on fol. 4[a] with an extract from the Diwan of 'Ali bin Abu Talib.

The above is followed by a Persian extract from the Diwan of Kamal Isfahani.

The colophon is dated, Saturday, 19th Zulhijja, A.H. 1019.

Shah Nama

An exceedingly valuable copy of the famous epic poem Shah Nama by Abu'l Qasim Mansur surnamed Firdausi, who was born in Shadab near Tus about A.H. 321 or 322—(A.D. 933 or 934) and died in A.H. 411 (A.D.1020). According to some the poet died in A.H.416 (A.D.1025) or A.H. 421 (A.D.1030).

The work has been frequently lithographed and printed.

This copy contains the introduction written in A.H. 829 (A.D. 1426) by order of Mirza Bayasangar.

The preface concludes with a list of the ancient Persian kings from Kayumurs to Yazdijird described in the text.

The second half of the Shah Namah, which begins on folio 263[b] is entitled here Kitab Lahrasp Namah.

A very fine specimen of eastern ornamentation containing some quatrains written in golden letters on foll. 1[b] 2[a].

Many of the folios contain richly illuminated illustrations.

Written in fine Nasta'liq, within four gold and coloured-ruled columns. The headings are written on gold grounds.

Not dated, aparently 16th century.

Khamsa-i-Nizami

A very interesting and valuable copy of the five poems of Nizami.

1. *Makhzanu'l-Asrar.* A mystic poem, composed A.H. 572 or 573 (A.D. 1176 or 1177) and dedicated to Fakhrud-din Bahram Shah (d.A.H. 622—A.D. 1225), son of Da'ud, king of Armenia and Rum.

2. *Khusrau wa Shirin.* The loves of Khusrau and Shirin, composed A.H. 576 - (A.D. 1180).

3. *Layla wa Majnum.* A poem on the loves of Layla and Majnum, composed A.H. 584 (A.D.1188) and dedicated to Shirwan Shah (d. A.H. 584).

4. *Haft Paikar.* "The seven stories" related by the seven favourities of the king, Bahram Gur, hence its other name Qissa-i-Bahram Gur.

This poem was written for 'Ala-ud-din Arstan, a descendant of Aqshanqar Ahmadili. He was governor of Maragah, where he was besieged in A.H. 602—(A.D.1205). It was completed 14th Ramzan, A.H. 593—(A.D. 1196).

5. Iskandar Namah or "The Book of Alexander." The poem is divided into two parts; the first part, called Sharaf Namah-i-Iskandari, or Iskandar Namah-i-Barri, treats of Alexander as conqueror, and records his battles on land. The second part, entitled variously Khirad Namah-i-Iskandari, Iqbal Namah-i-Iskandari or Iskandar Namah-i-Bahri, described the king as a prophet and philosopher, and relates his adventures at sea.

Khawar Namah

A very valuable and exceedingly interesting copy of the Khawar Namah, an epic poem in the measure and style of Firdausi's Shah Namah, relating the warlike deeds of 'Ali in battles fought with

Qubad, the king of Khawaran, and with other heathen kings, most of who embraced Islam, by Shams-ud-din Muhammad bin Husam-ud-din, better known as Ibn-i-Husam, who composed it in A.H. 830—(A.D. 1426) and died according to the best authorities in A.H. 875—(A.D. 1470).

This valuable copy is written in a very beautiful bold Nasta'liq within four gold-ruled columns with a profusely illuminated '*Unwan.* It contains 146 highly finished illustrations in the best Indian style. The headings are written in red throughout.

Not dated, apparently 17th century A.D.

Tazkirat-ush-Shu'ara

A very old and exceedingly valuable copy of the well-known biography of Persian poets by Daulat Shah bin 'Ala-ud-daulah Bakht Shah of Samarqand (d.A.H.900—A.D. 1494) composed in A.H. 892—(A.D. 1487).

A very excellent edition of the work with prefaces and indices, by Prof. E.G. Browne, appeared in London, 1901 Hammer's 'Schone Redekunste Persiens' are chiefly based on this work. It is divided into an introduction, seven Tabaqat and a Khatimah.

This copy, excellently written in learned Naskh, is dated Friday, the 17th of Jamadi I, A.H. 980.

Kimiya-i-Su'adat

A very valuable copy of the popular ethico-mystical work treating of the religious and moral obligations of a true Muslim, the external and the spiritual lives, man's duty to God, the qualities conducive to salvation, etc., by Muhammad bin Muhammad-ul-Ghazzali-ut-Tusi who was born A.H. 450—A.D. 1058, and died A.H. 505—A.D. 1111.

This work, which may be considered as a popular abridgment of the author's own Arabic work Ahya-i Ulum ad-din, to which he refers in the preface to the present work.

It has been printed in Calcutta, without date, and lithographed in Lucknow A.H. 1279 and 1282, and in Bombay 1883. Dated A.H. 903.

This unique and exceedingly valuable work, of which no other copy seems to be extant, is no doubt the most valuable possession of this Library. It gives, on an elaborate scale, an accurate account of the city of Heart and the Malik Kings of the Kurt race who ruled there, and treats of all the important events of historical interest which took place there between the years A.H. 618-721 (A.D. 1221-1321) Mu'in Asfizari, the author of the Rauzat-ul-Jannat (a popular history of Herat, composed A.H. 897 (A.D. 1491), who quotes this work as one of his sources, not only freely borrows from it, but bases his entire account of the aforesaid period exclusively on it.

The author who calls himself in the preface Saif ibn Muhammad bin Ya'qub-ul-Harawi but later on simply Saifi, says that after composing the ethical work Majmu'-ah-i-Ghiyasi, which he dedicated to his patron Malik Ghiyas-ud-din Kurt, the fourth king of Herat of the Kurt race, who reigned from A.H. 708-729 (A.D. 1308-1328), he was ordered by the said king to write a history of the events which took place in Herat after Chinghiz Khan's death in A.H. 624 (A.D. 1226) down to his own time. Hence the composition.

This part of the work comprises 136 zikrs or chapters, fully enumerated in the beginning; but from the preface we learn that the author divided the entire work into 400 zikrs. We are further given to understand in the concluding lines that the present volume is the first *daftar* and that if chance favours, he (the author) would have written a second. It seems quite probable that the author did not live to fulfil his promise.

Of the 136 chapters comprised in this volume, the first is devoted to the account of the foundation of Herat and the second to the pre-eminence of Herat, based on those Traditions of the Prophet which refer to this city. The history itself opens with the third chapter relating to the expedition sent by Chinghiz Khan under Tuli Khan against Khurassan in A.H. 618 A.D. 1221 and the general massacre of the inhabitants. In Chapters IV to XI the author gives a vivid account of the sanguinary expeditions of the Mongols against Merv, Mishapur and Herat and the ravages wrought by them. In concluding the eleventh chapter the author observes that after the destruction of Herat, as there were only 16 Survivors who he enumerates by name, and as the city remained in desolated condition for 16 years. Viz., A.H. 619-634—(A.D. 1222-1236), and no king or governor came forward to rebuild it, he has given a summary account of these years under chapters IV-XI. He has, however, dealt elaborately with the history of the remaining period, narrating the events year by year. Chapters XII-XX treat the history of the rulers and governors who ruled in Herat from A.H. 634-642 (A.D. 1236-1244) before the Maliks of Herat of the Kurt race of Ghor.

The remaining chapters are devoted to the history of the first four kings of Herat of the Kurt race covering the period A.H. 643-721 (A.D. 1245-1321). The history ends with an account of the expedition sent against Farah by Malik Ghiyas-ud-din in A.H. 721, the year in which the former went on a pilgrimage to Mecca, leaving Malik Shams-ud-din in charge of the Government.

The MS., is not dated, but the nature of the handwriting and the general appearance of the copy tend to suggest that it was transcribed during the lifetime of the author or immediately after his death.

The MS., is worm-eaten, mutilated and loosened from the original binding, but fortunately no folio seems to be missing.

ARABIC MANUSCRIPTS

Sharh Mishkat-ul-Masabih

A concise commentary of the *Mishkat-ul-Masabih* based chiefly on At-Tayyibi's commentary by Ali bin Muhammad bin 'Ali known as As-Sayyid ush-Sharif-ul-Jurjani, died A.H. 816, (A.D. 1413). 'Ali-ul-Kari in his commentary of Mishkat-ul-Masabin, had deñied the authorship of this commentary by As Saiyid Ush-Sharif ul-Jurjani and has given two reasons in support of his statement. The first reason is that this commentary is not mentioned in the list of the works of Al-Jurjani, and the second that it is inconceivable that an author of such erudition and distinction could have been satisfied with merely abridging the work of At-Tayyibi without adding any comments of his own.

I am personally inclined to ascribe the authorship of this commentary to Al-Jurjani, not withstanding the above two arguments which 'Ali-ul-Kari puts forward against such an assumption, for the following reasons :

As-Sakhavi in his work Ad-Daw-ul-Lami' mentions, on the authority of a great grandson of Al-Jurjani, this book among his other works. Then, again, it is not correct to say that the book is a mere abridgment of At-Tayyibi's work. Al-Jurjani has added remarks and comments of his own, though, indeed, their number is small. Further Hajji- Khalifah, Vol. V., p. 568, remarks that As-Sayyid-ush- Sharif wrote a commentary on Al-Mishkat.

It is noted on the title-page that Sayyid Jamal-ud-din is the author of this work.

Not dated. Circa 18th century.

Qurb-ul-Isnad

A collection of Shi'a Traditions. Biographers differ about its authorship. Some attribute it to Abu'l Abbas'Abdallah bin Ja'far bin-ul-Hussain bin Maliki bin Jami-ul Himyari-ul-Qummi, and others to his son Abu Ja'far Muhammad bin 'Abdallah bin Ja'far-ul-Himyari-ul Qummi. The former was the author of several works. He came to Kufa about A.H. 290—(A.D. 902) and many people heard traditions from him. He is regarded as a trustworthy authority by Shi'a Traditionists. The date of his death, is not known.

The latter viz. Abu Ja'far Muhammad bin 'Abdallah was also a reliable authority on Traditions. The date of his death, also, is not known.

It narrates those traditions which the author has attributed to Al-Imam Ja'far as Sadiq, died A.H. 148, (A.D.765), who was the eldest son of Al-Imam Muhammad al-Baqir (born A.H. 57, A.D. 676 and died in A.H. 113, (A.D. 731), or A.H. 114, (A.D.732) or A.H. 117 (A.D.735) or A.H. 118, (A.D.736), vide Ibn Khallikan, Teheran edition, Vol. II., p. 23). This part commences with various kinds of prayers which the Imam Ja'far has narrated on the authority of his father. Towards the end it deals with miscellaneous religious subjects.

The second part begins with Traditions which Al-Imam Musa Kazim has narrated. He was the son of Al-Imam Ja'far as-Sadiq and is considered the seventh Imam. He was born in Al-Madinah, A.H. 128, (A.D.745) or A.H. 129 (A.D. 746); and died in A.H. 183 (A.D. 799) or A.H. 186, (A.D.802).

The third part narrates the Traditions when the author attributes to Al-Imam 'Ali-ur-Riza bin Musa al-Kazim. He was born in Al-Madinah, some say in A.H. 151, (A.D. 768); and others in A.H. 153, (A.D. 770) and died at Tus, A.H. 202, (A.D.817), or A.H. 203, (A.D. 818). He is considered the eighth Imam.

Written in ordinary naskh. Not dated. Circa 19th century.

Kifayat al-Athar Fi'n-Nusus al a'l-A'immata'l-Isna Ashar

A work dealing with those Traditions which are exclusively applicable to the twelve Imams and show their superiority over others. With regard to the authorship of the work, reliable authorities differ in their opinions.

(1) Some say that Abu Ja'far Muhammad bin 'Ali bin-ul Husain bin Babuya-ul-Qummi as -Saduq (died A.H. 381, A.D. 991) was the author of the book.

(2) Others consider Muhammad bin Muhammad bin un-Nu'man al-Baghdadi, known as Ash-Shaikh-ul-Mufid, to be its author. Ash-Shaikh-ul-Mufid was born in A.H. 336 (A.D. 947) or A.H. 338 (A.D. 949). When young, he accompanied his father to Baghdad. He became a great orator and debater. He is a recognised authority among the Imamites. He died in A.H. 413 (A.H. 413, (A.D. 1022).

(3) But according to *Muntaha'l-Maqal* (page 224) the real author of the book is 'Ali bin Muhammad bin 'Ali-ul-Khazzaz ur-Razi ul-

Qummi. He was a pupil of Ash-Shaikh us -Saduq, (died A.H. 381, A.D. 919) and was an indisputable authority in matters connected with religion. He is also the author of *kitab al-Idah fi Usul-ud-din.*

This third opinion is corroborated by Rawzat at-Jannat, page 388. Dr. Ahlwardt in his Berlin Catalogue No. 9675 has been quite misled about the authorship of this work.

The author, in the preface, says that he had found a class of people of ordinary learning who thought that there were no reliable Traditions about the eminence and superiority of the Imams, and consequently he composed the present work from trustworthy sources in order to prove their eminence.

Written in Naskh. Circa 19th century.

Kitab-ul-Hadith

A portion of a work on Imamite Traditions, defective both at the beginning and end. It is most probably a commentary on the famous work of Muhammad bin Ya'qub bin Ishaq -ul-Kulaini, died A.H. 328, (A.D. 939), or A.H. 329, (A.D.940), which is known as Al-Kafi fi 'Ilm ud-Din.

Written in good Naskh. Not dated. Circa 17th century.

Nahj-ul-Mustarshidin

A short treatise on the Fundamental Principles of the Shie'a creed by Jamal-ud-din Hasan bin Yusuf bin 'Ali bin-ul-Mutahhar-ul-Hilli, died. A.H. 726, (A.D. 1326). He was born on the 20th Ramazan, A.H. 648, (A.D. 1250), at Hilla. He studied religious subjects under his father, and philosophy, logic, etc. under Nasr-ud-din Abu Ja'far Muhammad bin Muhammad-ut-Tusi. He was the greatest Shi'a doctor of his time, and was commonly designated Al-'Alamah. His works. chiefly dealing with religious subjects, are often referred to as authorities of undisputed merit. Muhammad bin al-Hasan-al-Hurr ul-'Amili in his work *'Aml-ul-'Amil* (page 40) enumerated no less than 69 works of this learned author.

Written in fine Naskh. Not dated. Circa 17th century.

Al-Iktifa Fi Fazl-Al-Arba'at Al-Khulafa

A work in praise of the virtues of the Companions of the Prophet, especially of his first four successors, chiefly based on the Traditions by Ibrahim bin 'Abdallah ul-Wassabi ul-Yamani ush-Shafi-i. From a perusal of the work it appears that he was an inhabitant of Yemen, and a follower of the Shafi'i school. He flourished in the latter half of the 10th century, A.H.

Written in Nastaliq. Not dated. Circa 19th century.

Miftah un-Naja fi Manaqib Al al-'Aba

A work on the virtues and excellences of the descendants of the Prophet, chiefly based on the Traditions, together with a short account of their birth and death by Mirza Muhammad bin Rustum Mu'tamad Khan ul-Harisi ul-Badakhshi. He belonged to an illustrious family which served the Mughal Empire in various capacities. His grandfather, Kubad Beg, a native of Qandahar, received the title of Diyanat Khan from Aurangzib, and died in Delhi, A.H. 1083, (A.D. 1672). His father, Rustam, received from the same monarch the title of Mu'tamad Khan, and fell in the Deccan War, A.H. 1117, (A.D. 1705). Our author was a scholar of great reputation and served Kutb-ud-din Shah 'Alam I (A.H. 1119-1124, A.D. 1707-1712). He is the author of a Persian history called Tarikh Muhammadi, and several Arabic works, such as Tarajim al-Huffaz and Tuhfat al-Muhibbin bi Munaqib ul-Khulafa ur-Rashidin, mentioned in Rampur list. p. 668.

From the preface it appears that the author began the work in Ramazan, A.H. 1123, (A.D. 1711), and the colophon indicates that it was completed on the 7th Muharram A.H. 1124, (A.D. 1712)

Written in the fine Naskh. Dated A.H. 1126.

Manaqib Ahl al-Bait

A work on the lives and virtues of the twelve Imams of the Imamiya sect by Haidar' Ali bin Mirza Muhammad bin al-Hasan Ash-Shirwani. He was an Imami scholar, and wrote several treatises and books. One of his works, called *Kitab ul-Mujalis*, is well-known. His father Muhammad bin al-Hasan, known as Mulla Mirza, was a pupil of Aqa Husain bin Muhammad al-Khunsari, who died in A.H. 1098, (A.D. 1686). The date of his death is not known.

Written in Naskh. Not dated. Circa 19th century.

Tabaqat-ul-Hanbaliya

A biographical work dealing with the eminent scholars of the Hanbali sect by Abu'I-Husain Muhammad bin Muhammad bin-al-Husain Abu Ya'la ul-Farra ul-Hanbali. He was born in A.H. 451, (A.D. 1059), studied under his father and others, and became one of the most eminent scholars of the Hanbali sect. He was murdered on the night of the 10th of Muharram, A.H. 526 (A.D. 1131) on account of his wealth.

The biographies are preceded by a short introduction, in which the special merits of Al-Imam Abu 'Abdallah Ahmad bin Muhammad bin Hanbal, with his genealogical table going back to the Prophet Ibrahim are given. The work is divided into six chapters, called *Tabaqat.* The names in the first two are arranged alphabetically, and in the rest chronologically.

Written Nasta'liq. Not dated. Circa 19th Century.

Zahr ur-Riyaz Wa Zulal ul-Hiyaz

A biographical work chiefly based on Ibn Khallikan's *Wafayat ul-A'yan* by Hasan bin 'Ali bin al-Hasan bin 'Ali bin Shadqam ul-Husaini ul-Madani ush-Shi'i. He was born in A.H. 940 (A.D. 1533), and was a pupil of Husain bin 'Abd us-Samad ul-'Amili, who died A.H. 984, (A.D. 1576). He visited Hyderabad, Deccan, and wrote a work called Al-Jawahir un-Nizamiya for Nizam Shah. The date of his death is not known.

Written in different hands of Naskh. Not dated. Circa 17th century.

20

Muslim Contribution to Libraries During the Medieval Times

MUHAMMAD RUSTAM ALI DIWAN

The love for learning and education of the early Muslims necessiated the establishment of libraries and in the second century of the Hijra, hundreds and thousands of public and private libraries were established all over the Muslim empire.

Islam has placed primary emphasis on acquiring knowledge. The Quran has equated uneducated persons with dead-bodies while the educated ones have been accepted as living beings. The Prophet (SM) of Islam has declared the superiority of the ink of a scholar to the blood of a martyr. A road to an educational institution has been called by the Prophet (SM) a road to Heaven. When Allah wants to do favour to a man He bestows the knowledge of religion upon him.

These and similar other teachings of Islam (which can be multiplied times without number) have left such a deep impression on the minds of its followers that within a short span of time it produced scholars like Ibn Shihab al-Zuhri, Muhammad bin Jarir al-Tabari, and a host of others. The great scholar, al-Zuhri of the early Ummayad period, so deeply absorbed in his books that one day his newly married wife entered his study-room and remarked: "By Allah ! these books are more my eyesores than three co-wives put together."

The great historian and a commentator of the Quran, Mahammad b. Jarir al-Tabari of whom Nicholson says, "For forty years, he wrote forty pages a day, started writing his history from the time of the early creation till his day. When the book was completed it was so voluminous that people refused to read it. He then made an abridgement of the book which is now known as Tarikh-i-Tahbari or Tarikh al-Rusul wal-Muluk. It is said that this encyclopaedic savant used to write his history with reed-pen, which he required to mend from time. The cuttings or his reed-pen were collected in the corner of his big library. Before his death, this savant advised his people to use the cuttings as fuel which would be required to boil the water needed for washing the dead-body.

The *First* Muslim who founded a library and managed to get all available sources of knowledge to be translated into Arabic, was Khalid b. Yazid (704 A. D.) the son of Muawiya. He was the first chemist in Islam. He learnt alchemy from a Greek monk Niryanus and wrote three books on chemistry. Ibn Nadim (987 A. D.) personally visited this library and found many books of great value on medicine, surgery, astronomy and chemistry. The royal library of the caliphate of Caliph Omar b. Abdul Aziz might have had its origin in the library of Khalid b. Yazid (704 A. D.).

Since then collections of books were on a continuous process among the Muslims. Poems of the pre-Islamic days descriptions of their conquests and their genealogy, were collected and put in book forms. New books were written by the Muslim scholars on Tafsir, Hadith, Jurisprudence, history, biography and Kalam. In 87 A. H., Abdullah b. Malik translated the official record of Egypt into Arabic at the instance of Walid-I (705-15 A.D.). At the time of Hisham b. Abdul Malik (105-125 A. H./723-742 A.D.) the official Syriac records were translated into Arabic. He also ordered his Head Clerk Salem for translating the history of Persian Kings in 113 A.H./731 A.D. The portraits of the Persian Kings were also in it.

During the Abbasid period, the Muslims made tremendous improvements in the field of intellectual activities. Big libraries were established in large numbers; new branches of science and humanities were cultivated; inventions were made in the field of Geography, Chemistry, Medicine etc.

Caliph al-Mamun (754-75 A.D.) was a great patron of learning. At his command, the literary and scientific works in the foreign languages, were collected and translated into Arabic. During his Caliphate, hadith literature were collected and was shaped in book forms. Books on fikh (Islamic Jurisprudence) were also written at his time. An ancient history of the Iranians-Sakiki, a sacred book to the Persians, was translated into Arabic. A large number of scholars including the Christian ones were engaged in translating Persian books into Arabic for further research. Mani's (215 A.D.) seven books were also translated into Arabic. Ibn Nadim in his Fihrist mentions the names of many reputed translators.

In addition, letters, circulars and ordinances of the Persian Kings—Nawshirawan, Hormuz, Ardashir and others, were collected and translated. Though the Muslims of those days, were not interested in Novels, yet they did not leave this field of literature untouched. Hindu scholars from India flocked to the court of the Abbasid Caliphs, in Bagdad. With their encouragement, several Sanskrit books were collected and translated into Arabic for the library. Hindu scholars were appointed to the higher posts. In 773 A.D. an Indian work in astronomy-Sidhanta was translated into Arabic. By al-Farazi and about one thousand original books were also written.

Caliph Harun Al-Rashid (786 A.D.) made remarkable improvement in the field of library. He also established in Bagdad his famous library named, "Bayt-Al-Hikmah" (House of Wisdom)—a library academy and translation Bureau, and gathered eminent scholars such as Asmayee—the grammarian, Shafeyee, Isa ibn Funus, Sufian b Thauri, Ibrahim Mosuli the musician and Gabriel—son of Bakhtishu—the physician. Caliph Harun-al-Rashid also collected many Greek manuscript and oriental literature and got them translated into Arabic.

His Prime Minister, Yahya b. Khalid Barmeki deputed ambassadors to India to invite distinguished scholars, well-known physicians and philosophers to the court of Harun-al-Rashid. Thus the city of Bagdad became the site of learning. In appointing the translators, the Caliph made no distinction of creed and colour, race and religion. Harun Al-Rashid appointed I'ian Sho'ubi to his library as an officer even though he was an anti-Arab. During this time, the Arabian historian, Omar al-Waqidi (736-811 A.D.) had in his library one hundred and twenty camels-load of books.

Caliph al-Mamun (813-847 A.D.) whose reign is known as the golden age of Islam, enlarged the "Bayt al-Hikmah" founded by his father. His court was crowded with reputed scholars, poets, physicians and philosophers from every part of the civilised world of diverse creed and nationalities. He extended, without any racial differences, a lavish patronage to the historians, philosophers, grammarians and collectors of traditions who were assembled in his capital. He treasured many records of the "Days of ignorance" of the Arabs and enriched "the Bayt al Hikmah" to a great extent. Besides poems of the Arabs, he collected letters, documents and materials on archieves.

One of the pioneer translators of this institution, was Abu Yahya b. Batriq (796 A.D.)—a Greek. This period witnessed the most momentous intellectual awakening in the history of Islam. This awakening was marked by translations into Arabic.

Mamun appointed Hunan b. Ishaque (809-877 A.D.) Superintendent of his Library—Academy. He was a great translator and Mamun paid him in gold, the weight of the books he translated from Persian, Sanskrit, Syriac, Coptic and Greek.

Another remarkable translator of this great institution was Yuhanna. He was a great philosopher, translator and Hunayn's teacher who translated 121 (one hundred twenty-one) books of Galenus (100-200 A.D.). The great philosopher, Al-Kindi (813-874 A.D.) was also a member of this institution.

In addition to his translation works, an impetus was also given to original research and contribution by eastablishing special departments under qualified professors. Authorship was encouraged by munificient allowances. Innumerable works on Arithmetic, Geometry, Philosophy, Astronomy, Meteorology, Optics, Mechanics,

Medicine etc., were compiled and issued to the public. Al-Razi (d. 925 A.D.), the great physician wrote over two hundred books for 'Baytul Hikma'. Ibn Abu Harith—a well-known bookbinder was appointed for binding books in this library. The vastness of Mamun's Library and its vast number of books, can easily be imagined by the fact that though the city of Bagdad was devastated many a time along with its stock of literature yet the number of books that survived upto the Seventh Century A.H., was colosal. Luckily, Ibn Abu Asiba got these books and mentioned them in Hussain b. Ishaqs translation.

From Mamun's time the practice of collection and compilation of books became a common feature throughout the length and breadth of Bagdad. Most of the Ministers, Courtiers and even the Generals had their individual big libraries and they spent much wealth for their collection. Fateh b. Khaquan, the Minister of Mutawakil (847-61 A.D.) who had built a vast library, had appointed Ali b. Yahya Munajjin (d. 888) as its librarian. This library was considered unique during those days. Muhammad b. Adbul Malik Zayyat, the Minister of Wasiq Billah (841-844 A.D.) spent monthly ten thousand rupees for translation and copying of book. Al-Waqidi (d. 822 A.D.) had six hundred almirahs of books. A few days before his death he sold a portion of his library at a cost of two thousand gold coins.

'Darul Ilm', at Musil was a public library founded by Abul Qasim Jafar b. Muhammad b. Hamadan al-Musili (854-934 A.D.).

Hamanid Saifuddowlah (944-67 A.D.) was both a scholar and a soldier. He was an ardent lover of education and there was a great crowd of poets and scholars in his court. Saifuddowlah had a great hobby for literary activities and as such he was more inclined to collect books on literature for his library. Ibn Hashem and his brother the two renowned poets of the day were appointed Manager & Officer of his library respectively.

Adud Al dowlah (977 82 A.D.), the Buwayhid Sultan was a great poet and scholar, founded a magnificent library in Dhiraz.

He ordered for collection of all books on various subjects beginning from the advent of Islam till his time.

Allama Bashshari described it as a paradise on earth and a wonderful library within the palace in a vast building where almirahs were filled up with numerous books. Each of these almirahs, was three yards broad and a man's height in length. The woods of the almirahs were very skilfully designed, decorated and illuminated with gold. Separate rooms and catalogues were maintained for each subject. One manager, one treasurer and a few clerks were appointed for running the administration of this library. General entrance into it was forbidden. He had another library at Basra which remained open for the study of the scholars and there was arrangemnet of stipends for the readers and the Calligraphers.

A library known as "Khizanah Al-Waqf" at Basra was founded by Ali b. Sawwar Al-Katib, who was in the service of Adud Al-dowlah (d. 982-A.D.). His library which contained some rare books remained intact until the time of Al-Hariri (d. 1122 A.D.) who mentioned it in his great work, "Maqamat-i-Hariri.

Probably in 922 A.D., Shapur b. Ardashir a Buwayhid Governor founded a Public Library in Bagdad named 'Darul Ilm' (House of knowledge), and donated huge number of books for public use. This is so far known, the first Public Library of the Muslims in the medieval world.

In 1004 A.D., Hakim Amr Billah, the ruler of Egypt, built a big library for the general public. Its opening ceremony was celeberated with great pomp & grandeur. Papers, pen, ink-pots and other things were supplied to the readers from this library. This library was also known as "Dar-Al-Ilm". In 1009 A.D., many buildings and shops were bequeathed to it for recurring expenditure.

From this time onward, establishment of Public Library became a common practice, and innumerable libraries were established throughout the whole Muslim world. During the eleventh Century there grew up a tendency for the establishment of the colleges and universities in the Muslim world and a library was unavoidably attached to each college and university. Nizamul Mulk (d. 1092) the word renowned Prime Minister and a patron of learning, gathered round him a galaxy of scholars consisting of astronomers, poets and historians. He also founded the Nizamia University in Bagdad and a library was attached to it. He issued general orders all over the Islamic world to establish a library adjacent to each Academy. As a result of this royal order there sprang up hundreds of libraries throughout the country. Every mosque and even a small primary institution where there was a single teacher had a library attached to it.

A library known as 'Khizanah Al-Kutub fi Mash-had-i-Abu Hanifa was attached to a Madrasah founded by Mansur Al-Hamid Al-Khawarizmi in 1066 A.D. This library was still in the same place three miles north of Bagdad, near the tomb of Imam Abu Hanifa. It contained a huge collection.

"Khizanatul Masjid of Zaidi" (a library) was founded by Al-Shareef Zaidi (1134-1179 A.D.). He received two thousand dinars as gift from the Caliph for his personal expenses but he purchased a plot of land in eastern Bagdad and founded another library.

Khizanah Al-Rabat Al-Khatuni Al-Saljuki, was bequeathed by Caliph Al-Nasir-li-dinillah (1180-1225 A.D) and kept at the tomb of his wife—Saljuka Khatun at the Basra Gate in Bagdad. Books contained in this library were the Caliphs personal cellection. Almost all the Wazirs of the Abbside had their personal libraries.

Caliph Mustansir (1226-1242 A.D.) founded the Mustansiriah University and a library in 1233 A.D. in Bagdad. A number of buildings and landed property were appropriated by the Caliph for the University and a library valued ten lakhs gold coins. It was unique in those days in the whole world, stated Ibn Al-Athir. The number of books in the library was eighty thousand volumes. The city of Bagdad only, possessed thirty six public libraries. The last library of the Abbaside period was that which was established by the last Abbaside Wazir Ibn Alkami. This library contained ten thousand books. Total number of collections was fourteen lakhs and these were public libraries during the times of the Abbaside Caliphates. All these destroyed during the sack of the city Bagdad by the Mongols in 1258 A.D.

Libraries created great interest in the minds of the people in the West also. In Spain, Hakam II's (961-76 A.D.) was the greatest of all. Ibn Khaldun (d. 1406 A.D.) and Al-Makkari (d. 1631 A.D.) wrote much about it. Ummayad's famous Caliph Hakam was a far-sighted ruler and a scholar of the first rate. His desire for collection of books was so great that the whole revenue of his State was not at all sufficient for this purpose. In the cities of Spain, Syria, Egypt, Bagdad, Persia and Khorasan, he had appointed several officers and merchants for the collection of rare and valuable books, new and old. When Abul Faraj Ispahani (d. 967 A.D.) completed his 'Kitabul Aghani', Hakam deputed a special messenger asking him to register the book first in his library before its cirulation in the country. So the book was purchased at a cost of rupees four thousand and was brought first to Hakam's Library. Ibn Khaldun and Ibn Abbar stated, "in addition to the pages required for the enlistment of its four lakhs books on various subjects, for enlisting books on poems only covered a space of eight hundred eighty pages of the catalogue of this library. Under Hakam (II) the University of Cordova founded in the principal mosque rose to a place of pre-eminence among the educational institutions of the world. It preceded both Al-Azhar of Cairo and the Nizamia of Bagdad and attracted students—Christians and Muslims, not only from Spain but also from other parts of Europe, Africa and Asia. His imperial Library was the largest and richest of all.

Hakam (II) spent lavishly on collection of manuscripts. His agents ransacked book-shops and libraries of Bagdad, Damascus, Cairo, Alexandria and other places. He also got books written for his library. Many books were dedicated to him. Among such books was a booklet on Calendar—the Kitab-Awqat al-Sanat composed by Abul Hasan 'Arib b. Sayeed (d. 980-1 A.D.) of Cordova in 961

A.D. and edited and translated into Latin by Dozy in 1873 A.D. Contemporary Arab scholars have spoken highly of the library Hakam II, its huge collection and its valuable books. This was (according to them) the biggest collection that a royal library ever possessed in the medieval world.

Alongwith these huge collection, Hakam (II) had a great love for their systematic arrangements, classification, techniques, decorations etc. So he gathered many reputed experts, calligraphers, revisers and skilful book-binders and several rooms were set apart for the work of copying; illuminating and binding books which were written in golden letters and decorated with beautiful paintings. In addition, to this, Hakam was a studious scholar who made copious notes on the *fly-leaf* and added valuable footnotes relating to the authors and the works. In the beginning or at the end of every book, this sagacious Caliph wrote the names, surnames of the family, tribe, date of birth & death of the author. None other than Hakam had such knowledge of the history of literature. His influence was so great that the later scholars accepted his footnotes as authentic. Hakam (II) collected at least four lakhs of books at the time when printing and publication was unknown and books were copied by the calligraphers and copyist.

During the reign of Hakam (II), women too, did not fall back in cultivating knowledge. Experiencing the honour of education, they devoted themselves in studies. Many of them earned reputation for writing good essays, poems and calligraphy. One of his slave girls, was well-educated in Grammar, Arithmetic and other sciences. She loved poems also. Nobody in Hakam's palace could speak like her in eloquent language. Fatema, a daughter of a court slave, Zakaria, was a fine Calligrapher, and she copied many manuscripts for the Caliph. Ahmad b Muhammad of Cordova had a daughter—Ayesha by name who was famous for her oration and composing poems. She had a beautiful library. During Hakam's reign there were seventy public libraries attached to the big mosques of Cordova. Ibn Abbas, a Minister of Almeria in Spain had, in addition to several booklets, four lakh books in his library. It is said that during his time, the whole country turned into bookshops. Manuscripts were largely sold in the markets like other commodities.

Hajib Al-Mansur followed Hakam II and patronised scholars. He spent lavishly on collection of rare books for his library. It is said that he spent five thousand gold coins for only one book, namely, *Al-Fusus* written by Sa'id of Bagdad (d 1021 A.D.).

In Bokhara, Nuh b. Mansur (976-97 A.D.) was the most powerful king who established a library which in those days were considered unparallel for many respects. Ibn Khallikan relates: "All kinds of books relating to industries, Arts & Science, were stored in the unique and rich library. Besides this, there were many such books which were not found elsewhere." Ibn Sina (Avicina, 980-1037 A.D.) states, "whatever treasures of philosophical materials I have seen in this library, neither I nor anybody else has seen them elsewhere. It is a gigantic building which has many rooms and in every room, there are numerous almirhs where books on each subject are separately arranged in and out of every almirah.

Nuh b. Mansur invited the eminent scholar, Sahib b. Abbad (938-95 A.D.) to Bokhara to become his Minister but he refused this offer on the ground that it would require four hundred camels to transport his books from his personal belonging. The personal library of Saihb b. Abbad was so big that its catalogue filled ten volumes. He was interested in Philosophy, Science, Techniques and was generous with scholars.

In Egypt the Fatemides also established a huge number of libraries. The libraries of the Fatemedes in fact, excelled all other libraries established by their counterparts in different parts of the world. The first library in Cairo was established by the Fatemide Caliph Al-Aziz, (975-96 A.D.) in connection with his Darul 'Ilm where thirty-five students were supported from endowment. This school library had one lakh volumes (some others say six lakh of bound books, among which, were two thousand four hundred Koran beautifully illuminated in gold and silver, and stored in a separate room above the library proper. The rest of the books on Jurisprudence,

Grammar, Rhetoric, History, Biography, Astronomy and Chemistry, were kept in large presses around the walls, which were divided into shelves—each of which had a door with a lock. Makrizi (1346-1442 A.D.) remarks on it saying: "This library was a part of the Imperial Palace and was included with those separate forty libraries each contained 18,000 books, only on ancient knowledge & science." Al-Makrizi further states that he found in it,the pens of the Calligraphers like Ibn Moqla and Ibn Bawab. The hand made globe of Batlimus which was made 2250 years ago, was preserved in this library. Another globe—purchased for Aduddowla at a cost of rupees fifteen thousand was also kept in it.

The desire for the establishment of libraries was not confined to the kings and rulers only but in those days, most of the scholars and officers of the country felt it a great honour to have a personal library. Abu Nasar Sihat b. Mazarban, the reputed Ameer of Nishapur, exhausted all his wealth for compilation and collection of books and frequently used to go to Bagdad in search of rare books.

Muhammad b. Hossain Al-Bagdadi established a library which was considered unparallel in respect of its rare and valuable collections. Ibn Nadim states, "I never found such a library elsewhere. I got an access to Muhammad b. Hossain when I won his confidence, he brought before me a big bag filled with innumerable poems, Qasidas, records & documents of the ancient Arabs which were written on hides and papers of Khorasan Egypt and China. It also contained several letters of Hazrat 'Ali (R). Imam Hasan (R), Imam Hossain (R) and Prophet Muhammad (SM) to the leaders of different tribes. Sufian Thauris and Auzayee's own hand written traditions were also found in it. In this library I learnt that 'Ilm Nuhwa was the invention of Abul Aswad.

The Persians Muslims also showed great enthusiasm in search of most ancient books. Abu Mash'ar Falaki states, "Long before our time, there was a big library in Ispahan established by the Iranians. It contained such ancient books that when a part of this library was building ruined, many books in old Persian of the ancient times, were found in it. Only a few of us who were acquainted with that language could read them. Ibn Nadim states, "In 350 A.H./961 A.D. many books were brought out from the ruins of the other parts of this building but nobody could read them. I saw Ibnul `Amid sending many books to Bagdad in 340 A.H./651 A.D. which were found kept in the chests of Ispahan. These books were written in Greek language. Yuhanna b. Masuvia (750-850 A.D.) and others who knew this language read them.

More than four hundred scholars, literatures and poets, such as Al-Beruni, Ferdousi, Dakiki, Unsuri, Asjadi and many others rallied round Sultan Mahmud (996-1030 A.D.), the great conqurer of Ghazna. He founded a big library. During his reign arts & learning flourished to a great extent. The rise of Persian Seljukides and their tastes for scholarship and science, rivalled that of the golden days of the Abbasides. Tugril, Alp Arsalan, Sanjar and others, were also distinguished patrons of learning. They established many libraries.

Volumes are required to give the full accounts of the glorious contributions of the early Muslims to this field of knowledge (Libraries) but fearing the monotony of the readers, I am concluding my essay with the names of some libraries of the medieval time from Maulana Shibli Nomani's Safarnama where he says, "In Turkey Constantinople was the greatest center for Arabic publications. There were forty-five libraries in the city of Constantinople. The libraries which were in the palace of Humayun were the most ancient. The total number of books in those libraries, were 85 thousand. Though this number is not so big yet Constantinople is prefered for its rare and best books. The names of some of those libraries are: Kutub Khana Jame Bayezid, Kutub Khana Jame Yul, Kutub Khana Hamidia Qadim, Kutub Khana Ashir Afandi, Kutub Khana As'ad Afandi, Kutub Khana Jame Muhammad Fateh, Kutub Khana Hamidia Jadid, Kutub Khana 'Ali Pasha Shahid, Kutub Khana-i-Lala Bai, Kutub Khana-i-Akhli Pasha, Kutub Khana Muhammad Pasha, Kutub Khana-i-Qalij 'Ali Pasha, Kutub Khana-i-Waliuddin Afandi, Kutub Khana Salimia, Kutub Khana Faizullah

Afandi, Kutub Khana-i-Sultan Muhammad Qazi Zada, Kutub Khana-i-Atif Afandi, Qutub Khana Shahzana Damad Ibrahim Pasha, Kutub Khana Khusru Pasha, Kutub Khana Meherbhan, Kutub Khana Muhammad Afandi, Kutab Khana Mustafa Pasha, Kutub Khana Taufiq Afandi, Kutub Khana Solaimania, Kutub Khana Muhammad Afandi Murad, Kutub Khana-i-Raghib Pasha."

The Maulana further states, "These libraries as their names indicate, were founded by the ancient Pashas and Ameers. All these libraries were bequeathed to the general public. Properties were donated adjacent to each of these libraries. Most of the highly educated Turks not only bequeathed libraries but also donated their own hand written books to these libraries and collected there many best and rare books. Full administration of these libraries were vested in the hands of the Government. The significance of the ancient library of Hamidia is this that the papers of most of the books were gilted or sprayed with gold-water and the margins of the books were embroidered with golden decoration."

In view of the above facts, one may easily come to a conclusion that nine hundred years ago the early Muslims had a great revolution of their credit in respect of the establishment of personal and public libraries when printing was unknown. The modern world has nothing new to this field except some technical progress due to scientific and mechanical advantages of the last two hundred years. Actually the Muslims were the real torch-bearers in the field of library.

